WE'RE THE FAMOUS MAN UNITED
OLD TRAFFORD IN THE EIGHTIES
THE PLAYERS' STORIES

By Andy Mitten

VSP

Vision Sports Publishing
2 Coombe Gardens,
London, SW20 0QU

www.visionsp.co.uk

This First Edition Published by
Vision Sports Publishing in 2006

Text © Andy Mitten

All rights reserved. No part of this publication may be reproduced,
stored in a retrieval system, or transmitted in any form or by any means,
electronic, mechanical, photocopying, recording or otherwise, without the
prior permission of the publishers.

This book is sold subject to the condition that it shall not, by way
of trade or otherwise, be lent, re-sold, hired out, or otherwise circulated
without the publisher's prior consent in any form of binding or cover other
than that in which it is published and without a similar condition including
this condition being imposed on the subsequent purchaser.

All pictures by Empics

Typeset by Palimpsest Book Production Limited,
Grangemouth, Stirlingshire
Printed and bound by Creative Print and Design, Wales

A CIP catalogue record for this book is
available from the British Library

ISBN 10-1-905326-14-9
ISBN 13-978-1-905326-14-3

In '77 it was Doc-her-ty, and now it's Atkinson in '83.
And everyone will know just who we are,
'Cos we'll be singing que sera, sera.
U-ni-ted, Man U-ni-ted,
We're the boys in red and we're on our way to Wem-ber-ly,
Wem-ber-ly, Wem-ber-ly, We're the Famous Man United
and we're going to Wem-ber-ly.

This book is dedicated to those good red souls who've followed them far, and followed them near . . .

Contents

Introduction vii
1 **Gary Bailey** The Graduate 1
2 **Billy Garton** The Salford Lad 29
3 **Bryan Robson** Captain Marvel 51
4 **Gordon McQueen** The Social Convenor 69
5 **Arthur Albiston** Reliability 95
6 **John Gidman** The Scouse Flyer 117
7 **Clayton Blackmore** Mr Versatility 139
8 **Frank Stapleton** The Consummate Professional 161
9 **Alan Brazil** The Raconteur 189
10 **Arnold Muhren** The Dutch Master 207
11 **Ron Atkinson** The Manager 223

Introduction

This book is about those players idolised in a different era. Manchester, and United have changed beyond recognition from the 1980s, a decade when players had mullets and perms, often both at the same time. And in the same Liverpool midfield. Shirts didn't have sponsors at the start of the decade and shorts were just that. Despite never winning the league, United were the best-supported club in Britain, although they were not commercially sophisticated: the club's attempts to increase revenues amounted to a Sunday market on number one car park and a failed basketball venture. Players didn't have agents and the finest talents left for Italy and Spain – which was no surprise given Mark Hughes, United's top scorer, earned just £250 a week. You were lucky if there was one televised game a week, and even European Cup finals didn't make it onto British screens unless they involved English clubs.

At Old Trafford, the view of the pitch was obscured by steel fences topped with spikes to cage fans in and some of the vitriol from the tightly packed mass of bodies on the terracing was stinging, like asking Neville Southall or Peter Shilton where their wives were,

We're The Famous Man United

following well-publicised separations. At other times, it was pernicious and sickening. The QPR defender Paul Parker, upon hearing the chant 'Trigger, trigger, trigger, shoot that nigger', reacted by pretending to shoot himself. Parker, one of the most pleasant people in football, became a United player two years later. Anyone attempting such a chant within Old Trafford these days would be cuffed well before the stewards could get near them.

Manchester wasn't the city of glass museums, soaring apartment blocks with grandiose names and sleek Calatrava bridges over the Irwell that it is now. Crippled from the effects of Thatcher-enhanced post-industrialisation, whole swathes of the city centre lay derelict and dying. Visitors were not impressed and these perceptions took time to change. While inter-railing in 1993, a lady in the tourist information office in Munich asked where I was from. Upon hearing Manchester, her expression changed and she said: "I'm so sorry. My husband was sent to work there a few years ago and he told me about it." I might as well have said Chernobyl. Or Liverpool. The cheeky get.

You might not have been able to get a cappuccino in Harvey Nichols, but Manchester has never been about aesthetics. The legacy of the city in the '80s endures through the music of The Smiths, Joy Division, New Order and the latest Hacienda spin-off, which are still bought in huge quantities. That first seminal Stone Roses album was written in '80s Manchester, no doubt inspired by the virtues shown by Terry Gibson or John Sivebaek.

Non-Reds may not talk about the great Manchester United teams of the '80s, but with United fans accustomed to a lack of league titles and a Merseyside domination, success was relative and there were plenty of highs. Such were the limited expectations that United recorded an attendance jump of 13,000 over two games in 1989 because the team had a chance of moving up to fourth *if* they beat Chelsea in a November league game. The game ended 0–0.

Fans of a certain vintage remember the '80s as fondly as any other decade, though, and it's partly because of that that I wrote this book. I also feel that not enough has been written about the players from

Introduction

that time: a decade that prompts mixed memories from United fans. There isn't the identity or romance of the '70s, nor the success of the '50s, '60s or '90s to reminisce about, but it was an intriguing period of turbulence and transition.

Another reason is that I kept interviewing former footballers and found them far more engaging than their present day counterparts, Roy Keane excepted. Too many modern players are unable or unwilling to speak candidly for fear that their words will be twisted by a voracious media. Former players aren't so restricted and many interviewed in this book have great anecdotes that are safe to go on the record because events happened two decades ago. Former players can also look back at their careers with the benefit of both hindsight and greater life experience. Certainly, some of the players in this book could never have expected what came after leaving M16. I also feel that some of them deserve a truer representation. Some might not be big enough names to have had an autobiography published and most of their interviews with the press amounted to a few minutes. Fans then formed opinions of personalities based on a series of anodyne quotes. Occasionally they would admit to liking steaks and Luther Vandross in a question and answer interview. When you sit down with a player for a full day, often over a few beers, you get a lot more than that.

With a mother born and bred in Old Trafford, an auntie who dated George Best, a father named after Charlie (my great uncle who played in Matt Busby's first great United side after the war) and my first five years living in the Stretford End end of Stretford, I didn't really have a choice which football team I would support. I've been fortunate enough to watch United play in over 30 countries spanning six continents, but by the end of the '80s I'd never seen them play outside Manchester, save for a trip to Nottingham's City Ground – the £4.40 junior admission fee prompting an angry letter to *Football Today* magazine. Yet I seemed to spend more time in the '80s obsessing about United than at any other stage in my life. Age meant I wasn't at Wembley or Old Trafford for key moments, yet some of my most vivid moments as a United fan were from that decade.

We're The Famous Man United

I looked forward to Sunday afternoon trips to see our great grandma at her semi-detached house on Seymour Grove, Old Trafford. Uncle Charlie lived there too. After an assault on their chocolate biscuits, my brother would go and play football in the garden, our sister would be fascinated by Charlie's electric organ in the front room, while I'd sit and listen as he re-told stories from his life in football. Tales about playing with Stanley Matthews during the war, winning the FA Cup with Manchester United, moving to Colombia to compete against Alfredo Di Stefano and managing Newcastle United. He would be stinging in his criticism of how much the players of the '80s earned, bitter even, because despite having been a star for United he finished his career without enough money to buy a car – though the greyhounds, which he still raced well into his 70s, probably had something to do with that.

On one visit, Charlie gave me Matt Busby's autograph which I proudly took into primary school the following day. The head teacher, who wasn't a football fan, held up the cherished squiggle in assembly – and explained that it was the signature of Busby the Bird who featured in the British Telecom advert. I was crushed.

Another time, Charlie lent me his 1948 FA Cup Winners' medal. Again, I took it into school, where my mates were more obsessed in completing their Panini '85 sticker album than with a little piece of metal, although the medal did bring a physics lesson to a premature end as the elderly teacher stared at it, fixated. He'd been at Wembley in '48 as a fan and there was reverence in his eyes that I'll never forget. My grandparents went to watch that final, too, travelling to see Charlie on a coach from the Gorse Hill pub in Stretford. Grandma hasn't returned to London since and she hasn't been to Old Trafford for four decades, but she still dissects the current United team in minute detail when I see her. Until Granddad, once a professional footballer himself, chips in and then they'll argue about Wes Brown's best position.

Charlie, meanwhile, died in January 2002. I went to see him a month before in a nursing home by Manchester Airport. Cheeky as ever, he told me he was the main man in the home. He asked if it

Introduction

would be possible to travel to Bogotá to meet friends last seen in 1950. He also told me angrily that the former United chairman Martin Edwards still owed him £100 from 1949 (Edwards was four at the time) and asked if I could arrange for Ferenc Puskas and Di Stefano to visit, because he had some 'business' to discuss. I smiled and said I'd try, but I knew I'd never see Charlie again.

I was six at the turn of the '80s, but one of my first memories is of a poster of Joe Jordan's gnarled expression above my bed. I asked my dad continually about going to the 1983 FA Cup final, but it wasn't happening. He explained that tickets would go to those who deserved them, but deep down I knew he was a footballer and not a football watcher. For me, that meant a pre-teen life of trawling the non-league grounds of the north most Saturdays.

I was at home in Urmston watching the 1985 Cup Final, when United lifted the cup against all odds. I dreamed of being there, but the closest I got to that team was an autographed menu from the banquet held by Trafford Council in their honour. Mum had helped serve the food at the town hall that night while working 'a foreigner'.

Old Trafford used to have a roar. I could hear it from my paper round if the game was big enough; the wind caught the noise right off the Pennine Steppes. I was allowed to go to games with my mates from the age of 13 onwards, travelling on the 255 bus, and getting to the ground at 11.30am on a Saturday for a 3pm kick-off. The bus was always full of like-minded locals, the £1.10 admission fee for Old Trafford half what I got on my paper round. The bus is empty now. We'd wait patiently for the turnstiles to open and then run through to *our* space in the Stretford Paddock, before graduating to the Stretford Groundside proper (right-side).

The news that Ron Atkinson had been sacked was a 'where were you moment' in school, while I made a 'Sparky Come Home' banner (eight sheets of A4 paper stuck on a Simple Minds poster from *Smash Hits*) when Mark Hughes returned for Gary Bailey's testimonial. Until I spoke to him for this book, I had no idea how upset Bailey had been by people like me singing for Hughes on his farewell day.

Away games were off limits for a few more years. Me and our

We're The Famous Man United

Joz were listening to Piccadilly Radio's match commentary in our bedroom when Gordon Strachan equalised at Anfield in '88. Not even Liverpool v United was televised then. We ran out of the house and down the street telling everyone. A year later I started the *United We Stand* fanzine with mates at school, not for a second thinking that it would still be going 17 years later, with over 150 issues produced.

This book wouldn't have been possible without the help of the following: Jim Drewett and Toby Trotman at VSP. They were the first publishers approached and agreed straight away. They were asked because they are true football fans who watch AFC Wimbledon home and away and understand the game's nuances when so many don't. Joyce Woolridge was unstinting in wading through copy, often at short notice. I appreciate her efforts immensely. The following all chipped in with useful comments, advice, numbers and suggestions: Jim White, David Mitchell, Grant Cass, Danny Taylor, Seb Ewen, Francis Keenan, Hugh Sleight, Paul Moreton, Jonathan Northcroft, Derek Balment, Adam Renton, Graham Hunter, Oliver Holt, Paul Davies, Ian Hawkey, Rob Moore and Paddy Barclay. The lyrics of Paul Heaton helped, as did the words of Kevin Sampson. I must also thank my family for their continued love and support.

But most of all I'd like to thank the players and their former manager, without whom this book wouldn't exist. Two players approached couldn't do it, but I understand and respect their reasons why. The eleven who did were paid what amounts to beer money, yet I found it refreshing that none were motivated by financial gain. They didn't have to be as honest as they have been. Every interview was an absolute joy, all of the interviewees exceeding my expectations of them as people as they looked back at their often remarkable lives. I hope I've done your stories justice. You were the famous Man United . . .

Andy Mitten
September 2006

1
Gary Bailey

The Graduate

GARY BAILEY
MANCHESTER UNITED

Gary Bailey's frustration was unbearable. After leading 2–0, United had shipped three goals away to Nottingham Forest in December 1984. The tension had been building for weeks, with his fellow players critical of his performances, yet Bailey felt that he wasn't the only culprit responsible for United's mediocre form.

"I walked into the dressing room and said, 'I am sick and tired of our defence giving away silly goals'," says the former United keeper in his distinctive South African accent. "I had conceded fewer goals than any other goalkeeper four seasons in a row and was very proud of my record, so I took it personally when things didn't go right."

The strain was acute between Bailey and Gordon McQueen.

"Gordon and I had had words before," he recalls. "He had a lot of positive abilities – he was tall and would win headers – but one of his weaknesses was his positioning. I was very frustrated with Gordon because whenever I tried to organise my defence he wasn't where he should be, so I was forever having to cover. I was frustrated with him and he was frustrated with me."

The defeat against Forest would be the catalyst for what happened next.

"I had a go at Gordon and told him that he was all over the place defensively," explains Bailey. "He told me that I wasn't good enough, adding that he thought I was a coward." Bailey took umbrage at that. "I wasn't a coward. I put myself all over the place and had the bumps to show for it. So I walked across to confront Gordon." But the pair were from different worlds. "In classic university style, I wanted to debate the issue. In classic working-class style, he punched me hard in the face," grimaces Bailey. "One person held me back and twelve held him back. Thank goodness they did because he would have killed me."

Later that night, Bailey sat with his girlfriend Kathy Plowright, daughter of Granada Television's managing director David.

"Kathy said, 'You know what? You are just a mild-mannered, sweet little university boy. You have no idea how tough the boys in your team are, no idea where they've grown up. You'd better learn how to fight.'"

The following day, Bailey headed into Manchester's Chinatown and enrolled for a kung-fu class.

"It didn't do the fancy karate, but did street fighting," he explains. "Over four years I worked my way up and was just short of black belt by the time I left United." No team-mate challenged him to a fight again.

Bailey's background was far removed from the archetypal working class upbringing of his team-mates. Educated at a top university, Bailey grew up in apartheid-era South Africa, living in a house with a maid and a swimming pool. Yet while he has spent most of his life in South Africa, a country he returned to when leaving United in 1986, he is English by birth.

Gary Bailey

"I was born in Ipswich, where my dad, Roy, was a goalkeeper under Alf Ramsey. Dad was a south London boy who served in the army in Germany. His brother David was considered the better goalkeeper of the two and got offered trials at Crystal Palace. He agreed to go but only on the proviso that my dad could go too. Dad, who was six two and well built, ended up in the first team while David was released after a year.

Ramsey took Roy Bailey to Ipswich.

"On his first day of training he drove up to Ipswich and waited around for the other players to arrive – and he carried on waiting. Eventually, he walked into the changing-room and Sir Alf asked him where he had been. He said that he had been waiting in his car for his team-mates, yet they were already in the changing-room. They'd all cycled as none of them had a car."

Bailey's first memories are of seeing his dad play football.

"Ipswich won the league in 1961/62, and I remember seeing Dad play against the great Spurs double-winning team a few years later. I was about five and Ipswich got hammered. I saw Jimmy Greaves kick my dad in the head and I burst into tears. That was my introduction to goalkeeping. Dad had a couple of very good seasons and reckons he would have played for England if there had been a squad system then."

After more than 300 Ipswich performances, Bailey Senior decided he would take his family to either South Africa or Australia to make a fresh start, rather than play in a lower league.

"My mum preferred the idea of South Africa as it is closer to England, so we moved in 1965. South Africa was going through a decent spell as a country and there was a good offer for him to coach there. I was six when we flew there on a BOAC plane and I can remember walking around Johannesburg for the first time. It was hot, sunny and there were lots of African guys dressed in their traditional robes. I loved the sunshine from the moment I got here. There were lots of English people and my school was called King Edward's, so it felt like a home from home."

With the advantage of parental coaching, Bailey played football at primary school, but at high school the Afrikaans government decreed rugby to be the main sport.

"I refused to play rugby," says Bailey. "So they wouldn't let me take my A-level equivalents. The compromise in my final year was for me to play in goal for the hockey team – only then was I allowed to sit my exams."

Hockey took some getting used to.

"I remember flying out with my hands to claim the ball and the game came to a stop. Everyone said, 'You can't do that or you'll get yourself killed, you have to come out on your knees in hockey.'

"I got a bit of stick at school. Soccer, as they call it, is considered a girls' sport in South Africa, and I got stick from the so-called hard men playing rugby. They called me a softie and, in fairness to the rugby players, football is soft by comparison. But the abuse toughened me up and it was a good grounding – I was never intimidated getting a whack by the big centre forwards in England because I'd seen bigger lads playing rugby."

Roy Bailey became national coach in South Africa before managing a now defunct Cape Town City in the early '70s.

"There were a hell of a lot of English lads playing under him, people like Geoff Hurst, Frank McLintock and Gordon Banks," says Bailey. "They used to get 20,000; it was a golden age for South African club football. Bestie played in Johannesburg so we got to see some greats."

From High School, Bailey went to Witts University – "Or 'half-wits' as Stevie Coppell called it" – where he played in the university football team in the South African third division. He spent two years studying civil engineering and excelled. "I was an academic and had great results," he says. At 18, his dad called him up to the national squad.

"He didn't play me though, saying that if I played for South Africa then I could never play for England. He said, 'Look, you are in the national squad on merit but you've got to get overseas because there is no serious future for you in South African football – you're going to stagnate.'"

Gary Bailey

Bailey had already ventured to England a year earlier.

"I trained with Ipswich and Bobby Robson for nine weeks," he says. "And I hated it. It snowed for seven weeks and I couldn't wait to get home. I vowed never to go abroad again."

But after being selected for his country, he realised he'd have to travel again if he was to realise his dream of making it as a professional footballer.

"I didn't want to go to England after the Ipswich experience, so I went to Holland instead," says Bailey. "I could speak Dutch, coming from South Africa, and I went to AZ Alkmaar where they offered me a junior contract. I went to Hamburg too, where Kevin Keegan played, but that didn't work out. I had two days left in Europe before going back to South Africa. The agent who was sorting out all the these trials said, 'Give it one last shot. What is the club of your dreams?' I said, 'Man United.' So he said, 'Ask your old man if he knows Dave Sexton.'"

Roy Bailey did indeed know the United manager and gave him a call.

"That opened the door for me, and I spoke to Dave. He said, 'We're playing West Ham in London, come to the team hotel and then the game'. Martin Buchan was the first player I saw at the hotel. I told him that I had come to see Dave Sexton and he said, 'Yeah, you and everyone else.' I insisted that I had an appointment but he didn't believe me. Eventually he called Dave across and I got on the bus to West Ham with the team."

Instantly, Bailey was the butt of the United players' jokes.

"Thinking that I was a smart arse from university, they started saying things like, 'I wonder where the Post Office Tower is?' Falling right into their trap I would say, 'It's over there, can't you see it?' I remember thinking, 'I know these lads left school early but hell they must be thick.' I was diving headlong into all the wind-ups because I just didn't understand the British sense of humour."

Bailey travelled back to Manchester with the team after the game and followed Sexton's instruction to go to training on Monday morning, where he "dived about a bit" and impressed Sexton enough to be asked to play for the reserves that night against Everton.

We're The Famous Man United

"Apart from giving away a penalty in a 1–0 defeat, I didn't do too badly. Afterwards, Dave said, 'I need to see you tomorrow in my office.' I thought he was going to say that I'd done well, but not well enough to play for Manchester United. He surprised the hell out of me when he asked me to sign a four-year contract. I phoned my old man. Money-wise it wasn't great, but he told me not to worry about that because my foot was in the door. He told me that he wanted to put a clause in my contract which allowed me to study every Wednesday so that I could finish my degree. Dave agreed to that and for three years I went to Manchester Polytechnic every Wednesday where I finished my science degree."

Bailey stayed in Manchester, although his initial impressions of the city were mixed.

"I was put in digs near Moss Side, a stone's throw from Maine Road. There were three of us and I had to share a room with another young player. I'd always lived in a massive house and eaten wonderful food. I was used to housekeepers and had never washed clothes in my life. Then I was sharing a room at the top of a terraced house in a poor part of Manchester. I moved there in December 1977 and didn't see the sun for four months. It was freezing, wet and miserable."

"The one thing that got me through was the people," he adds. "I found Manchester folk so friendly and they helped me settle, but it still wasn't easy. I had to catch two buses to get from the digs to training until I could afford to buy an old beat-up car.

"I remember going into town, a gangly 18-year-old with a few spots on my face. I went to a disco and not one person spoke to me all night. Girls didn't believe me if I told them that I was a goalkeeper at Manchester United."

Bailey moved to new digs in Prestwich, near Heaton Park, where he felt more settled. "My landlord's nephew used to take me out for a few drinks with his mates which was fun. They were very working-class lads and we'd go out around north Manchester and then into town."

Yet at the Cliff, he didn't gel with the other young players.

Gary Bailey

"I struggled to fit in at United, full stop," he offers. "Coming from university was a bit of a problem for me. The lads were from very working-class backgrounds, in fact the whole class system really threw me because it's completely different in South Africa. Anyway, I thought they were really thick because I'd been told that. They would read the *Sun* and be stuck on page three for half an hour. And yet they were far quicker than me in many ways; they were so streetwise and I felt like an idiot for years because they were always quicker to the punchline. They always read situations better. In every sense they were bright lads and they had to be to get to that level of football, but academically they weren't and there was this constant conflict for me. I wanted to talk about my physics course and astronomy, but it was a pointless exercise trying to talk to the lads about these subjects. I felt very out of it, and I don't think anyone, not even the manager, appreciated how difficult it was for me to come from a country of sunshine and beaches and live in Manchester. I really struggled and it was a very tough beginning."

When it came to training, Bailey's expectations were different from the reality too.

"I was brought up on an American-style culture of sport. I wanted to train twice a day, I wouldn't drink, went to bed early and believed that we should study videos. Harry Gregg came in as a goalkeeping coach and we used to analyse videos together in the afternoon. I liked that, but the other players thought that I was a bit of an idiot. Harry was good for me. My dad made me a goalkeeper and I was already good technically, but Harry worked me and got me stronger physically and mentally. He got me coming for high balls because he was a very arrogant goalkeeper who had done that himself. He dominated his area and that's what I tried to do. Schmeichel used to throw the ball out quickly but I was doing that before him. My handling was great and I don't think a ball went through my legs in my entire career at United."

Bailey was frustrated by the amount of free time he had in the afternoon.

We're The Famous Man United

"You couldn't watch videos every day and I used to go to the pub and sit there as the other lads played snooker. I was useless at pool, let alone snooker, and felt like an idiot. They would have a pub lunch and then go shopping and yet it was only three in the afternoon. I just couldn't do that. I had to be active and finishing work at midday drove me crackers."

It wasn't as if he had a home to go back to, either.

"It was depressing going back to my digs at four in the afternoon and it was already dark. Today they would have sports psychologists looking at things like this. I just had the coach Tommy Cavanagh saying to me, 'You have to be tough to survive in this game. If you can't be tough then piss off'."

Bailey was lonely and felt isolated.

"Almost every player was married except me and the only advice the club gave me was, 'Get yourself married.' I had friends outside of football – but it was difficult to find young single guys with money who could afford to travel or whatever.

"I told my dad that if I didn't make it within a year I was coming home; it was only my passion for football and United that got me through."

Three weeks before the year was out he packed his bags.

"I hadn't made it and I was prepared to go back to South Africa. Then Alex [Stepney] got injured. Paddy Roche was still ahead of me and I was third choice, but after Paddy played in a 5–1 defeat at Birmingham and was roasted by the manager I thought I was in with a shout for the next game against Ipswich."

Bailey was expecting good news when he was called into Dave Sexton's office on the Thursday before the Ipswich game.

"I thought, 'This is it, I'm getting the call up,'" he remembers. "But he actually said, 'I'd like to introduce you to our new keeper Jim Blythe.' I couldn't believe it; he'd gone and signed a new goalkeeper."

Despondent, Bailey called his father and revealed that he was now Manchester United's fourth choice goalkeeper, as a £440,000 fee was agreed for Blythe.

"We agreed that I would go back to South Africa where I would

Gary Bailey

finish my studies," he says. "I had given United my best crack and it was time to leave."

But Sexton wanted to see Bailey again the following morning. "We've got a major problem," said the United manager. "Jim Blythe has failed his medical and you're playing tomorrow. The press want a few pictures of you."

"I thought, 'Holy shit!'" recalls Bailey. "The game was against Ipswich, where I was born and where Dad played. That must have been the good omen."

The prospect of playing for Manchester United, even if it was just once, was enough for Bailey.

"There was talk of signing the Argentine World Cup 'keeper Filiol, but I was happy to play the game then return to South Africa, at least I'd have played once for United.

"The lads were great beforehand. They gave me a lot of support. It was raining and in those days goalkeepers had green cotton gloves rather than those lovely latex ones they have now. The cotton ones were useless in the rain."

But the rain did not diminish the experience of walking out in front of 42,000 at Old Trafford.

"It was the most awesome feeling in the world," he says. "The first song the fans sang was, 'There's only one Gary Bailey.' I absolutely loved it. Early on I headed a ball clear that was intended for Paul Mariner early in the game and the whole crowd went dilly. I thought, 'That's it, I'm here.'"

United won 2–0 and everyone was delighted with Bailey after the game.

"Louis Edwards said, 'Son, you've saved us £500,000.' If I was a bit quicker I would have said, 'Well, don't you want to share some with me?' But I was only 19, on £70 a week and he was the chairman of the club so I didn't say anything. Then Bobby Robson asked to speak to me. He said, 'So sorry, son, that I never got to see you play at Ipswich last year, you've done well.'"

Bailey was still in the team to play Everton at Goodison Park midweek.

"Big Joe Royle and Bob Latchford were their centre-forwards and I got pounded by high balls, kicks and elbows," he recalls. "We got beat 3–0. The press got hold of me after the game and I didn't know what to say. After the Ipswich game they had given me an umbrella and said, 'Come on, let's do a picture of you dancing in the rain.' They used the same pictures a week later with the line: 'Drowning in the rain, Bailey has a nightmare.'"

That episode prompted a warning from captain Martin Buchan.

"He pulled me to one side and said, 'That's what the press will do to you. Keep your mouth shut in future.' That was good advice. We played Chelsea at Stamford Bridge the following Saturday. The press were saying that if I didn't play well then I'd be gone. We won 1–0 and I did all right. From then on I managed to survive. We lost that famous game 5–3 to West Brom but I managed to pull out a couple of cracking saves from Cyrille Regis. Whenever there were question marks about me I followed up with a good game. I stayed in the side and we were soon in the FA Cup semi-finals against Liverpool."

From being a nobody to becoming United's first choice goalkeeper, Bailey's life had changed on and off the field.

"To the lads I'd go out with in Prestwich, suddenly I was a United player. Being Gary in the reserves was good to them, but being Gary in the first team was very different," Bailey remembers. "They changed completely towards me. I had a six-wheeler transit van because I intended to go travelling around Europe that summer, so one day I drove the lads down to Didsbury. We walked into one pub and the lads were chanting United songs. Some City fans were in there, too. I always wore T-shirts and denim jackets, which was quite a student look in South Africa, but they still recognised me, especially after the United fans – my mates – started bowing in front of me. It was all extreme, but fun. Then the City fans were calling me a 'spotty shit' and saying, 'Who does he think he is?' Suddenly a fight started. My mates got stuck into the City fans and, brave as a lion, I sneaked out to my six-wheeler and left."

Dave Sexton got to hear of the incident and called Bailey in to see him on Monday morning.

Gary Bailey

"He accused me of wrecking a pub in Didsbury and he was angry," says Bailey. "The owner of the pub had called claiming that I had started a riot and asked United to pay for the damages.

Dave said, 'Here's the deal. You're wearing jeans and denims but you're a Manchester United player now. Do you know what that means in this city?' I told him that I was a normal guy who wanted to dress normally, but he gave me a load of cash and told me to go to Phil Black's shop in town to kit myself out with new clothes. And he gave me £6,500 to buy a car – which was an awful lot of money then. So much that I thought he was joking."

Bailey went into Manchester to spend his unexpected windfall.

"I walked around wondering how I'd spend the money. I went into Bauer and Millet, the luxury car place at the bottom of Deansgate, to buy a car. I liked Alfa Romeos because they were big in South Africa. I hadn't bought the new clothes yet and the owner of the dealership ignored me as I looked at the car. Eventually, I said that I'd like to chat about the car. He said, 'What do you want to chat about?' He didn't believe that I was interested in the car and told me not to waste his time as he had a business to run. I wanted electric windows and when I mentioned that he looked at me incredulously, more so when I told him I wanted to take the car. I said, 'I was told to give you this card by Les Olive at Manchester United.' He was looking seriously fed up with me by this time. I told him to call Les Olive. He did. He came back full of apologies. I realised then that people would behave towards me not because of who I was, but what I was – a United player."

The students at Manchester Polytechnic treated Bailey much the same as before.

"They were upper-working-class and lower-middle-class students; they were there to work like me and would always help out with notes if I couldn't make a class. The last thing I wanted to do was talk about United and they appreciated that."

When it came to the opposite sex, though, Bailey's life changed completely.

"I'd always noticed the groupies hanging around the club but when I became a first team player they were all over me. I remember thinking, 'Wow, I'm the man.' But then I realised that they were all over every first team player. In discos there was a totally different response. Suddenly I was pulling the best birds around. I really had to keep my feet on the ground and bear in mind that being famous was a huge attraction to women. I had to look a bit deeper than that."

When he wasn't playing the field, Bailey's girlfriends still tended to come from South Africa, until he met up with Miss UK, Della Dolan.

"She was modelling furs at Old Trafford for a company owned by the director Mike Edelson and we started going out," he says. "She was runner-up in Miss World and was beautiful, really stunning. She was a lovely person with a lot of depth and I really enjoyed going out with her.

"I thought I was a little bit of a Georgie Best," adds Bailey. "Della and I were in the papers together and people thought we were some kind of celebrity couple. But she had someone else in her life and it soon petered out."

At United things had gone well for Bailey, even if his pre-match preparations caused raised eyebrows among team-mates.

"For a game at Fulham away in the FA Cup fourth round in 1978/79 I roomed with Jimmy Nicholl. I took a tennis ball with me to away games to throw against the hotel room wall. I'd then dive across the bed to save it as a way of testing my reflexes. Nicholl said, 'Bloody hell, son, what are you doing? Save your energy.' But I was really sharp for the game in a 1–1 draw."

United beat Fulham 1–0 in the replay and then Colchester United by the same score in the fifth round.

"I started to really grow in confidence," says Bailey. "People compared me to the goalkeeper Mervyn Day. In the semi-final, I made a couple of good saves against Liverpool at Maine Road. We were 1–0 up but they were putting a lot of pressure on us and there was a high cross near the end. I didn't know whether to stay or to go out and claim it. I dived out but couldn't get two hands on it and only managed to tip it away from danger. As luck would have it, it went straight to Alan Hansen who knocked it in."

Bailey was left under no illusion about the impact of that mistake in the Old Trafford grill room a couple of days later.

"Sam McIlroy said, 'We were six minutes away from Wembley and we'll probably never get there now.' I felt like I'd let everyone down," says Bailey. "McIlroy turned and said, 'Don't worry, you had to come for the ball.' It was the first time that I'd felt really gutted. I was 20 years old and I felt a huge burden of pressure. I don't think Alex Ferguson would have a 20-year-old keeper today; it's too much pressure and responsibility for someone so young."

Bailey repeated a mantra before the semi-final replay at Goodison.

"I kept saying, 'Don't screw it up again,' and I vowed not to go for any crosses."

Jimmy Greenhoff scored the game's only goal and United were at Wembley.

"I saw the parties after and realised what it meant to the fans. I knew I had to be strong and that a goalkeeper just couldn't afford to make a mistake. That's why the '79 Cup final was such a real blow – because the third and final goal for Arsenal was not a bad mistake. I came for a cross that was curling away. It wasn't like I dropped the cross, I just didn't get there. Alan Sunderland got the other side of Arthur Albiston and knocked it in. Somebody had to take the blame. You could have asked about our marking for the first and second goals, but the clinching moment was the third goal and the defining aspect of it was me going for a cross that I didn't get. I took dogs' abuse after that.

"The abuse toughened me up and I had a blinder the following season, '79/80. We came second behind Liverpool in the league and I'd like to think that a lot of it was down to me and the back four. I was calm and confident and was loving my football. I was visiting a lot of grounds for the first time too, places like White Hart Lane that I'd seen on TV and dreamed of playing in. It was absolutely awesome."

But United couldn't surpass Liverpool in the league.

"Liverpool were at their peak," says Bailey. "If they hadn't been then we would have won the league. We didn't have players like Ian Rush who could slot in goals. We had players like Joe Jordan, who had a lovely touch but was not a prolific goalscorer."

Bailey's progress had not gone unnoticed and he was selected for England at U21 level.

"After playing for England at that level, I was classed as English. Perhaps it was a mistake to play for England at a time when there was Joe Corrigan, Phil Parkes, Shilton and Clemence. I don't think you could have picked a harder time to be England goalkeeper and maybe it would have been a better idea for me to play for Scotland; they had Alan Rough and I'm sure I could have played for them through a family link or having a Scottish wolfhound or something. I would have played in a very good Scottish team and would have had a hundred caps or more."

Bailey was called up for the full England squad at the end of the 1979/80 season. That's when he started to feel the pressure. "Someone really should have helped me out and said, 'You are 20, you've had a gruelling season. Go back home and take a rest.' Instead, I did a tour of Europe with new players who I didn't really know. I wasn't part of the gang and was a bit of an outsider so it was tough mentally. I hadn't recovered any of my energy by the start of the next season.

"Season '80/81 started well though, until we got knocked out of the FA Cup in the fourth round by Nottingham Forest. Trevor Francis got the winner, a header at the near post. It wasn't my fault, but I was so proud of how I was playing and my record that I took the blame for any defensive errors, saying that I should have marshalled the defence better. I stupidly told the press that I took responsibility for the goal and the headlines the following day said: 'Bailey Blames Himself.' My stomach turned when I saw those headlines and I thought, 'Oh dear, now the world is against me.' Yet it was every man for himself when the ship started sinking."

Bailey stopped enjoying his football.

"I found it a real slog for about two years," he says. "Even up to beating Brighton in the 1983 FA Cup final, I wanted to pack in

Gary Bailey

football and return to South Africa. I missed the weather and my family and my batteries were running low. Being involved with England meant I hadn't had a break from football for three years, and I was struggling to fire myself up for games. I was mentally tired and was getting hit in every game by big centre forwards who considered me fair game as I wasn't a kid anymore. I'd had a couple of off years and the press were on my back, team-mates too. People started to crap all over me. The glitz and glamour had gone. The glory boy status had gone, the crowd were on my back and the players were at each other's throats.

I had nobody to turn to because my family were abroad. It was bad when my team-mates turned on me when my form wasn't good. Naively, I thought that they would support me, but I was wrong. It was their living and I could feel the energy change against me. I ended up having treatment for ulcers because of the tension of trying to survive this tough environment. Martin Buchan was very hard on me when I was young too. And I remember Tommy Cavanagh being hard on me. Once, in five-a-side, I let him get the ball before kicking him so hard that he hit the ground. The other players said, 'You nearly killed him.' He said, 'You did that on purpose didn't you?' I said, 'Yes, because I'm sick and tired of the way you treat me.' He never spoke to me again. But, more importantly, the abuse stopped. Maybe it was because I had toughened up; maybe it was because I wasn't worth the trouble to him. Andy Ritchie didn't toughen up and we lost a wonderful talent when he left."

Bailey thinks that United's approach didn't get the best out of genuine talents.

"Look at Nikola Jovanovic, a lovely guy and a very, very good footballer – better than anyone else there in defence. He'd played for a brilliant Red Star Belgrade team, yet entered a screaming, shouting culture that destroyed so many good talents. He took a lot of stick during the Cavanagh era. Dave Sexton was such a mild and meek lovely person who wasn't involved in the shouting, but he was manager and was ultimately responsible. I often envied players at Arsenal under Don Howe. To listen to him and Bobby Robson talk about tactics with England was fascinating because we never had that at Old Trafford."

It was a girl who helped Bailey out of his despair. "I started going out with Kathy Plowright, daughter of David at Granada TV and niece of Laurence Olivier," he says. "She was a bit different, a powerhouse of energy and an awesome personality."

But England's class system still left him confused.

"However, I was studying with middle-class students, playing a working-class game and dating an upper-class girl, so I was all over the place. Kathy drove a gold Mercedes and insisted that she drop me off at the front of Bisham Abbey one day when I was going training with England. I wanted to be dropped around the corner but we were meeting at six and it was five to. The car came screeching to a halt in front of all the players and manager Bobby Robson outside the hotel. The roof was down and pretty much every player went, 'Bloody hell, son, that's some bird!' I stepped out of the car feeling very self-conscious. I told her that she had to go but she insisted on introducing herself to Bobby Robson. They got on like a house on fire."

"Kathy was great for me," Bailey continues. "She told me to believe in my ability and showed me how to have fun again, how to enjoy living in Manchester. Every time we played in London we'd stay at Laurence Olivier's place. She showed me the finer aspects of London that I'd not seen. She took me to shows and we did things that were a little more cerebral. We lived together for four years and built a house by the River Mersey on the Northenden golf course. I designed the house myself based on South African architecture. I built it 18 feet above ground and had a lake built beneath the house. It was the most ridiculous thing I did. I would return from a London away game at two in the morning, only to be woken by the builder five hours later. I started to feel sick and was under terrible strain. The football wasn't going well and the house was a problem, so Kathy took control of that."

A party held at the house caused much amusement to Bailey's team-mates, even though hardly any of them were actually there. The

Gary Bailey

story, which still has the likes of John Gidman and Bryan Robson giggling, was that Bailey held a housewarming party for his posh mates. He gathered his guests and announced a toast to his relationship with Kathy, before a dozen ducks, intended for their new lake, were released. The only problem was that Bailey had forgotten to clip the wings of the ducks which, upon release, immediately flew away.

"The duck story is not true," he says, laughing. "John Gidman told Bruce Grobbelaar who told it on *Wogan*, but the ducks didn't fly away and I had clipped the wings. What happened was that someone left a gate open by the lake and they walked out of the gate and into the river. Whatever, everyone thought I was a prick!"

Bailey considers the Brighton FA Cup win a turning point in his United career.

"It was very important for me psychologically. Two months before that game we lost the Milk Cup final against Liverpool after a long-range effort from Alan Kennedy skipped off the ground and over my hands. Questions were again asked about me. I really had my back to the wall going into the Brighton match. It was 2–2 and Smith had that famous chance right at the very end. I just kept my eye on the ball and came flying out. What made it a good save was that a lot of goalkeepers close their eyes when they come out. I've done it myself. But this time I kept them open and I was able to get there before Gordon Smith or Michael Robinson. When the whistle went, I walked off thinking, 'You've just saved United. You've made one or two errors but you've paid them back.'

"In the replay I kept a clean sheet and made one or two nice saves. My dad had come over from South Africa to watch the match. They are big into witchcraft there and he had seen goalkeepers use a lock and key. My mates had said, 'Gary, you're a nightmare at Wembley; you've conceded seven goals in three games', so Dad gave me a lock and key with a red and white ribbon on. I was to lock the goal before I played in it and then unlock it at half time to allow my team to score in the second half. I said, 'Yeah, yeah, bullshit.' But I went with it and kept a clean sheet against Brighton in the replay, then another one against Liverpool in the Charity Shield and another against

Everton in the 1985 final. So, draw your own conclusions. The other players had their own superstitions. Whether it got me focused or not, it was worth doing."

Off the field, Bailey rarely socialised with his team mates, but he genuinely got on with the more 'professional' of them.

"Ray Wilkins was a lovely person," he says. "Frank Stapleton too, a bit quieter, but a lovely guy. The three of us and even Stevie Coppell shared similar values. We were hard-working pros, and thinking players who wanted to create a thinking culture of how to outmanoeuvre other teams.

"We certainly had the players to do it, Norman Whiteside was a genius of a player for example. If he had had pace he would have been one of the greatest players of all time. Whenever a young apprentice came into the first team dressing-room to collect the boots to clean, one of us would say, 'There's a broom in the corner, go and ask it for a dance.' The timid apprentice would then ask the broom for a dance and the whole dressing-room would shout, 'No, fuck off you ugly bastard.' The kid would creep out of the room as we all laughed. Norman Whiteside came in when he was 15 and it was my turn to tell him. He was a skinhead from Belfast. I said, 'Son, go and ask that broom for a dance.' He said, 'You're fucking kidding me.' I insisted and he told me to get stuffed. He wouldn't budge, so I said again, 'Go and ask the broom for a dance.' I was getting angry and he replied, 'Are you going to make me?' I tried to turn it around by laughing and saying, 'You'll make a footballer one day, son.' But in truth I was really taken aback.

"Three years later, I was in Spain for the World Cup when Norman became the youngest player to play in the competition. I asked him about the incident and why he hadn't asked the broom for a dance. He said, 'Gary, I grew up on the Shankhill Road. I saw people get drills through their knee caps. Do you think that I was scared of you?'"

This all happened, however, before Bailey started martial arts after the incident with McQueen.

"People's response to me changed when they saw I could fight. I broke Colin Gibson's ribs just before he joined us. He was playing for Villa and I came out of the box and went for the ball. He just beat me to it but I did a straight leg challenge, like a karate kick. I heard this crash. They carted him off the pitch and my team-mates were saying, 'Jesus, Gary. We know you do karate but did you mean that?' I didn't mean it at all, but I said, 'Of course I did.' They were so impressed. I realised that you had to fight to impress in England. Gibbo joined us a few months later and when he first walked into the dressing-room, he said, 'Holy shit, my ribs are still sore.'

Whenever we went on tour with United after that, when we went for a drink I'd say to the bouncers, 'Look, I'm with United. If there's any trouble with us don't touch the players, but come to me and I'll sort them out. I actually said to a few of my team-mates, 'You cause trouble and I'll take you out.' I could fight and I had the respect of the players for that. I could be aggressive if I wanted to and take people out."

Bailey played his 300th United game in 1985, yet was still plagued by insecurities after mistakes.

"In the '85 semi-final against Arsenal at Villa Park I was still going through a dodgy patch where I wasn't playing consistently well. Their goal came from a shot which I parried. Tony Woodcock was really quick and put a toe out, deflecting the ball, from which someone scored. It looked really bad on my part, but it was a small error. I thought 'Shit' after that game, even though Robbo and Norman had scored the goals which got us to the final."

Although most of United's success in the '80s came in the FA Cup, they experienced significant highs in Europe.

"We did well, against Barcelona for example, but I was bitterly disappointed on two occasions when we lost in Europe," Bailey says. "Losing to Juventus in 1984 was more acceptable because we were easily outplayed in Turin, Paolo Rossi was superb. But we should have buried Videoton of Hungary and made the UEFA Cup final in 1985. We were a much better team and lost on penalties. It really pissed me off that we kept missing out on the championship and in Europe."

Bailey played in all of United's ten straight victories at the start of the 1985/86 season.

"We should have won the league and Ron should have been the man to make it happen. I felt sorry for Ron that it didn't."

So what went wrong?

"At the start of the season I was playing well and I was excited about United. Paul McGrath was a superb centre-half, so that made a difference defensively. I remember sitting with Gary Lineker before I made my England debut in November '85 and he said, 'United are going to walk the league this year.' We looked the business and I believed that. Then we started leaking goals and not performing. Mark Hughes had agreed to sign for Barcelona and we lost his focus. The spark, and Sparky, disappeared from the team."

What else?

"The drinking culture was a problem, no question. It wasn't a problem for people like Bryan Robson who enjoyed the drinking and still performed perfectly well. But it created a culture that other players were not comfortable with. I believe in looking after your body, watching what you eat and being physiologically stable. I bumped heads constantly with the 'you cope or piss off' home approach.

"During that ten-game run Robbo arranged a session in the Four Seasons in Hale. I thought, 'I'm going to try and be one of the lads. I can fight now and I'm playing well, so I'll give it my best shot.' Well, they drank so quickly – Robbo, Norman, Paul McGrath and Kevin Moran – that I had to stop them buying me drinks. I got to pint number four after an hour before saying, 'Please guys, I can't keep up. I need a break.' Then we had lunch. I hoped that the lunch would sponge up the fluid. After lunch they were on their ninth pint and I was on my fifth. I couldn't take it and stupidly got in my car and drove home, where I was sick. I propped myself up in bed with a jug of water and went to sleep before waking up at 6pm with a stinking hangover. The lads had told me to go back to meet them, so I drove back to the Four Seasons. They were on their 16th pint and were talking a different language, all falling over laughing. I tried to have one more drink but it was the most horrible taste. So I went

Gary Bailey

home again and went to bed. I said to myself: 'Gary you are not part of this culture. You're a loner, you're different and had better get used to that.' I think they cracked 20 pints each that day.

"Ron had the approach that if you got up in the morning and did the business you were OK. I didn't agree. I felt that heavy drinking would do you long-term damage. If it didn't damage Robbo then it certainly damaged Norman Whiteside's and Paul McGrath's careers."

Despite differences of opinion and philosophy, Bailey liked Atkinson.

"He was a good person. He threw a party the night he was fired as United boss. Norman, Strachan, Robbo and I were the only other players who turned up. I thought it was the most terrible sign of disrespect by the rest of the players, many of whom he had brought to the club. I felt very embarrassed by the behaviour of my fellow team-mates that day. I think Ron could have done with a Don Howe to make them more tactically astute. Ron was a great people's person and Mick Brown was not a tactical guy. A lot of games were on a wing and a prayer because we had such great players. Ron had the ability to make it happen; he really did, but needed someone else. I enjoyed Ron but was frustrated that we couldn't have a goalkeeper coach. I wanted a tactical man to discuss how to line free kicks up. I was almost anal about it and wanted to stay after training to practice. That put me in a very bad light with the players. I needed a technical coach to say, 'Hey, you are staying behind after training to practice and work as a unit.' I wanted a Thursday afternoon session with defenders but that didn't happen."

February 1986 saw Bailey pick up a serious injury.

"I was training with England at Bisham Abbey. I dived one way and my leg got stuck in the ground, tearing my cartilage. I had an operation and worked hard to get fit for the World Cup in Mexico, but I pushed it too hard. I told Bobby Robson that I was fine to join the squad and we went to America to acclimatise. On the first day, the goalkeeping coach gave me a gruelling session. That night, I looked at my knee in the bath – it was up like a balloon. The following day the specialist said, 'Don't even think about playing.'

But I stayed with England as an emergency goalkeeper. I was the music man, responsible for the tunes for six weeks. It was so bloody frustrating."

Bailey gained an insight into government intervention in football during the World Cup.

"Before the quarter-final against Argentina we were told, 'Don't stir anything up. The Falklands War is just over and we don't want to cause problems.' The order had come from above. That's why hardly anyone complained when Maradona handballed. That England side was good enough to win the World Cup too."

After the World Cup, Bailey had to endure a second knee operation.

"I had come back from the first operation too quickly and a piece of cartilage had come loose and was ricocheting around my knee like a bullet. That was sorted out the second time."

Bailey then spent a year rehabilitating in Manchester. But what could have been an intensely frustrating period on the sidelines proved to be the opposite.

"I began to enjoy Manchester for the first time. I was on the treatment table and knew that I had a long journey ahead of me and that my knee might never recover. I was having treatment with Robbo and Norman. Without the pressure of playing I started to relax. I had been at the club long enough to be accustomed to the English humour and I had learned to have fun with the players – I was even cracking a few jokes myself. Bryan Robson once made me eat an egg in its shell. He told me that un-peeled eggs were good for you and I pretended to believe him, then as the shell hit the back of my throat I started spitting it out. They were in stitches."

Away from the Cliff, Bailey made good use of his free Saturdays.

"I started to go away for weekends, something I'd not been able to do because I'd always been playing – I'd only missed seven games in seven years. I started going out for meals and would go to the Lake District with Kathy or to London for shows. I started seeing the beautiful parts of England.

"I became a different person. I had become very aggressive in '85/86, partly because of the martial arts. I didn't like the person I

Gary Bailey

was becoming, it wasn't me. I am a gentle and mild person at heart and I became that again when I started to chill out."

The change did not go unnoticed.

"Robbo said to me one day, 'We all said that you were going to moan like hell about your injury but you haven't. I've lost a bet because I thought you'd be throwing your toys out of the pram.' They thought that I was a typically arrogant South African, but maybe they saw a different side of me."

Ron Atkinson said of Bailey, "He always had this burning ambition to be the number-one goalkeeper. At one point he was really paranoid and we had to teach him to relax a little and be patient. It's one thing to be ambitious but it doesn't help to get uptight about it."

"That was fair," says Bailey. "Each of us will beat our own drum 20 years later, but if you had taken Shilton and Clemence away I would have got 100 caps for England. In the end I got two caps – a joke. The timing was wrong for me. It was a shitty feeling when everyone at United was playing internationals, some for very poor teams, and I was the only one left behind while they got the exposure in international weeks. Schmeichel is the greatest 'keeper of all time because he had everything, but Shilton was the best before him. He was such a worker on the pitch.

"It was annoying at England; I'm second behind Gary Owen in the number of U21 caps. I watched players go past me and into the first team, but if you are third-choice keeper you are not involved. It really frustrated me but I couldn't do it. I made my England debut in '85 against Ireland – seven years after getting into the squad. Liam Brady hit a shot in the dying minutes which I would have saved nine times out of ten. But I didn't save this one. We won 2–1 but after the game the crowd were singing: 'There's only one Peter Shilton.' I thought 'Damn'. So it's ironic that my career was curtailed by a knee injury picked up while training for England."

Two decades have given him time to reflect on his time at United.

"My problem was that I couldn't sustain the energy levels into my third and fourth seasons and my form suffered. Harry Gregg was judged by how I played and he suffered too. When Ron came he wouldn't give me a goalkeeper coach which infuriated the hell out of me. Ron wanted his own men and Harry was a Dave Sexton man. That was a real pity because I enjoyed working with Harry.

"I don't think I had a weakness technically," he continues. "People said that my weakness was crosses, but my problem was that I came for crosses I shouldn't have come for because I wanted to get other people out of trouble. I tried to be the greatest goalkeeper in the world but I was too confident sometimes. I should have been shrewder and stayed on my line, but I wanted to help people. Out of ten crosses, I'd get nine of them. But for the tenth someone would hit me, foul me or I'd drop the ball and I'd end up getting nailed. That's why I found it very harsh when people said I wasn't good on crosses. Once I had Paul McGrath there, I felt better. He would cover for me and that helped."

By the time Bailey had recovered from his most serious injury, Alex Ferguson had been at the club three months.

"I was working hard and was very fit," he says. "But at the same time I was questioning what I wanted from life and whether I wanted to be an aggressive goalkeeper anymore. I'd changed as a person during my rehabilitation. I hesitate saying this because fans will think I'm crazy, but I was tired of football and wanted to do something else with my life. I wanted to get home and see my family properly and do something different."

Bailey had split with Kathy.

"I had met my wife to be, a South African girl in Manchester. My sister had called and said, 'I've got the perfect girl for you. She is coming to England. She has relatives in Manchester.' She was involved with someone but I showed her around, we got on well and it went from there. She didn't like football – one visit to Old Trafford was enough for her – and she didn't like money. I knew that she didn't love me because I was a footballer."

Alex Ferguson impressed Bailey too.

"He was sharp and far from a fool," he recalls. "I wanted to play for him but my knee needed to be A1. There was no kidding this man. Alex came to me in March 1987 and said, 'Chris Turner is injured and I need you to play. Also, I need to know what your future is.' That was fair to ask. I told him that my knee wasn't right. He said to give it another go, to see how it went, so I did. I played five games for him and didn't do too badly. I was getting sharper game by game, but my knee was hurting more each time I played. After the fourth game I couldn't train all week and I knew I had a problem because Alex wasn't going to retain a goalkeeper who couldn't train. After the fifth game I couldn't get out of bed the following morning. I knew then that if I was ever going to play again it was going to cost me in terms of my long-term health. I have seen Roy Keane get over worse injuries, but I thought I've done everything I'd wanted to in football. I'd played for the greatest club in the world and I'd been to a World Cup. I wanted to retire at the top and maybe start a new career doing something different."

Bailey spoke with Ferguson, who advised him to see a specialist.

"The specialist told me to pack in the game; that physically I wasn't going to win the battle. Mentally, my heart wasn't in it. So I went back to see Ferguson. He looked me in the eyes and said, 'Son, I'm gutted for you. You're only 28, you've played nearly 400 games for United and you could have gone on to do wonderful things for me. How can I look after you? Why don't you stay on as a goalkeeper coach?'

"I had to decide," remembers Bailey, "but my heart wasn't in it. I had to go home for my personal growth. Alex said, 'Travel back to Old Trafford with me.' So I left my car at the Cliff and went with him. In the car, he said, 'You are no longer a Manchester United player. So what would you do with this club?' Nobody had ever asked me that. I gave him all my ideas. I'm pretty sure that they were crap, but when I got out of the car I really wished that I could have played for that man. I felt that he engendered a wonderful spirit. I wanted to fight and battle for him."

At Old Trafford, Bailey said goodbye to Martin Edwards, with whom he had enjoyed a good relationship.

"I said to Martin, 'There's something about Alex. I think you are going to have a wonderful time with him.' His principles were sound."

Edwards, who had appreciated Bailey's work representing the club in the community by visiting hospitals and schools during his rehabilitation, reminded Bailey that he was owed a testimonial.

First, he held a farewell party at the Northenden house which he put straight on the market.

"Only Gordon Strachan and Norman Whiteside turned up. Ray and Frank had moved on. Strachan got everyone around me in a circle at the end of the evening and sang lovely songs like Auld Lang Syne. I'm not surprised that he has gone on to be a success because he had a lovely nature about him."

The testimonial could have gone better too.

"I was a bit upset at my testimonial," he says. "It's a silly reason really, but Mark Hughes came back to play in it. That was wonderful because it put people on the gate, but at the end the fans weren't singing my name but his. I felt quite hurt, but I understand they also wanted him to come back. Maybe it was just me and, as Ron said, I did get a bit uptight about things. These days you would have advisers who choreograph those things."

Bailey returned to South Africa.

"Ironically, I left Manchester on one of its rare sunny days and arrived back home in the middle of winter. That destroyed my whole image of going back to the sunshine."

A more serious reason for unease was the property market crash.

"I'd invested all my money into properties in London about two months before the market collapsed, so I lost a lot of money there," he says.

Financially, he had benefited from an insurance payout at the end of his career, which stipulated that he couldn't play football again in any country under FIFA regulation.

"But South Africa weren't in FIFA because of the apartheid regime," Bailey explains.

Not that he had any intention of playing again.

"I spent six months in Cape Town without playing any sport, doing a two-year computer science degree in six months. But I was a 31-year-old former England and Man Utd star sitting with university students. I thought, 'You are trying to turn the clock back here, son, and you can't do that.'"

Bailey's knee felt fine, too. "I contacted my dad and said that I thought I could play again. He said, 'Play for Kaiser Chiefs. They are one of the biggest clubs in Africa.' I phoned the owner and he said come up to training. I worked damn hard to play again."

Bailey was the only white player for the Chiefs. "All the black players had heard that I was the Man United goalkeeper and expected a miracle worker," he says. "It was just before Mandela was released and I played in all the black areas and felt proud to be part of that whole pre-Mandela era."

White friends weren't so enamoured.

"I got a lot of stick from whites for playing with blacks," he says. "Just as I'd got a lot of stick in England for being from South Africa – people called me a bloody racist even though I refused to join the army, refused to fight against blacks and get involved in apartheid at all. My white friends accused me of being a sell-out to the blacks, yet most whites didn't know that I played for Kaiser Chiefs because they didn't follow soccer – yet every black in South Africa did."

The culture at the Chiefs was in stark contrast from that at Old Trafford. "I turned up for the first training session on time, but I was the only one there," he recalls. "The custom was that the better player you were, the later you were allowed to turn up. So the star player turned up 90 minutes after me. There was no way I was going to put up with that bullshit so I had a right go at them. They must have thought, 'Who the hell is this guy?'"

Kaiser Chiefs were runners-up in Bailey's first season, 1988/89, and in his second won five of the six trophies possible.

"I was really relaxed," Bailey says. "We played in front of 100,000 on seven or eight occasions. Towards the end of my second year I bumped heads with the coach and decided to start a new career."

The year was 1990, and South Africa was about to go through a cataclysmic period in its history.

"I had met all the ANC people, the soon-to-be black elite, and it was tricky because I lived in a white area with white people who were scared of blacks. Yet I was happy in the company of both. It got very tense before Mandela came out of prison. I was pro-ANC which annoyed whites around me, who felt I was wrong. Yet it all seemed to work out well. There are still problems with whites accepting change, but generally I think it's been a miracle. Hopefully the final couple of steps to complete that miracle will come in the next ten years."

Bailey's first job outside football was in radio, where he hosted a morning show on the credible non-government 702 station.

"They wanted a sports editor and when I went to see them they said, 'On one hand you are over-qualified, on the other you have never done radio.'"

For three years Bailey got up at 4am to go to work.

"That was really tough and financially it was a struggle as the value on my property in London had been wiped out, yet I still had to pay the mortgage payments as rents halved and interest rates doubled. I chipped in a lot from my savings and eventually sold them for what I'd bought them for. That was a drain on resources because I hadn't earned a lot of money playing in South Africa."

After radio, Bailey moved into television when he approached a channel in 1990 about screening English football.

"I said, 'You don't have any English football and I am sure it would be popular.' The guy said no, but he did give me a three-minute slot every Friday to do a preview on the weekend's games. I talked to camera with no help at all."

Bailey's three minutes attracted such acclaim that they became a 30-minute programme.

"Then we did the 1990 World Cup which was shown on TV in South Africa. After that a pay channel approached and asked me to join them. I started off part-time and became full-time. I've been doing that ever since. We go to 46 countries across Africa and I am a household name throughout the Continent. I love it – it's my passion, not my job."

2

Billy Garton

The Salford Lad

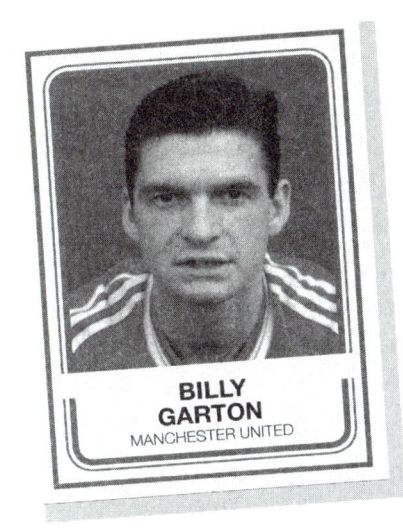

Billy Garton played just 51 first team games for United in his six years at Old Trafford, between 1983 and 1989, yet he's included in this book at the expense of more decorated red-shirted heroes because he was a local boy whose life story demonstrates the harsher side of life as a professional footballer.

"I was born in Salford in 1965 and had a real working-class upbringing," explains Garton, whose Salford accent – a harsher, more nasal blend of Mancunian – remains strong, despite his current life being a world away from where he grew up in Ordsall, a hard estate close to the old docks, a mile from Old Trafford. When Garton was five, a lecturer at nearby Salford University made a film of the living conditions in Ordsall. In two parts, it was entitled *Life in the Slums* and *Bloody Slums*.

Salford, one of the reddest areas of Greater Manchester, is the subject of the Ewan MacColl's song *Dirty Old Town*, famously covered by The Pogues. Yet it is a city in its own right, something its residents are proud of. Vast areas of Salford were re-developed in the '60s and '70s, with the traditional terraced housing replaced by forbidding tower blocks and functional concrete buildings. Yet Ordsall had redeeming features, like Salford Lads' Club, famous for its appearance on the cover of The Smiths' *The Queen is Dead* album. Several Busby Babes would stop at the Lads' Club after games, usually led by local boy and club member Eddie Colman. Colman – a half-back who struck an irresistible understanding with Duncan Edwards in Matt Busby's thrilling young side – lived on Archie Street, across from where Arbuckle's restaurant now stands in the gentrified Salford Quays. It was the street that used to be shown at the start of *Coronation Street*, but successive attempts to regenerate Ordsall mean that only a street sign remains.

Salford Lads' Club still stands. The club opened its doors on the night of 6th February 1958 for locals to mourn the victims of Munich, especially Colman, who died in the air disaster aged 21. He is buried in nearby Weaste cemetery, his grave marked by a black headstone. The statue of a footballer which stood on the grave was vandalised and removed, but his name lives on, not just in the memories of older Reds, but on a Salford tower block, now used as student accommodation by the University of Salford.

"Ordsall was a huge United area and I'm proud to come from there," says Garton. "Eddie Colman went to a school 100 yards from my house. It was great to grow up living so close to Old Trafford, and the culture of United was a big part of my upbringing."

From his bedroom in a two-up two-down terraced house, Garton could see the glare of the floodlights and hear the United crowd.

"Fans used to park their cars in our street and I'd mind them with my mates. Now kids would say, 'Mind your car mate or we'll brick it,' but there was more integrity to it in my day. We'd get 20p or 50p, and if someone gave you a pound you'd run around and tell everyone. That was how we got our pocket money. I didn't get to the match a lot because the deal with the cars was that the guys wanted to see

Billy Garton

you back at their cars after the game. Some of them would only pay then. I would stand by my row of cars with my hands behind my back and say, 'Everything was all right, Mister.' I'd pretend that I'd stayed by their cars, yet I would have been playing football for hours.

"Ordsall was impoverished, and the people were underprivileged. Dad was a painter but he was in and out of work and we often lived by the week on dole cheques. There were four kids and times were hard. Sometimes we didn't have electricity because we didn't have money. We always seemed to be without electricity when there was a game on the telly, so I'd knock on mates' doors and watch the match at theirs.

"Mum and Dad were very family orientated. They taught us good manners and to be respectful, like a lot of working-class people in Salford. We were never scruffy bastards and took pride in our appearance; although I remember taking the studs out of my football boots and using them as trainers. Well, they looked like trainers when you stood on a carpet, but I didn't appreciate that the bottoms were made of plastic and was like Bambi on ice when I tried to run outside. I can't ever remember having a new pair of football boots."

Despite the poverty, Garton is convinced that the bonds forged and standards learnt growing up in Ordsall were vital in later life.

"A lot of great people went on to better things from Ordsall because they had good values," he says. "Take my best mate Les. He is two years older than me, and when he was 16 he used to pay for me because I had no money and he had a job. He'd die for me – you get a bond like that when you come from a place like Ordsall. Where I live now is like paradise on earth, but there's little loyalty. People want to be an acquaintance but it would be tough to get close to people. Where I grew up my mates stuck together through thick and thin. If you were ever on your arse mates would help you out, either financially or emotionally. That did and still means a lot to me. Mates were like family and any scallies who just looked after themselves ended up with no mates."

There was a flip-side.

"Les would get up to all the rogue stuff," admits Garton. "When

We're The Famous Man United

I was at United I'd finish training with the first team at the Cliff and go to see him in this shitty house he bought in Broughton. The house was full of villains and likeable rogues, but I never removed myself from that because I didn't want to. Those people were my heritage."

Despite the distractions, Garton remain focused on his football career.

"I was really into football," he says. "I knew every player from every team and read loads of books about football. I would buy the books from jumble sales for about 3p. My mates would look at toys, but I was into books. Mates liked United and knew that you had to follow them, but they weren't really into the memorabilia and the statistics like I was. I would read about football every night, soaking up facts. I had a book about the history of the World Cup which was like my bible. I loved that. I would learn the teams in the competition going back to 1930. I could still name the Uruguay team from 1930. I saw the World Cup as the pinnacle – that was the highest that you could go as a footballer."

He also has a confession to make.

"Ordsall was so red that everyone knew the only blue family in the area were the Murphys. Yet there was a period in the late '70s when City had a great team and for a while I toyed with the idea of supporting them," Garton says. "I wasn't the type of person to follow a team because everyone else did. I loved Colin Bell and the way he played football. He was elegant and always looked like he was in control – I wanted to be like him. Eventually I saw the light and my support for United never wavered. City? I can't stand them now!"

Garton played football too, yet a loyalty to his friends meant he rejected offers to play for the best junior teams in the Salford district like Bar Hill, or Deans – the Swinton-based club Ryan Giggs would play for.

"I wanted to stick with my mates at Salford Lads' Club. We didn't have a good team and I was the best player, but I didn't want to leave them. The Lads' Club was an escape from the mundane, underprivileged and upsetting lifestyle for most of us. For me it was an escape from the problems at home, where Mum and Dad were not getting on. The club was a community where you could play

Billy Garton

indoor football and table tennis. I would pay my subs and go every night. The idea was to get the kids off the street and keep them on the straight and narrow. That was a pipe dream to some degree because kids still got in trouble away from there. We had some rough families, but if you weren't prepared to conform and behave yourself then you wouldn't be let in the club.

"Nobody vandalised the Lads' Club," he says. "We protected what we loved. And if anyone robbed from their own in Salford then the handy lads would fill them in or they would have to move out. I thought that was right.

"I probably played at Salford Lads longer than I should have, and eventually my focus switched to playing for Salford Schoolboys. The scouts from United were watching and I was quickly signed up and began training at the Cliff in the school holidays."

Garton realised that he had a serious chance of being a footballer and his emphasis switched from football statistics to winning an apprenticeship with Manchester United.

"I was worried that I wasn't going to get offered an apprenticeship, but I was and I signed it in 1981, the year I left school. I was on £16 a week and my mum got a brown envelope every week from United with another £25 in for my keep. United were good like that and I thought it was very respectful that they gave my mum the money. Mum was by now living alone next door to one of the real heavy families called the Dansons. It was great for me because I played football so they were fine with me, and they used to say, 'Don't worry about your mum, she'll be fine. Nobody will rob your mum's house.' That gave me comfort knowing that someone was watching out for my mum. It wasn't a case of only the strong surviving in Ordsall, because the old and infirm were protected. There were hard people in Ordsall who were ruthless at times, but there were unwritten rules that were not broken."

Ordsall was in effect a self-governing estate, where problems were sorted out internally. Outsiders, and authority, were distrusted. It even had a 'Grasswatch' van which contained messages to deter potential informers to the police and social services.

"I knew the bloke who did that," says Garton. "The police had no authority in Ordsall. Rightly or wrongly they were perceived as the enemy. The people policed the estate themselves and the police were aware of that. They knew that the gangsters would rule with an iron fist and sort the troublemakers out."

One advantage of living in Salford was that he didn't have to move away from home like the majority of youngsters who sign for United.

"I would get the bus to the Cliff every morning. Norman Whiteside and Clayton Blackmore were the same age as me," he recalls.

The trio, along with Mark Hughes and Graeme Hogg, played in the 1982 team which reached the Youth Cup final, losing out to Watford 7–6 over two legs.

"Clayton is a great guy and we had a tight relationship. He wasn't really streetwise when he arrived from Neath. You needed to be streetwise when you came to Manchester and he had the piss taken a bit at first."

Blackmore could take a nod from Garton, a young casual who wore the right clothes and listened to the right music. "I would wear Fred Perry T-shirts and black Slazenger jumpers," he says. "I had a big fringe which I used to flick across, and I was into The Jam big time. I still listen to their music, but you have to be in the right mood. It was moody music and very political because Paul Weller was political. Weller was writing about the things I was going through and I could relate to his criticism of government and poverty – songs like 'That's Entertainment'."

Politically, Garton never wavered.

"I voted Labour because my dad voted Labour and his dad did too. Even when I was getting well paid as a footballer, I voted Labour. People couldn't believe it, because I was in the high tax bracket, but I wasn't voting for myself but for the people. Voting Conservative would have been a betrayal of my people."

Yet Garton would still have to overcome substantial obstacles before he could become a well-paid footballer.

"Everyone was scared of Eric Harrison," he remembers. "He was a great coach but he ruled with an iron fist and that was his style. I couldn't see the method in his madness at the time. I went head to head a few times with Eric. He was fighting material and he wanted you to be like that too. He later said that he did things on purpose because he felt it was character building; that he was teaching you about life as well as football. Eric would make me feel so small sometimes that I'd go home and cry. There were times when I thought that he didn't rate me as a player or a person. He was talking to all the young lads at the Cliff one day and he caught me looking across to where the first team were training. He slaughtered and ridiculed me, saying, 'You're a fucking million miles from that. You keep your eyes on me, you fucking wanker.'"

But Garton did progress, at a very young age.

"I got in the reserves for one game when I was 16, without having played a single game in the A or the B teams. It was a neat experience, playing at Old Trafford. I was a snotty-nosed kid from Salford playing with internationals like Jimmy Nicholl, Nikola Jovanovic and Paddy Roche. United must have thought something of me to play me in the reserves at 16. And because I had this knowledge of all the players, I knew that I was marking John Richards for Wolves in that game and knew all about him. Maybe some of the other guys wouldn't have known who he was, but I knew how many goals he'd scored in his career and what his weight was."

Garton puts his progress down to his ability to listen.

"I was quite a smart kid academically and digesting information came easy to me. I always tried to be more knowledgeable about how to play the game and whenever I was asked to step up a level, I was usually able to do it. I had good positioning and was pretty quick, but what really helped was that I listened to every word that Eric said and tried to absorb everything he was teaching us. I was able to implement information easily."

At 17, Garton travelled to Hong Kong and Australia with the first team on a post-season tour. "The older guys looked after us," he remembers. "United wanted to short-change the younger lads with the spending money and gave all the senior pros £1,000 but tried to give us £200. Gordon McQueen and Robbo made sure that we got the same as them – and then wouldn't pay for any drinks."

Garton signed professional terms in 1983, aged 18.

"I'd striven to be a pro and again I was very nervous about getting a contract. Although I think I knew I was going to get one because I was playing in the reserves quite regularly. Big Ron had intimated to me a few times that I was doing all right and told me that if I kept doing what I was doing then I'd be in the first team soon. I travelled to a few games with the first team just to get used to the experience so I knew I was doing pretty well. When I was called into the office and told that I was going to get a pro contract that was the high point of my career so far."

Garton admits that the money, about £220 a week, wasn't fantastic.

"But that didn't matter as it was almost all spending money. I didn't have a mortgage and I bought a car off a kid in Ordsall, a mark two Escort 1600 Mexico. It was red with sports wheels. I painted the inside of the wheels red and black so that they would go with the car. Gordon Strachan used to rip the piss out of me for that and called me 'the Devil'. It was a bit boy-racerish and I had it for two years until the club gave me a car."

He made his first team debut against Burnley in the Milk Cup in 1984. "I found out I was playing, with Ron at his flippant best. I was walking to the canteen at the Cliff and he was walking into his office. He just walked past and said, 'Fancy playing tomorrow night?' 'Fancy playing where?" I asked. 'We've got a game tomorrow night, the first team,' he said. 'Right, I fancy playing.' I think Ron told me that way before putting the team sheet up so I could start getting my head round the idea."

Fans expect players to list trophy-winning moments or great goals as their career highlight, yet many, be they Steve Coppell or Billy Garton, list it as their first team debut.

"It was the greatest day of my life," Garton remembered. "You dream and work towards becoming a pro and when you play one game, just one game, you've proved that you can do it. I'll always thank Big Ron for giving me my debut. There were certain parts of his personality that were not to everyone's liking, yet for me he was very knowledgeable about the game."

Billy Garton

Garton's mode of transport to his debut game was straight out of a Roy of the Rovers' script.

"I got the 58 bus from Ordsall Lane to Trafford Bar and walked to the ground from there. It was 3.30 in the afternoon when I got on the bus and there was a guy in front of me reading the back page of the *Evening News*. The headline was 'Billy the Kid to make debut'. I was sitting behind him with my boots in a bag.

"I walked the final 20 minutes to the ground in my suit. Nobody knew who I was. But it was tough to go unrecognised from then on."

His debut was an occasion for the family to enjoy.

"My nana, my mum's mum, had watched me in every youth and reserve game so I was delighted that she got to see me play for the first team a year before she died. We won 4–0 and Sparky scored a hat-trick. We didn't concede a goal and I did pretty well. The game was a blur, but the feeling and emotion were so special. Afterwards, I went in the Jubilee [an Ordsall pub] for a pint. Everyone was congratulating me, but with that came a level of expectation. People were thinking that I'd become a first team regular so there was an added pressure."

Garton didn't become a regular, but one appearance for United's first team was enough to give him a high profile locally. With that, he saw a different side of having a high profile, of being a local boy who'd done well. Anthony H. Wilson once commented that Mancunians always like to piss on their own. And Noel Gallagher, when defending his decision to leave Manchester for north London after making it with Oasis, once said, "If I go into my local in Manchester and buy everyone a drink then I'm a flash bastard. If I don't, I'm a tight bastard.'"

"I'd try not to be big time," explains Garton, "try just to be one of the lads – and yet you'd still get the odd knobhead saying, 'What are you doing coming in here, Flash Harry?'

I think it is a lot worse now for footballers. People don't have the same respect and it's not cool to have a hero who's a footballer, to be seen to kiss arse. And I used to get one or two jealous bastards saying things like, 'Our Johnny was better than you and he could have been a pro,' or 'Our Joey was on United's books but he walked away from it.' They were from the type of people who sit at a bar slating players on the box. To this day, I hate it when I'm in a pub and someone says that so and so is a crap player and that they could do better than them. If I know them, I am not scared of saying, 'No, you couldn't do better; he's playing at the highest level.'"

Garton's connections meant he didn't have too many problems.

"I grew up with a lot of lads who became villains. I'd get the hero status and the lads were fine with me because I was the local boy made good, the working-class hero. Most of them were proud that I played for United, but there were one or two arseholes who made playing for the club a double-edged sword. My dad was the proudest man around when I played for United and for me nothing changed. I'd still go down to the Jubilee with him after playing at Old Trafford. I didn't have pretensions of going to Worsley to sit in the Bridgewater [a canal-side pub frequented by footballers and perma-tanned babes]."

Garton's roots were something that Ron Atkinson put to good use in the dressing-room.

"United were getting criticised in the mid-'80s by people who said that the players did not appreciate what it meant to play for Manchester United," he explains. "So Big Ron used me as an example and got me to tell the players what United meant to the people of Manchester and Salford. It was dead easy. I told them that there were people who would go without food and spend their last penny to watch United. They'd travel to Newcastle on a Wednesday night when it was freezing, take the following day off and risk getting the sack. I believed strongly in what I was talking about. Further down the line, when we got our arses kicked 5–1 by City in September '89, that was the only reason why we lost. There was no-one in that team who really knew what the Manchester derby meant. We lay down and got what we deserved that day. If you had a Keano or a Robbo in your team and you were getting your arse kicked, they would break someone's fucking legs.

"I wasn't a hard player or a hard person. I was very streetwise; you

Billy Garton

can't help that where I'm from. I could have a fight, but I didn't go looking for trouble. I boxed when I was at school, so if I had a fight I'd get a few good early punches in and try and win that way. As a player I was quite fast, smart, I read the game well and I could play.

"I used to go to a lot of games and watched United away at Liverpool, City at Everton. I had a couple of situations where my mates were involved in hooliganism and there were skirmishes. When I was an apprentice, I would go to games in my jeans and regular clothes. I would hang out at the top of Warwick Road with my mates who were looking out for away fans, but I had to be careful not to get involved in any trouble. Then I would use my player's pass and go and watch the game from my seat. It was a mad existence. I had to stop that when I was in the first team."

He didn't drop his mates though.

"I'd meet my mates in town after the game and they would be looking for Scousers or whatever. That was the culture. It was a buzz, being with your mates as they talked about the events of the day. I had to be so careful because I knew the dire consequences if I was involved in trouble."

Garton avoided trouble, but once dropped his brother in it, badly.

"I got my brother seats for Everton away," he explains, pronouncing 'Everton' as 'Ever'on' in the most Salfordian of accents. "They were in the main stand and he went with his hoolie mates. They were clocked for being Mancs straight away and started fighting before being chased outside. Our Dave was like, 'You could have told us that the tickets were with the Everton fans!'"

Following the 1985 FA Cup final win, Garton travelled to the Caribbean with the first team for a post-season holiday, which he remembers for Gordon McQueen's antics.

"Gordon McQueen was so funny. We went on a glass-bottomed boat one day. It's fair to say that [assistant manager] Mick Brown was never going to be a male model. So as we stared at the fish through the glass, Gordon said, 'The fish are paying to come and see Mick.' Gordon was ruthless. We were hanging off a raft in the ocean off Trinidad. There were a few birds around and Gordon dropped his trunks and had a shit in the water. The shit was floating around the raft near people's feet and that. He was such a fucking lad with a real unique sense of humour."

There were problems with the accommodation on the trip.

"We were booked into the shittiest hotel to start with in Jamaica," he says. "And Gordon wasn't having it. He said, 'We're the famous Man United and we're not staying here.' We had a team meeting in this crappy hotel with Les Olive [United's club secretary for 30 years and later a director, Olive died in May 2006], who held the purse strings. All the senior pros said, 'We've just won the FA Cup, we're not staying here.' Big Ron was already staying in the five-star Royal Caribbean so he was sorted. Les agreed with us and we moved out. As we sneaked out of the hotel, the hotel owner was just putting the finishing touches to his 'Welcome Man United – FA Cup Winners' banner by the front entrance. The poor guy was devastated.

"You lived and breathed your team-mates. It was more like a family than work because you spent so much time with them. You really became close and there were never any secrets. If anyone had something on anyone then everyone in the dressing-room knew."

Yet injuries blighted Garton's early United career and he featured infrequently in Ron Atkinson's final two seasons at the club.

"I had problems with my hamstring and that's one reason why my early career floundered," he says. "I think United had big expectations for me, but I kept pulling hamstrings. Later on, I found out it was because I had a protruding disc which was pressing against my sciatic nerve. I had this pain down the back of my legs. I had a back operation to sort this out and that kept me out for six months. The injuries got me seriously down. Every footballer will tell you that. I wasn't a good watcher; I wanted to be out there playing and not sat on my arse."

In March 1986, he was fit enough to go on loan to Birmingham for three months.

"Birmingham was the perfect escape because I wasn't getting in the first team at United and I needed to be playing at a high level. Birmingham made me a better player. I went from being young Billy

Billy Garton

Garton in a team of internationals at Old Trafford to someone who they looked up to at Birmingham. I was a bigger fish in a smaller pond and it made me grow up really quickly. They were fighting relegation and I played five games there from which we won three. We beat Villa 3–0 which made the fans very happy. John Bond was manager. I had heard loads of bad things about him but he was great with me."

Birmingham wanted to make the move permanent but Brian Whitehouse, United's reserve manager, watched Garton's five games for the Brummies. "I played really well and went straight back into the first team when I went back to Old Trafford," he says. "Birmingham ended up getting relegated which was sad."

Garton's face seemed to fit when Alex Ferguson arrived at the club in November 1986 and he played in Ferguson's first FA Cup team, a 1–0 victory over Manchester City in January 1987.

"We were confident of beating Coventry at home in the fourth round, and I really fancied us to get to Wembley that year, but that was the year they won it," he remembers. "I played against Cyrille Regis and bounced off him four or five times. It was as if I was a fly and he was swatting me. If I have one regret as a player it was that I wasn't physically strong enough. I didn't do the weights to build myself up until much later in my career."

United's defensive muscle came from elsewhere.

"We had Kevin Moran, Gordon McQueen and Paul McGrath. My make-up was different to those players because I was more of a footballing centre-half. I loved playing there because there was always action and a kudos from playing in that position. If you play well against a great forward – and more often than not the forward is the other team's best player – then you get the plaudits. I played against Andy Gray a few times and played him really well.

"Yet I loved the freedom of playing full-back because you could get forward and get crosses in. If I'm honest, I don't think I had the speed to be a great full-back. It was tough for me when I came up against a fast winger. Newcastle had a Brazilian player called Mirandinha – he had blazing speed. Mickey Adams was very quick for Coventry too. I would have rather marked someone like Trevor Steven who was a jinker than quick players."

Garton's highs and lows on the field were mirrored off it.

"My private situation wasn't ideal," he says. "I was living with a girl and we had a baby, my daughter Lauren. But I wasn't happy there. In some respects being a young professional footballer was really exciting. The social scene was good and there was a great attraction. I was playing for Man United, had a nice car, wore the right clobber and went out with my superstar mates. I had a great time, but I have some regrets. It all came too soon. I settled down too soon and wasn't faithful. I regret that.

"You have to be careful that you take the right path," he adds. "The social scene has slowed a lot of players down and yet some of my happiest memories were being with the lads on tours and in the pub."

Garton's best spell for United came at the start of the 1988/89 season. "I finally got over my back problems and I was in the team every week. Credit to Fergie, he said, 'Don't train all the time; get plenty of rest to make sure that you are fine for the matches.'"

Despite Ferguson's patience, a sporadically fit Garton was not going to offer a long-term solution for a manager who was under increasing pressure to win trophies. In October 1988, Ferguson did a deal for another defender, the veteran Ulsterman Mal Donaghy from Luton Town. In 1989, he bought five new £1 million-plus players, paying a record £2.3 million for defender Gary Pallister from Middlesbrough. It was clear that Garton's future was not at Old Trafford and he began to look at his options.

"I wasn't sure that Fergie was going to keep me. Arthur Albiston knew Mel Machin [the Manchester City manager] well and said that he wanted to speak to me. United agreed to sell me and I signed for City in 1989." The fee was to be decided by a tribunal with United asking £390,000 and City offering £150,000.

"You're always signed subject to medical," Garton explains. "My photo was on the back of the *Evening News* with Mel Machin and Wayne Biggins, another new City signing."

The contract, which he still has, was a good one.

"It would have been a great deal for me with a £60,000 signing-on fee. I was on to get a huge bonus if City were promoted, plus a contract of £700 a week for the first year. Leaving United and moving to City was a major decision for me, but I'd grown up by then. It was my livelihood, my profession. I'll always love United, but this was a great deal that would have meant that I could have stayed in Manchester."

However, Garton failed the medical. His voice trails off as he starts to explain why.

"By the time I signed for City, an illness had kicked in. I had started to suffer symptoms on a pre-season tour of Malta. I had the shits for about five days and didn't really feel myself. I was light-headed and always tired, but I thought it was a stomach bug. The symptoms stayed with me though. I had blood tests and they diagnosed me with having glandular fever and said it would be over it in a couple of months.

"I had already started having the blood tests when I did the deal with City who, understandably, said that they were not prepared to sign me until I had the all-clear medically."

However, the doctors struggled to find out what was wrong with him.

"For three years I just didn't get better, and eventually I discovered I had what they were now calling ME or 'chronic fatigue syndrome'. You get it when there has been a virus in your system and your body reacts like it is still there, with your cells acting like they are being attacked. I did not have a clue what it was. The worst thing was that I always felt light-headed and dizzy. I think I could have got away with working in an office, but I had to play football. I felt shattered all the time. I got bad advice too. One doctor basically dismissed my symptoms and said, 'Get on with it'. He told me to train and push myself through it. When I later spoke to specialists they told me that that was the worst advice that could have been given and that I should have rested.

"I had 18 months on my contract when I was first diagnosed and even though Fergie was very supportive, I was devastated. I was embarrassed driving to the Cliff every day. Alex was making me report in as I was under contract and I had to explain to people that I wasn't getting any better. I would waste away the morning, read the paper or walk around the field. It was embarrassing just being there. Nobody believed what I was saying. I felt like I was going nowhere, that nobody was listening to me and that I wasn't making sense. I went in to see Alex one day and broke down in his office. I demanded a second opinion and he agreed. It brought some relief when my condition was then diagnosed.

"I felt like a lot of people thought I was on the blag, that I was imagining things and people questioned my mental state. The problem was that I didn't look ill. If you have a broken leg people can see the evidence. I heard rumours about myself, based on ignorance rather than malice. The other players were great and I don't ever remember anything being said, but lads in Ordsall would say, 'What the fuck's up with yer? Just get out there and run.' I knew that a consequence of not recovering was that I was going to be released when my contract ended, and that's ultimately what happened.

"I had a mixed bag with Alex. I got into trouble a couple of times for coming in late. He wanted people to report players if they were out pissed up, misbehaving. He nurtured a grass mentality which put everyone on guard. I can understand why he did it because a lot of players were going off the rails by drinking in the afternoon. People reported me a couple of times. I came home one night drunk as a lord to my little apartment in Worsley. For some reason I needed to get a music tape out of the car, but I was that drunk that I walked out with nothing on except one big monster slipper. I walked into the car park and in my mind I was gone for five minutes. My mate came out and said, 'You've been gone about half an hour, what are you doing?'

"I was called into Alex's office after training the following morning. He said: 'Where's your other slipper?' I pretended to act daft but then he gave me a dressing-down and fined me two weeks wages for embarrassing the club. One of the neighbours had called in.

Billy Garton

"I played for three years under Alex and he gave me the chance to play and to prove myself after injuries. I fully respect him for that. He's a fantastic manager because he's so good at man-management. He turned that club on its head when he arrived and completely changed the mentality of the place. To do that at an organisation as big as United was a massive achievement. He did little things like trimming down the excesses on away games. We would be used to à la carte menus in five-star hotels. He would say that the set meal was good enough for us and banned room service. It felt more professional and better organised. I felt that I had to be more responsible. Players would load the club up with expenses and Alex just stopped all that.

"Alex sorted the training out too. We had to play by his rules, and if you turned up for training smelling of beer you would get fined. If you carried on, then you would be out of the club. Nobody could believe it when he got rid of Norman Whiteside and Paul McGrath – who was one of the best players in the country at the time. Alex took a brave decision, but he realised the damage that a drinking culture could have."

In May 1990, as Ferguson won his first trophy with FA Cup success over Crystal Palace, Billy Garton retired from professional football.

"I was depressed and seriously sad that my time at United was up. My first thought was, 'How am I going to survive?' I had a mortgage and a daughter. I needed to run a car, yet I was still sick and unable to do a proper day's work. Did suicide cross my mind? Yes. There were a couple of times when I was driving when I thought about it. I thought of my options and suicide was one of them. Then I started to think of how I would do it. I was so desperately sad, yet I'm not the type of person who would take his own life and that's why I didn't do anything. I felt that suicide was the selfish way out. I know that some people do it because they are not thinking rationally, but you leave everybody else with the hurt, pain and financial worry. It might have been the selfish answer for me, but it wasn't the answer for my daughter, Mum, Dad or other people close to me."

Manchester United didn't help his predicament by refusing Garton a testimonial game.

"The chairman at the time was making it difficult, and I don't know to this day if Alex had anything to do with the decision or not. I would have loved a testimonial, at Old Trafford, but I wasn't fussed about the money. It was the same year as Robbo's testimonial so maybe they didn't want to grant another. I think that testimonials should be for players who have had their careers curtailed through injury or illness and I think United got it wrong. Robbo was a millionaire and United gave me 20 grand to walk away."

A group of Garton's friends were determined that he should have a benefit game.

"The testimonial committee approached United about using Old Trafford and the request was turned down, saying that the game might only attract 15,000. So my mates decided to organise one without United's help. It really annoyed me that it came to that. I wanted my final send-off to be at Old Trafford; instead I was embarrassed because it was at the Willows in Salford [the rugby league ground]. Salford Rugby League Club were very helpful, but I shouldn't have done my final walk out at a rugby ground. It rained all day, it was freezing and I was seriously down. The players showed up and Alex did too, but I was angry that day at the circumstances."

Four thousand United fans attended.

"I was pleased with that," says Garton. "It rained so hard that I don't think I would have bothered if I was a fan."

Garton's next move was to enrol on an FA coaching course to do his 'A' badge, which was ironically held at the Cliff. He could cope with the theory, just not the playing. The course would benefit him in the long term.

"No matter how much you know, if you've not got that piece of paper saying that you are qualified then it means nothing," he attests.

Garton researched his illness thoroughly.

"I'd spend hours in Central Library reading medical articles. I needed to know how long it was going to go on for. I wrote a couple of articles about my condition in the medical journals. The bottom

Billy Garton

line was that the only cure was time. People reacted differently to different treatments and for me it just gradually went away over time. I did a few articles in the papers about my illness and a lot of people wrote letters to me. There was an organisation which had literature and meetings so I attended those. There was a big article about my illness in the *People*. It was a double-page spread about what I was going through. Pallister and Bruce had just become a defensive partnership and they weren't quite doing it, with Pallister looking a bit rocky. There was an article about this right under mine. At first glance, it looked as if I was questioning whether Pallister and Bruce were good enough for Man United. The press can stitch you up like that sometimes."

Garton would find out what Alex Ferguson thought of the article on his next visit to the Old Trafford.

"I had just left the club and I had to go to Old Trafford to pick something up," he explains. "The first team were training at Old Trafford. I was walking down the tunnel to the dressing-rooms and Fergie came flying at me. He was really angry, saying, 'You fucking coward, tell them [Bruce and Pallister] to their faces what you think about them.' I was in no mood for him at the time because I was angry with all the testimonial shit. So we ended up going head to head in the tunnel under the main stand. We both went for each other. Keith Kent, the groundsman, split it up, then I went straight into the dressing-room and said to Pally and Bruce. 'He thinks that I wrote that article and you have to tell me now that you don't think I wrote it.' They said, 'We read the article and knew quite well that it wasn't you, that it was by the reporter.' Fergie came in and he had calmed down. I told him, 'These two don't think that I've written the article.' He admitted, 'I've not even read the article, somebody told me about it. I'm sorry. I apologise.' He called me later that afternoon to apologise properly."

By 1992, Garton's health had started to improve to the extent that he was able to take the manager's job at Salford City in the North West Counties League.

"I loved it there," he remembers. "I was never big time and didn't have ideas that I was going to manage a pro club, I just wanted to be involved in football again. I knew a lot of the lads who played and loved the craic in the dressing-room. The camaraderie and togetherness of the team were what I had really missed after leaving United.

"It was a challenge being a manager but I loved it. I was playing too. I was sent off in my first game for fighting! A big crowd had come to watch as it had been all over the papers that I would be manager. Things weren't going well on the field and I got frustrated. A lad tackled me and half threw a punch as we fell. I smacked him in the face and was sent off.

"Then Mike McKenzie, a great local semi-pro manager, called me and asked me to play for Witton Albion, who were in the Unibond Premier division. I loved it there too and was earning really good money. I was at university doing a degree and getting £250 a week to play football. Being a mature student, a high percentage of my mortgage was being paid too. I was doing better financially than when I played for United."

McKenzie went to Hyde United, whose Ewen Fields ground currently stages United's reserve team games, and asked Garton to go with him as player coach.

"I had some of the best years of my football life at Hyde and we twice got to the semi-final of the FA Trophy. I was playing against tough nuts that had just come off the building site so I needed to do the weights. I should have done them earlier in my career. We were beating good teams like Stevenage who had Barry Hayles, who later played in the Premiership with Fulham, playing for them. We played in the FA Cup first round against Darlington, a great highlight for the club."

After completing his degree, Garton did some voluntary work in local schools to see if he would take to a new vocation – as a school teacher. He liked it and got a job teaching at a primary school in Altrincham in 1994. He met Francine, a Liverpool girl, in Bojangles, a Manchester bar that wasn't named after Ron Atkinson. Francine was a dancer at ballet college in Manchester. They dated and later married. Life was definitely on the up.

"I got promoted really quickly at school and was soon deputy

Billy Garton

head," recalls Garton "The head teacher was fantastic and taught me a lot about man-management and how to deal with people, which has come in very useful."

Arthur Albiston tells a story about Garton from that time.

"I was on the Metrolink back from Manchester when I overheard two posh ladies talking about the new deputy head at their kids' school," recalls Albiston. "They were all excited, saying that he was really good looking [Garton was known as 'Brylcreem' by some team-mates] and that he used to play for Manchester United in the 1980s."

Albiston leaned forward to listen into their conversation, but no name was mentioned. Vexed, he spent the rest of the journey back to Altrincham thinking of who it could be before concluding that someone must be telling a few lies.

"I couldn't think of anyone who played in the '80s who was capable of being a deputy headmaster and was good looking too," says Albiston. Yet the story was true.

"A month later my wife told me that Billy Garton had been made deputy head of a primary school in Altrincham. Then the penny dropped."

In 2001, Garton's life took another twist, thanks to Jeff Illingworth, his former PE teacher from Ordsall High School. Illingworth had lived in San Diego for 20 years, coaching football. Garton had stayed close to him and had been out to California on holiday a few times to help out with coaching.

"The last time I went out, he told me that he was thinking of starting a soccer club, and asked if I was interested in moving out there and being a part of a new club called Carmel Valley Manchester Soccer," explains Garton, who uses the word 'soccer' throughout the interview – and apologises each time for not saying 'football'.

"We moved in 2001 and it has gone well ever since. We have three kids, Billy and Bobbie Leigh and Frankie, and my daughter Lauren comes to visit from England. I have a programme with 600 kids and 27 teams. My wife has a dance studio with 700 kids. Things are going really well financially, and the way of life here is great for a family.

We're The Famous Man United

The weather is fantastic and we live by the ocean on a golf course. We have worked hard to get where we are – I'm a believer that you get out of this life what you put in. We are never complacent and we are honourable with the staff that we employ and we get on all right with them. The values I was taught as a kid are still the values I have now.

"I'd love to get to the stage when I can semi-retire and enjoy life without worrying about the financial implications. Too many people I know have got to retirement age and have never had the chance to enjoy it because they've died a year later. I want to enjoy my kids and do a bit of travelling."

He keeps in touch with friends in Manchester.

"I still see the likes of Robbo, Big Norman and Arthur when I am back in Manchester. Kevin Moran's son came out here last year and stayed with us. Most footballers tend to move on, it's the nature of the beast that you are nomadic and are always moving on and building new relationships with people. You are friends, but at the back of your mind you know that you are colleagues too."

And life by the ocean gives him time to reflect on his time at United.

"I still look back at every moment I spent at United. I have some good memories and some not so good ones. Because I was a Salford lad, it meant so much more for me to play for United. It was a worldly experience where I went from playing on the streets to travelling the world. It brought me fame in my own little world where I signed autographs and posed for photos on the streets. It was a great life and the most significant thing was that without my time at Man United, my reputation here would just be the same as everybody else's. The knock-on effect of being a former United player is always there. I want my kids to know that their dad played for the biggest club in the world as they get older. I've tried to get my eldest son into football and I've bought him some factual books on football hoping that he'll get the same pleasure out of it that I did. My books are still at my dad's in Ordsall. My room is almost untouched from when I left the house when I was 15. It's like a little shrine to Manchester United."

3

Bryan Robson

Captain Marvel

BRYAN ROBSON
MANCHESTER UNITED

March 2006 in a blustery West Bromwich, and the then Albion manager Bryan Robson is under pressure. Days earlier, Manchester United had beaten his struggling side, reducing its chances of another late relegation escape. During the game, the travelling United fans sang, 'There's Only One Bryan Robson'.

Naturally, he waved an acknowledgement. That didn't go down well with the frustrated locals, just as it hadn't done with Birmingham City fans when Steve Bruce responded in the same manner months earlier.

At the time this book was being put together, Robson and Bruce, two heroes of past United successes, found themselves in control of struggling Midlands' sides and readily admitting to conspiring to drag other teams into the relegation zone in the slim hope that one of them would avoid the drop.

We're The Famous Man United

On this Friday afternoon, a tracksuited Robson is giving his weekly press conference to the local and national media in an executive lounge beneath the Halford's Lane Stand at the Hawthorns. The former United captain, who made 457 appearances and scored 97 goals in a 13-year spell at the club, doesn't shirk any questions and appears to have a good relationship with those from the fourth estate, but he can't disguise the situation, and clichés like 'points on board' litter his answers to the dozen or so hacks.

Photos of Robson a quarter of a century ago in a West Bromwich Albion kit adorn the walls around him – stress-free days when he didn't have the burdens and responsibility of management. Of all the people interviewed for this book, Robson was always going to be the most difficult to pin down. Time is tightest for him and there was no expectation of getting the three hours minimum spent with most other players. There would have been little surprise had he rejected the request for an in-depth one-on-one interview. Managers can never keep everyone happy – Celtic's Martin O'Neill had a waiting list of 85 journalists at one time during his Parkhead tenure.

It was pleasing when a 30-minute interview slot was agreed with the West Brom press office. Robson may not be Roy Keane when it comes to entertaining copy and forthright opinions, but he was such a central figure for Manchester United in the '80s that any time with him is a bonus. After he has spoken with the media for an hour, it's time to meet him. Ninety minutes later, Robson, having made two cups of tea, is still talking about Manchester United. He never was one for doing the minimum.

"I was a Chester-le-Street lad who was obsessed by football," he says, recalling his childhood. "I always loved it. I had a cousin from Birmingham who used to visit and we'd always go out and play football together; that was one of my earliest memories. He always said that I had good technique, even when I was two or three!

"I supported Newcastle as a kid but the first professional match I saw was at Sunderland – an FA Cup replay against Manchester United in 1964. Dad took me because United were a big glamour team and the cup holders. I was mesmerised by the whole occasion and the atmosphere. The game finished 2–2 but United won the second replay."

Robson was hooked.

"From then on I went to every Newcastle home game when I wasn't playing. A perfect day for me was playing in the morning and supporting Newcastle in the afternoon. I'd go with my dad and we'd stand on the Leazes End. Bobby Moncur and Wyn Davies, a big no-nonsense centre-forward who just battered everybody in his path, were my heroes. Davies made me realise how important aerial power could be in football, but even though he was a forward I preferred playing as an attacking midfielder from a very early age. I just wanted to be involved in the play as much as possible and would chase the ball all over the pitch.'

Robson had made his school team aged seven.

"I scored a lot of goals from midfield. I got eleven in one match but it cost me – my dad stopped giving me 50p a goal after that game. I knew that I wasn't a bad player at school, but you never know how good the opposition really is when it is at local school level."

Football, Robson says, kept him on the right side of authority.

"I was never in too much trouble as a kid because I was always playing football. I did go bird nesting and had a great egg collection, but I sold it to a lad for £15, which was an awful lot of dough then. I wasn't very big, but I wouldn't be pushed around and I did have a few fights. Two ginger lads from school picked on me once. They had waited for me on the way home from school and while I had a good scrap, I ended up with a right shiner. My dad asked me what had happened when I got home. He said that I should go down to the field where we played and get them one at a time. I said that I'd get them at school and I did, separately."

Robson went to secondary comprehensive school in Birtley, by the A1, south of Newcastle, where coach-loads of Manchester United fans are still met by police before away games at Newcastle and Sunderland. However, academic studies were never really his forte.

"I was very average when it came to doing schoolwork and Mum was always telling me off for not doing better. My parents were very influential though. They gave me the right morals in life and supported me. Dad was a continental lorry driver and he would be away a lot. I didn't miss him because you got used to it. He used to bring me loads of presents back from Europe, he really spoilt me.

"As a footballer, I didn't really realise that I was good until England Schools came in for me. When I was 13, I had trials at Burnley and Coventry, a week at each. I stayed in a hostel at both. Sheffield Wednesday, West Brom and Newcastle also showed interest. I was a Newcastle fan but it just didn't feel right there. West Brom was completely different. They put me in a hotel and took the triallists to games and even the theatre. I loved the atmosphere at the club and found it very friendly.

"I was lucky enough to be among the last of the 15-year-old school leavers. The next age group after me had to stay until they were 16, which was a result for me.

"But well before I left school I would spend my holidays training with West Brom."

In 1972, Robson was offered a two-year apprenticeship at the Hawthorns, with the new Baggies' manager Don Howe delivering the news.

"Don Howe was a great coach. He taught me some basics which stayed with me for the rest of my career. So that's why youth team coaches are so important – they can have such a big influence on a player's development. The good habits they teach will stay.

"At 15 I was quite small and it took me quite a time to develop. I was too small to play regular for the youth team. I was 5ft 4 inches and very light so they had me doing weights and circuits in training. I was also put on a diet of potatoes and meat, as well as a bottle of Mackesons every night with my evening meal. It tasted horrible, but maybe because of that I just shot up."

Robson was 18 when he made his debut for West Brom at York, away. He was picked for the England youth team's trip to Switzerland for the mini-World Cup soon after.

"I had a really good competition and my confidence was sky high," he says. "I really felt that I could be a player after that."

Bryan Robson

Over the next few years he established himself in the Baggies' first team. From three appearances in 1974/75, he made 16 the following season, then 23, 35, 41, 35 and 40 by 1980/81. His goals tally also crept up; he netted ten in his final season at West Brom.

Robson had been selected for England Under 21s in 1976/77, the same year that he scored during his first appearance at Old Trafford in a 2-2 draw for West Brom. Ron Atkinson, who would work with Robson for the best part of a decade, joined West Brom as manager in 1978 and took his new players on what would become a legendary summer tour of China, which was covered by a *World in Action* TV crew.

"It was an amazing experience for us," says Robson, "but one comment made the trip famous. We were taken to the Great Wall of China, and John Trewick was asked for his opinion. He really did say, 'Once you've seen one wall, you've seen them all.'"

Atkinson built a formidable side at the Hawthorns which included three black players known as 'The Three Degrees': defender Brendon Batson, winger Laurie Cunningham and striker Cyrille Regis. They beat United 4-0 in 1977/78 and knocked the Reds out of the FA Cup in the same season. Somehow, they topped it with a 5-3 victory at Old Trafford in 1978/79.

"I remember Sammy McIlroy scoring a cracker for Man United, but Len Cantello and Cyrille Regis scored two each for us," recalls Robson. "We were a decent side who were really finding our way and playing regularly in Europe. We had smashing players and it was great to put five past Man United at Old Trafford – teams just didn't do that. It shows what a memorable game it was because I used to get letters from Man United fans about that game, even as a West Brom player."

West Brom's brilliant rise would not last though, and in Robson's eyes it was self-inflicted.

"What disappointed me at West Brom was that they promised to sign a couple of top-notch players to add to the excellent squad we had. After being told that, I signed a four-year contract. But over time, Len Cantello, a very good player, was sold to Bolton and Laurie

Cunningham to Real Madrid. So instead of adding two top players, we lost two. That annoyed me. The 1981/82 season didn't get off to a great start when we got knocked out of Europe early on and Ron Atkinson moved to Man United and I decided to leave."

The transfer was protracted with West Brom pretending that they didn't want to sell Robson. By then, he had won the first of 90 England caps, having made his debut against the Republic of Ireland at Wembley in February 1980. He wanted out.

"I said to West Brom, 'You told me lies to make me sign a contract.' I knew that Liverpool and Man United had an interest in me so I told them that I wanted to move on. I was ambitious and wanted to play for a club that was ambitious. Liverpool didn't come up with the money; they wouldn't go above £1.2 million, whereas Man United went up to £1.5m which the Albion agreed to."

The final deal was worth £2m as United also signed the Mancunian midfielder Remi Moses.

"Remi was a top player," says Robson. "He was very quiet but a real fitness fanatic. He was a tough tackler who worked really hard. He was a little bit limited with his range of passing, but he was a very neat and tidy passer of the ball. He was going to be an England regular, but then he got his injury which forced him to pack the game in well before his time."

The huge price was a burden on the 24-year-old.

"I think the fee affected me when I first went to United. Maybe I was just getting used to my team-mates, but when you come through the ranks of a football club there are no expectations. At West Brom the home fans take to you because you have come through the ranks. But when you are bought as a record signing the expectations are higher from the crowd, and that meant more pressure. I took time to adapt, and it took another England competition, the '82 World Cup, to get my confidence sky high again. I had a good tournament in Spain, and it proved to me that I could be one of the better players in Europe. I came back and I was flying the following season."

Robson was made United captain.

"I never really had any problems with the responsibility of being captain. I was captain of the school team so I was used to it. I enjoyed being captain. People sometimes get the wrong end of the stick with football captains. They are completely different to cricket captains, for example, who have to make tactical decisions and are responsible for bowling changes, that type of thing; they have a role in selecting the team with the coaches. You don't get that in football. To a degree you tell people where you want them and what you want them to do, but you have more or less worked it all out on the training field. You are merely fine tuning."

Yet despite Robson's top form in 1982/83, the league championship which Atkinson so desperately wanted to win remained elusive.

"The United team got better, but the squad didn't, and as soon as we got any injuries we struggled. The squad members were not strong enough or good enough to replace the players who we'd lost. That's where Liverpool were great, because they had a great squad. Liverpool had great players and on our day we could match them, but they coped a lot better with injuries than we ever did. United had very good players. Liverpool had great players. That was the difference. Souness was a great, Dalglish, Hansen and Rush were too, while Lawrenson was bordering on being one. Dalglish was the main man, Souey was the hard player, but they had lads like Ronnie Whelan and Jimmy Case who could look after themselves. We didn't have great players.

"Liverpool were fierce, fierce rivals. They were the team to beat but while there was a great rivalry between the fans, we were normally quite civil with each other on the pitch considering the intensity of the rivalry. It was against Arsenal that the players cut it up."

United met the Gooners in the 1983 FA Cup semi-final at Villa Park.

"We played well that day," says Robson. "Tony Woodcock put them one up, but I had a shot that made it 1–1. Then Whiteside scored a great goal that put us in front. During that game, I remember thinking, 'This is why I left West Brom. It's because I want to play in cup finals and win medals.' Kevin Moran was carried off against Arsenal with five minutes to go. There was blood everywhere but he was putting his fists up to all our fans behind the goal, which they loved. When we went into the dressing-room after the game, we threw Mick Brown, the assistant manager, into the bath. He landed on Kevin, splitting his wound again which had just been stitched. He had to have it re-stitched."

Robson's first United trophy would come when he lifted the 1983 FA Cup after a replay against Brighton.

"Everybody says that it was a bad miss from Brighton's Gordon Smith in the first game but I thought Gary Bailey made a great save. Gary took a lot of knocks in his career, people criticising him for making mistakes and that, but he was brilliant that day."

United slaughtered Brighton 4–0 in the replay, with Robson scoring two first-half goals. As well as singing 'Shit on the Seagulls Tonight', the whole United end sang, 'You'll Never Walk Alone' – surprising given the contempt United fans now have for the traditional Liverpool anthem. United's number seven could have been the first player to score a hat-trick in an FA Cup final since the 'Matthews Final' of 1953 after a penalty was awarded, but Arnold Muhren had agreed to take spot-kicks before the game.

"Arnie asked me if I wanted to take it but I said no," says Robson. "Arnie was a very good player with great technique. His vision of pass and weight of pass was outstanding." Despite never having taken a penalty in his five years in England, Muhren made sure.

The cup win meant that United qualified to play in an eventful European Cup Winners' Cup run the following season.

"The game everyone remembers is the Barcelona one," says Robson. "We had played quite well over there, but lost 2–0. Graeme Hogg scored an own goal and I missed a couple of chances, one where I was clean through. For perhaps the only time in my career I switched off. I thought I was off-side and stopped. I never normally do that until I hear the whistle. But I just half flicked the ball and lobbed it casually. It hit the top of the cross bar and went over, but I wasn't really concentrating because I thought I was off-side, when actually I wasn't. To my horror the flag stayed down. That really annoyed me and revved me up a wee bit. The *Sun* did a big article saying that I owed United one because of the two chances that I had missed."

Bryan Robson

Back at Old Trafford, it wasn't just the players who were up for Barca.

"It was the best atmosphere of my whole career. The ground was actually shaking. They said the crowd was 58,000, but there were definitely more. The fans never stopped singing. They just wouldn't stop and because your adrenalin was flowing, that really pumped you up. There was a point in the match where Barcelona had completely gone . . ."

Barca had gone after Robson scored his second stunner to draw the tie level on aggregate in the 52nd minute. Returning to the centre circle after, he yelled, "Come on! We can do these." Sixty seconds later Frank Stapleton made it 3–2 to United.

"The danger for us then was we started to tire because we'd put so much effort into the game. Bernd Schuster could have wrecked the evening because he bent a shot which went inches past the post."

Robson's performance that night confirmed what the biggest clubs in Europe suspected: he was world class. It has been said that there's only one way for a player's career when they leave Old Trafford – down. As Ray Wilkins, who left for Milan might testify, that simply wasn't true in the 1980s. Top European clubs could pay five times what the top earner at Manchester United was making. And at Manchester United it was Bryan Robson on £2,000 a week.

"I had offers from Juventus, Milan and Sampdoria," says Robson, "but I was priced out of the market by United. Maradona had just gone to Barcelona for £3 million. Ron Atkinson said to me, 'You can go, but it will be for £3 million.' Milan offered £2.5million, but nobody would go above that. I would have earned a hell of a lot more than I was on at Man United, a hell of a lot more. Of course, that appealed, but what appealed more was that the Juventus team at that time was very, very strong. Michel Platini was my favourite player and they had seven of Italy's 1982 World Cup winning team."

Would Robson have left Old Trafford if a deal had been agreed with an Italian club?

"Yes, I would have gone there if United had accepted their offer."

Fortunately for United, no team bid the £3 million asked. It led to the club being called a one-man team, so dominant a figure was Robson.

"In this game you can never be a one-man team," he says, refuting the suggestion vehemently. "You need good team-mates around you and I usually had them."

Soon after, Robson signed a seven-year contract, worth £1m, to stay at United.

"The contract gave my family financial security and moving wasn't really an option from then on because I was tied to the club," he explains. "Plus I was settled in Manchester, as were all the family. I had a greetings card business too with Ronnie Wood. I played an active role in the business and we'd find the sites for shops together. But I wasn't running the shops or designing birthday cards or anything like that. I'm not the best drawer!"

By 1995, Birthdays was producing more than 100 million cards a year, employing over 2,000 people and boasting a turnover of £78m. When the company was sold the following year, Robson pocketed an estimated £1.8m.

It wasn't as if Robson was ever unhappy enough at Old Trafford to force a move either.

"I always got on great with Big Ron," he says, "apart from when he left me out of the semi-final for West Brom against Ipswich. I didn't even get on the bench, so I reminded him about that for years. He took me to United and our good relationship continued. His man-management was very good; he was always jokey and liked the banter. He actually joined in training. He told everyone that he was good, but he wasn't. He was so full of enthusiasm that he was always comparing himself to Bobby Charlton or some German player we'd not heard of. That enthusiasm rubbed off on the players in training and made it enjoyable. In matches, Ron's way suited those who wanted to play off the cuff. It didn't suit some players though, players who needed to do work on their technique and practise the systems and formations."

Few are surprised that the best player in England got on with his manager, but that wasn't the case for everyone.

Bryan Robson

"The way Ron worked," Robson explains, "he had this circle of players he was interested in, who he devoted all his energies to. This worked well for the players in the circle, but the fringe players felt left out a bit, and Ron's banter sometimes wasn't best for them. And when you got injuries, that's when it showed, because the fringe players always felt, 'Well, I'm coming in for a couple of games, but it doesn't matter how well I do. When they get fit again, I'll be left out.'"

And Robson had a lot of injuries.

"I did, and that was partly because of the way I played. But my injuries were blown out of proportion by the media because I missed two World Cup tournaments. That is inevitable when you are captain of your country. And I must admit, I couldn't believe it the second time, when I missed the 1990 World Cup. I didn't like some reports saying that I was injury-prone and making out that was an inherent weakness. Injuries are part of the game and the way I played left me open to the possibility of getting hurt. People kept telling me that I was too brave for my own good, but I wouldn't have changed my style or reined in my commitment. For a start, you are asking for trouble if you hold anything back in tackles and I wouldn't have been half the player I was if I had played any other way. I played something like 850 games in my career and finally retired just before my 40th birthday. That's hardly the record of an injury-prone player."

Robson stops to make another cup of tea.

"Sorry, was it one sugar?" he asks. He wants to know which other players have been interviewed for this book, and what the other lads are up to. Robson has to be more guarded in what he says – he was a Premiership manager when we spoke, but he is keen to hear stories of pranks recounted by the other interviewees.

"Macari was always cutting socks up and doing things like that," he says. "And McQueen was the king of the one-liner with a sharp sense of humour."

He refuses to accept Gary Bailey's version of events regarding the ducks that flew away from his pond and offers another story about Bailey.

"He paid a fortune for all this walnut wood in his house. He went away with the team, but when he came back his girlfriend had had it all painted white gloss!" The manager of West Brom starts giggling to himself about an incident two decades ago.

He tells another about Colin Gibson, who was convinced that he was good enough to play for England and kept pestering Robson to have a word with Bobby Robson. The United captain set up a sting. While the lads were having a beer in Paddy Crerand's pub, the phone went. Paddy shouted that it was Bobby Robson for Bryan.

"Is Colin Gibson with you?" asked Crerand from the other phone in the pub, pretending to be Robson.

"He is, gaffer," answered Robson.

"Well, tell him that he's getting a call-up."

Robson duly relayed the good news.

"Colin Gibson shouted, 'I knew it, I knew I was good enough,'" says Robson. "'I knew I was better than Kenny Samson!' He was the butt of a lot of jokes, but I don't want to destroy him because he was all right."

Robson was better than all right on the field. He describes his goal in the 1985 FA Cup semi-final replay against Liverpool at Maine Road as his best for United.

"I did a one-two with Strachan on the half-way line and Alan Hansen was chasing me. So I just let go and it went right in the top corner. You can do that 25 times on the training pitch and you will miss 24 times, but it was the one time when it went right for me. Then Sparky came up with a goal to win us that game. We were through to another final and our fans went crazy. I went towards them at the final whistle, but before I knew it I was surrounded by hundreds of them. They swarmed on to the pitch and lifted me on their shoulders. I didn't stay up there for long though because I fell off. Mounted police moved in to rescue me, but I was fine. Our fans made sure of that."

United were at Wembley against champions and FA Cup holders Everton, who were hoping to lift a second FA Cup in three years.

"They had an excellent, well-balanced side, and fancied their chances of making it a double. We had other ideas. Everyone knows what happened, with Kevin getting sent off and Norman scoring the winner in extra time past Neville Southall, one of the best goalkeepers in the business."

Robson didn't go on the celebratory tour to Montego Bay as he had to play with England, but he felt like he was there given the number of phone calls he received from his United team-mates.

"They were ringing me at 4am and all that shite. I was on international duty and I blame McQueen, definitely. He was having a great time and a few beers and rubbing it in because I couldn't. He was Scottish and wanted to sabotage England's plans."

Robson thought that United's ten-game winning start to 1985/86 would finally lead to the title coming to Old Trafford.

"You get off to a start like that and you think, 'This could be our year.' We were playing devastating football and the goals just flowed. But then the injuries started. Giddy broke his leg at Ipswich and Strach dislocated his shoulder. Remi Moses twisted his ankle crossing the ball. It seemed nothing at the time, yet it eventually ended his career because the muscle down the side of his leg never fully redeveloped. I played for England and did my hamstring really bad. Either Whiteside or McGrath had a serious injury too, so that hit us. By the time players got back from injuries everyone had caught us up and the confidence of some players was very low. Ron left Gary Bailey out and brought Chris Turner in, while Alan Brazil was having a hard time trying to please our more critical fans. Eventually, he had enough and decided that he couldn't take any more. We all felt for him. I liked Alan, he introduced me to horse racing and I really enjoyed a day out at the racing. It was a release for me, but I've not been too many times since becoming a manager."

United's 1985/86 season petered out, with Robson barely featuring because of hamstring and calf problems. The form didn't pick up the following season and by November, Ron Atkinson, the man who had brought Robson to the club, was sacked.

"When you are at a club like Man Utd, it's okay winning cups but the fans want the league," Robson says of Atkinson's dismissal. "People were getting frustrated, especially after the ten wins on the bounce in 1985 had come to nothing. The pressure was building in the media, too, and the rumours that there might be a change of manager.

"Ron reacted as only Ron could. He invited friends around to his house in Rochdale for a few drinks. Some of the injured players, who weren't going to be in the team that weekend, went along. I did, so did Norman and Strach, who took over as DJ belting out 'Big Spender' and 'Goldfinger'. Ron wasn't one to hide away, but I'm sure his sacking hurt him. He said at the time that he ought to have quit that summer, but his pride wouldn't let him."

On 6th November 1986, Sir Alex took over as Manchester United manager.

"Alex got all the players in the gym on his first day and made a very good first impression," recalls Robson. "He said, 'Everyone has got a fresh start and a chance. If you play well in training then you will make the team, I'll judge everybody as we go along.'"

Changes began quickly.

"Alex had a reputation for being really angry and having a go at players. He did that to find out their character. He would see how a player responded. If a player wilted then he would have got rid of them because he would have felt that their character wasn't strong enough to play at Man United."

When asked about the perception that Ferguson stopped the drink culture at the club, Robson disagrees.

"The talk of a drinking culture has been taken out of proportion," insists Robson. "Yes, it has definitely changed now. Players look after themselves a hell of a lot more and a lot of players don't drink at all. If a player had a reputation for liking a beer then most managers would maybe stay clear of him. I would. We'd have a drink, but it would always be well away from the game. The lads would maybe meet on a Monday lunchtime after training at somewhere like Paddy's pub, because you wouldn't get pestered there. Plus we knew we'd get looked after by Paddy. Some players did take it a little bit further and drank too close to games. Ron Atkinson found out and then Sir Alex found out. Obviously as manager you are not happy about

Bryan Robson

things like that and you sort it out. But in them days I used to have a rule that I'd never drink two nights before a game. Having a drink was important for team bonding, though. We enjoyed it, and you feel that you get close to each other and get to know each other as mates as well as footballers when you socialise together."

"Fans used to write letters to the managers saying that they had seen a player drunk in this bar or that club. A lot of the time they were wrong. You could have been in a bar and maybe you only had two pints. But according to the letters the manager got you were legless. After a while he brought me in for a chat because I was captain of the club. He said, 'I've heard the reputation of the lads but I'm telling you now that I don't want drinking through the week. I want people to start cutting down on the alcohol because I don't like the stories that I'm hearing.' I told the lads but he still heard stories about them, that's why he ended up getting rid of some of them. That was his way. He'd made it clear what he wanted and you either changed or you carried on what you were doing. And inevitably, if you ignored him, he'd move you on."

Like most new managers, Ferguson began to bring in his own players.

"You could see that the type of players Sir Alex was bringing in were starting to improve us," says Robson. "You had Brian McClair who started scoring goals straight away while Mickey Phelan had real good experience."

Robson watched and learned how his new manager dealt with situations in comparison with his old one.

"I picked up the good and bad points from Ron and Alex. They were both very good man-managers. Sir Alex was very good at preparation, while Ron was more off the cuff and didn't worry about the opposition. Alex would be in-depth with his preparation leading up to games. He would have identified strengths and weaknesses of the opposition players and that would help you approach a game. Yet he still focused more on your strengths and what we should do."

Ferguson's overhaul took time.

"Maybe the disappointing league positions didn't reflect what he was doing," muses Robson. "Sir Alex was changing everything about and you didn't get much cohesion because there were so many changes. Plus he had to deal with some players who Ron brought in towards the end of his time who were never good enough to be Man United players."

By 1990 there was pressure on the terraces for Ferguson to be sacked.

"Some fans were not happy, but according to some of the directors who I knew well and I used to get on well with, United had no intention of sacking Sir Alex. It was more a media thing."

The consummate club captain named 'Captain Marvel' by the press, Robson unsurprisingly enjoyed a good relationship with United's directors.

"I got on especially well with the chairman Martin Edwards," he says. "I always thought that he was a fair-minded guy because at certain times under Ron and Sir Alex we had commercial stuff which we weren't always happy about. I'd go to the chairman, maybe with another couple of players, and speak on behalf of the players and he was always very fair. I don't know why he was unpopular with fans because he always backed his managers with money. He gave them decent dough to spend and he wasn't one to sack and hire and sack a manager. He stuck by his men and gave them a fair crack of the whip."

Robson thinks that FA Cup in 1990 was the turning point for United.

"Once we won that it gave the players confidence," he says. "We won the Cup Winners' Cup the following season and, personally, I felt that I was more than playing my part in the team that won the league in 1993."

Robson's biggest frustration would come in what should have been his final game of his final year, the 1994 FA Cup final against Chelsea. It could have been his fourth FA Cup final win with United.

"Definitely my biggest disappointment," he says. "I had come on in the semi when we were a goal down and we drew. And I played in the replay when we put four past Oldham, so I was hurt not to be

Bryan Robson

involved because I knew that it would be my last game. Sir Alex said to me that he had to look after the players who were the future of the club, and he knew I was going to Middlesbrough. Maybe Alex was determined not to be swayed by sentiment, because I'd done well in the semi and given the club so much service, but United won the final 4–0 without me."

The two men did not fall out over this matter.

"I still stay in touch with United," says Robson. "And I've always kept in touch with Sir Alex. I spoke to Keaney when he was there and I keep in touch with Giggs because we share the same agent. And because my family is in Manchester, I see a lot of the lads I played with."

Clearly if he didn't like talking about United, Robson wouldn't have gone well beyond the allotted half hour for this interview.

"United are first class when I go back," he says. "They just let you walk through without showing a ticket. Well, they do with me anyway. The fans have always been great too."

And he's happier being involved in football than out of the game, as he was for over two years following his seven-year spell as Middlesbrough boss between 1994 and 2001.

"I'm enjoying life and I enjoy the role of manager," he concludes, "but I enjoy it a hell of a lot more being successful rather than struggling. The West Brom fans have always been good with me and you sense it walking around the town. But fans pay their money and if the team gives a bad performance they will attack the team and the manager because they want to see their team do well. I understand their frustrations."

On 18th September 2006, Bryan Robson left West Bromwich Albion "by mutual consent".

4
Gordon McQueen
The Social Convenor

"You've had a few," says Yvonne McQueen, raising her eyebrows, as her husband manoeuvres his 6ft 4ins frame with difficulty into their black BMW outside the Black Bull pub.

"It's close season, I'm allowed to relax," replies Gordon, as the car moves off through the cobbled streets of Yarm, a wealthy town situated in a loop of the River Tees, on its way to the station to drop me off. Yarm is home to several Middlesbrough footballers and the former United defender Gary Pallister – Middlesbrough footballers don't live in Middlesbrough.

Five hours earlier the McQueens, who have been married for almost three decades, had picked me up from the station, then Yvonne had dropped us outside one of her husband's favourite pubs on the High Street.

"It's on me today," said McQueen as he ordered the first pint in the pub. "No arguments."

McQueen's name had come up again and again in conversations with the other players, almost always endearingly.

"Tell me about the other lads you've interviewed," he demands, as he carries the drinks to a table adjacent to a group of elderly locals discussing Middlesbrough's progress to the UEFA Cup final. Each name brings a smile and a comment.

"And how is Clayton? Still playing is he?"

The one he doesn't ask about is Bryan Robson. The pair are still close mates and are about to take their families on holiday to America together. The lads matter to McQueen. United's long-time social convener and dressing-room wag, he was always quickest to the punchline, the king of the one-liner, a priceless commodity in a football dressing-room where the weak don't become heroes.

"I was always like that, even as a kid," he says. "It helped me settle at new clubs quickly. I wasn't one for the pranks. I didn't find them that funny."

The evidence suggests otherwise. Three players had already described one incident as the funniest thing they had ever seen before McQueen recounted it, "off the record". Unfortunately, it was already on tape from other sources and and very much on the record, much to McQueen's discomfort.

McQueen was rooming with Kevin Moran in London's Royal Lancaster, the night before flying to Majorca for a week's break with United. The Irish defender was lying on his bed, busy having a telephone conversation, as McQueen walked out of the bathroom wearing just a towel. The big Scot positioned his backside close to the face of the distracted Moran and removed the towel before attempting to squeeze out a "wee fart" while announcing, "Kop for a bit of that." But McQueen involuntarily followed through, spraying the Republic of Ireland defender's face with warm excrement. Moran did not immediately realise what had happened, before emitting a loud "Aaaarghhh!" then shouting: "You dirty bastard, you dirty, dirty bastard." Moran's pained cries were heard by the rest of the team, much to their delight.

Gordon McQueen

The trip to Majorca that followed wasn't without incident either.

"We had a wee bit of a run-in with the American Navy, who had come into Palma for a few days," McQueen says. "They were all like big gorillas. Paul McGrath, who was never the most subtle guy when it came to getting up and dancing, pushed one Yank aside and started dancing with his bird for a bit of fun. Two of his mates started laying into McGrath. I was with Robbo and we started thinking 'Oh no!' We went over and I left-hooked one with a big haymaker. Then I hit another one with a right-handed haymaker. They both felt it and I thought, 'I am going to get my head kicked in here.' Robbo thought the same. Except suddenly the military police stormed in and battered the living daylights out of the gorillas for causing problems."

As centre-forwards would often testify, McQueen was not to be messed with. Despite the anecdotes, McQueen isn't a polished performer like Big Ron. He's not into the after-dinner scene, either as a source of income or amusement, saying that he'd "much rather have a few pints with my mates in a pub than sit with ten strangers round a table". He's not being arrogant, he just likes the company of the "good lads".

"My problem was that I didn't judge players on their football ability, but whether they were good lads or not," he admits.

"Come on, let's go and get something to eat," he says, before walking slowly down the High Street to a restaurant called Chadwicks. It takes some time, partly because an artificial ankle means that movement is painful and partly because he knows so many people, who all want to stop and chat.

A day before the Trans-Pennine Express journey to Yarm, I'd got a similar reaction to his name on the supporters' bus of United's Glasgow branch, the regulars being a mixture of exiled Mancunians and Scots who eschew the Old Firm in favour of Manchester United. As the bus passed through Glasgow's impoverished east end and into Lanarkshire, a breeding ground for footballers which had yielded such red legends as Joe Jordan, Brian McClair, Jim Holton, David Herd, Jimmy Delaney and Sir Matt Busby, I canvassed opinions about

We're The Famous Man United

Gordon McQueen, who grew up in nearby Ayrshire and went on to captain Scotland. The fans were complimentary.

"I support Manchester United because in the 1970s we had so many Scottish players," said one. "Now there's only Darren Fletcher. That must piss McQueen off because whilst he loved Man United, he loved Scotland more."

McQueen is disappointed when we enter Chadwicks, a favourite of the Middlesbrough players, where Jack Johnson plays on a loop and Teeside's smart set discuss handbags and glad rags. His favourite chef isn't in. But not to worry.

McQueen is from a town with the same population as Yarm, yet the 8,000 residents of Kilbirnie in North Ayrshire, where property prices are a fifth of what they are in Yarm, live acutely contrasting lives. A trip to Kilbirnie, a predominantly Protestant town 20 miles south-west of Glasgow, a month after visiting McQueen, revealed a hard-bitten former steel town, the main evidence of life on the street being the wasted figures gathered outside the door of Ramage's Bar, a windowless pub no different from the hardened saloons close to Ibrox or Celtic Park.

"It's a tough place," states McQueen. "And I'm proud to be from there." McQueen's dad Tommy was a professional footballer who grafted in the steel works when he retired. Before that, he played in goal for Hibernian, Motherwell, Berwick Rangers and Accrington Stanley in the '50s, when Accrington sometimes took the field with an all-Scots team.

"Apart from a spell living in Accrington, our family stayed in Kilbirnie," explains McQueen. "It wasn't unusual for Dad to be away for long periods playing football and I was very close to my mum, who has passed away. My dad lives back in Kilbirnie where he's a well-known figure, not because of me but because he played in a junior cup final the first time Kilbirnie ever won it in 1952."

Nothing to do with the age of the players, junior football is the Scottish equivalent of English non-league. Junior cup finals used to attract vast crowds, an incredible 69,959 turning up for Kilbirnie against Camelon Juniors in which McQueen's father played and Alan Hansen's dad turned out for the Falkirk side.

Gordon McQueen

"The four teams which people in Kilbirnie supported were Kilmarnock, Rangers and Celtic, and Kilbirnie Ladeside. Kids there didn't dream of playing for Manchester United, but Rangers or Celtic, depending on whether they were Catholic or Protestant. It could get pretty lively there between the two groups. I was a Protestant so I wanted to play for Rangers. Although, while it wouldn't have been the done thing to go out with a Catholic girl when I was a lad, I never let sectarianism into my head."

McQueen's childhood heroes were Jim Baxter and Colin Stein of Rangers, as well as Kilbirnie goalkeeper Ernie McGrath. "He used to give penalties away deliberately because he was brilliant at stopping them. He was that good that he went to play for Aberdeen."

The young McQueen would visit Ibrox regularly and get lifted over the turnstiles into the enclosure of the stadium's stunning main stand.

"I'd watch Alex Ferguson and in later years ended up playing against him when he was at Falkirk and I was at St Mirren. The support Celtic and Rangers had and still get is unbelievable," he says, shaking his head. "It's far more substantial than a club like Newcastle and yet they're watching absolute rubbish."

McQueen wasn't academic at school, claiming he wasn't pushed. Organised football didn't offer a focus either, because there wasn't any.

"Of course I played football, but it was real rough and ready. I didn't play organised football until I was 15 when I joined a junior side where I actually got paid for playing."

The side was Largs Thistle from the Ayrshire seaside town where the Glaswegian working classes used to holiday before cheap trips to Benidorm and Magaluf. McQueen's height made him a natural centre-half and within weeks senior clubs like Rangers, St Mirren and Liverpool started watching. McQueen, naturally, was desperate to sign for Rangers.

"I went on trial there. Rangers told me that my boots were too scruffy because they were ripped and had holes in them. They gave me a new pair." The boots made little difference. "Training every day absolutely killed me. I realised after a week that I just wasn't up to it." Rangers thought the same and let him go, but not before they'd taken the boots back.

Bill Shankly, himself a son of Ayrshire, started his own playing career in junior football and had good scouts in the area. One arranged for McQueen to go on trial to Liverpool when he was 17.

"Shankly was keen on me signing but I didn't like it at Liverpool and came home because I was really homesick," he explains.

Instead, McQueen signed for St Mirren under manager Alex Wright, a friend of his father.

"They were part-time but I thought I would have a better chance of getting in the first team than at a bigger club and it worked out that way.

"Then a new manager took over called Wilson Humphries and he completely changed my life because he really believed in me and got me fit. He told me that I was a good player and that meant a lot to me. Some players need to know that more than others.

"Dad told me that I needed to be playing full-time so I went to see Mr Humphries and he simply said, 'Okay, start next week with me.'"

McQueen quit his job labouring at the nearby Glengarnock Steel Works. "It had been my job to empty ingots out of the railway carriages," he explains. "It was heavy physical work and I used to get a bad back. I'd wear a towel around my neck to avoid the heat of the furnaces. The wage as a full-time footballer was peanuts, but it was never about the money and never has been to this day."

McQueen was St Mirren's only professional. He trained with the manager on Monday, the part-timers on a Tuesday and so on. "We had a really good young side, we'd get crowds of 4–5,000 and I was feeling quite happy with myself."

Yet if McQueen was ever seen to be getting full of himself, there was always a reminder that suggested he shouldn't. "Lou Macari, who was in a brilliant Celtic reserve team with players like Dalglish, was a mate. I was in a very exciting St Mirren team and we thought we were the bee's knees. One morning Lou and me were at Paisley station and this young kid was hanging about. We gave him some money and told him to go and get us some fish and chips. He never did come back."

Interest in McQueen continued to rise. St Mirren were convinced that he was leaving and signed Ian Ure, another Ayrshire boy, from Manchester United in August 1972, ostensibly as his replacement. McQueen had a £35,000 price tag and his manager told him that five clubs had met the asking price.

"He gave me the number of all five managers and told me to ring each of them: Bill Nicholson at Spurs, Bobby Robson at Ipswich, Jock Stein at Celtic, Jimmy Sirrell at Notts County and Don Revie at Leeds United. Unbeknown to St Mirren, Don Revie had already been speaking to my dad, and with Bremner, Lorimer, Hunter, Giles, Charlton and 17 Scots at Leeds, there wasn't any doubt in my mind where I was going."

The reality of arriving at Leeds was as good as the expectation.

"It was like opening up a football magazine when you walked through the front door. It was unbelievable, and a really happy time in my football career. I was only 20, but I was always quite confident in myself and settled easily. I was always quite funny, with a quip and a line. I don't know where that came from, but I could handle myself in the dressing-room."

Jack Charlton was the Leeds centre-half and the intention was for McQueen to be groomed as his eventual replacement. Within a year, McQueen was a first-team regular and playing in the European Cup Winners' Cup final against Milan. The following season he partnered Norman Hunter, as Leeds won the league after remaining unbeaten in their first 29 games. There was another high in the summer of 1974, when McQueen was called up to the Scotland squad for his debut against Belgium.

In 1975, Leeds reached the final of the European Cup, beating the Barcelona of Cruyff and Neeskens in the semi.

"We won the first leg 2–1, and went to the Camp Nou where the atmosphere was incredible. We were drawing 1–1 and hanging on for dear life. There was 15 minutes to go when their striker, Clares, spat in my face. I counted to ten and then knocked him out, for which I was sent off. I sat in the dressing-room and as I cooled down it dawned on me: 'Oh, wait a minute, I'm going to miss the European Cup final here.' It was horrible missing that. My temperament was a weakness in my game."

Despite some Yorkshire revisionists claiming otherwise, Leeds lost the final 2–0.

"Leeds were probably the biggest club in the country in terms of names. It was 'Super Leeds' at the time. They averaged 42,000 at Elland Road and it wasn't until some of the great players got a bit older and started drifting off that I realised life at Leeds wasn't only about winning trophies all the time, that I'd been on a fantasy island.

"I had some funny times with Leeds too. Just after losing the European Cup we went on a break to Marbella. Joe Jordan had done well that season, especially in the final. Anyway, the waiter came down to the pool and said: 'Telephone call for Mr Joe Jordan from Mr Detmar Kramer in Germany.' He was Bayern Munich's manager. Joe looked around, and when he didn't see Billy Bremner and Johnny Giles – the two main jokers – he assumed that it was them ringing reception from their rooms. Joe gave me a nudge and said, 'Go and deal with it, Gordon.' I went to the phone and pretended to be Joe.

"The man said, 'We want you to join Bayern Munich. We've been really impressed by you and would like you to join this great club of ours.'

"'Yes, no problem but you have to sign McQueen too.'

"'McQueen is a good central defender but we have Beckenbauer and Schwarzenbeck who play all the time.'

"'They couldn't lace McQueen's boots. They are not in the same class. You don't know what you are talking about.'

"'OK, maybe we speak later but I'm not so sure.'

"Later on, just as we were all dressed up to go out to Puerto Banus, there was another phone call, claiming to be from Detmar Kramer. I answered it and realised that it really had been him earlier. Joe was mortified. He never did end up joining Bayern Munich."

Reassured by Don Revie's promise that Leeds were going to sign

Gordon McQueen

the best players in Britain, McQueen signed a four-year contract in 1977. He was quoted in *Shoot!* magazine saying that he wanted to stay at Leeds forever.

"The problem was that Leeds never did sign the best players," says McQueen. "Leeds broke a lot of promises – none of them financial – but more about the direction that the club was going. My best friend was Joe Jordan, who I eventually became best man for. We joined Leeds around the same time, broke into the first team at the same time and the Scotland team too. They let Joe go over what amounted to £15 a week in wages. They were talking about building a new Leeds and they let Joe, one of Leeds' best young players, go to Manchester United. That was the final nail in the coffin for me, and I became very disillusioned."

Leeds declined into mediocrity, while McQueen's standing as a player increased. A month after Jordan moved in January 1978, McQueen followed him to Old Trafford, moving west for £495,000. He knew that the Leeds fans wouldn't take too well to the transfer, but he didn't realise that they would hold it against him to this day.

"It was horrible," he recalls. "Firstly, a lot of the articles from *Shoot!* came through the post, with messages like, 'You bastard, this is what you said.' I gave up answering them because people didn't want to know my reasons. Everyone said I went to United for money. That's absolute shit. Leeds would have paid me more money, and I lost my club car when I joined United.

"My wife and I carried on living in Leeds for six months after I joined United and we couldn't go out. I made the mistake of going to a midweek game at Elland Road a few months after signing for United and I had to leave the ground after 20 minutes; the abuse was so bad. My garage was painted with the word 'Judas', and the hate mail continued to be intense. I wasn't like the modern footballer who lived in some private gated community; I lived in a semi-detached on the Wetherby Road.

"I went to Elland Road four or five years ago and saw T-shirts saying 'United Scum – Jordan, McQueen, Cantona and Ferdinand'," he continues. "They had them in kids' sizes for people not even born when I was around. For years I never went to Leeds, but I went to a dinner there recently and the people were all right with me. They were the well-behaved types, but after a few beers they were still saying, 'Why did you go?'"

As a player, McQueen would return much sooner.

"Second game of the 1978/79 season," he says with a smile. "The police came to us in the hotel before the game and said, 'Get McQueen and Jordan off the bus last because we want to make sure they're all right at the other end.' We got booed when we arrived and when we walked out onto the pitch. I scored United's opener after seven minutes. It came when we were awarded a corner in front of the Kop. As I moved forward the abuse got louder, and by the time I reached the penalty area missiles were being thrown. I headed a goal in and it didn't go down well. There was just a deathly silence. I was delighted, but I didn't overdo the celebration because I realised that wouldn't have been the brightest thing to do. Winning 3–2 was enough."

Manchester United's support had made McQueen notice the club long before he moved to Old Trafford.

"We played United in the 1977 FA Cup semi-final at Hillsborough, and I vividly remember walking out at Hillsborough and immediately feeling deflated. We were in Yorkshire, the ground was supposed to be split between Leeds and United, yet it was anything but."

Both teams were allocated 21,000 tickets with Sheffield Wednesday receiving the 'neutral' 13,000. After United's allocation sold out, Mancunian touts bought up many of these tickets. With Leeds not selling their allocation, one newspaper described the scene: 'Within 15 minutes Manchester United were two-up, delighting a crowd in which the red of Lancashire so dominated the yellow and white of Yorkshire that Hillsborough looked like an egg with a whole bottle of tomato ketchup poured over it.'

"I just thought, 'Jesus Christ, look at the support these lot have got,'" says McQueen. "I never thought, 'Right, that's it I want to join Manchester United.' But it swayed my decision when United wanted me to sign."

Yet McQueen had never really rated United as a team.

"I'd played against Man United many times. Leeds went to Old Trafford in 1974 and we beat them comfortably because they just weren't a good side then. And despite the fans hating each other, the biggest game for Leeds was against Liverpool."

The size of United staggered him, though.

"Leeds were a big club, but United was on a different level. You just had to compare the away support alone. There were no restrictions on travelling fans in those days and United would go to places like Norwich or Stoke and it was like carnival day. United fans would take over the whole stadium, and as a player you just felt very, very comfortable.

"Everything was bigger at Old Trafford – the ground, the crowds, your mail bag, the press conference when I signed. United were big, yet other clubs could compete for players with United. It was a more level playing field than now, where Chelsea and United can pay far more than the rest of the clubs."

McQueen's first full season at Old Trafford concluded with a goal in the FA Cup final against Arsenal, a game which ended in disappointment, despite his late equaliser setting up a memorably mad last five minutes. Many United players blamed Gary Bailey for Arsenal's late, late winner, but McQueen isn't one of them.

"Maybe Gary shouldn't have come for the ball, but everybody forgets what Mickey Thomas and Lou Macari did. Liam Brady was running with the ball and Mickey and Lou, who were both quick and very fit, lunged in when all they needed to do was stay on their feet for another few strides. They would have won the ball before he shoved it out to Rix. We had that game won, no doubt. We would have won 5–2 in extra time. They had been two up in a cup final before conceding two goals in the last few minutes. They had gone – then that happened. It was horrible."

Still, McQueen enjoyed life at Old Trafford and respected his manager Dave Sexton. "He was a lovely man and we had a good side, but we never won bugger all. There's a myth attached to the football Sexton played. People said that his football was negative, but he didn't have a negative thought in his head when it came to attacking. I cannot tell you how strongly I feel about that, because it was totally unfair.

"Dave's man-management was first class. He didn't have a selfish bone in his body. He wanted to improve players, improve Manchester United and he couldn't give a hoot about himself. Defensive? He used to say, 'Get the ball forward' and yet he got the sack because people said he was defensive.

"I was annoyed when he was sacked, but I wasn't the type to pick up the phone and offer commiserations. I've met Dave many times since and he knows that I like him. And I know that he likes me. Big Ron came in and he was ten times more defensive."

Sexton's assistant Tommy Cavanagh wasn't McQueen's friend.

"He said publicly that he didn't like me and I didn't like him. And he was a Scouser. But I liked Ron and got on fine with him. He was quite hard on me at times because there was a wee bit of indiscipline in my game, and I maybe wandered a bit out of position. Or maybe I took too many touches of the ball when I should have been more positive. Ron was good for Manchester United though. Maybe if there had been more funds available he might have been even better. But he signed Bryan Robson and he was one of the greatest players in the club's history. When United signed Bryan, I was a Glenn Hoddle fanatic, and I thought that Bryan had nowhere near the technical ability and the touch that Hoddle had. I sat in the stand with Robbo on the day he signed when Sammy McIlroy, the player he was bought to replace, scored a hat-trick. Robbo never flinched – he knew, he just knew, that he was a lot, lot better. Three games down the line I realised that Robbo was a bit different. He could tackle and score goals with his right and left foot. He protected the back four so much that I felt I could play and have a cigar – nothing got past Bryan. I started realising that Bryan was right up there with the best players I'd been with – Bremner and Giles at Leeds, Kenny Dalglish at Scotland."

Another player who didn't impress McQueen initially was Ray Wilkins, who signed from Chelsea for £825,000 in August 1979.

Gordon McQueen

"When Ray first came to the club I thought, 'Nah,'" says McQueen. "I wasn't so sure about him as a player but he grew on me. He used to come to us, take the ball and start playing. He always accepted responsibility, even when things were not going well. He never scored or made the killer pass because he played so deep. The season he left to go to Milan, he was fantastic – probably the best player at the club."

Despite the speculation linking Robson with a move abroad, he stayed at Old Trafford and McQueen's friendship with him grew.

"Bryan was a real modest lad, I don't even think he realised how good he was. I used to pick him up every day for a year when he had a driving ban in 1983. He was starting to get bigger and bigger and he would confide in me and tell me about the commercial offers he was getting. He was becoming a major figurehead in football, a Bobby Charlton type figure. He never changed one little bit. He was fond of a pint with the rest of us, but that was great for team bonding. I'm glad to say that he is still a great friend of mine. Bryan was a freak in terms of fitness, mind."

Not everybody could drink and play like Robson.

"The drinking was a serious problem but we never realised that it was at the time because it was pretty much the norm. You had pride in your performance, but you didn't have to stay super fit like you do now. The drinking was just wrong. When I think of the injuries I had, the boozing can't have helped. Would we have been a better team without it? Yes. It showed on some players. Look at Paul McGrath. You wonder what would have happened if Paul would have been more sensible. Him and Norman Whiteside, the drink must have taken the edge of their game, it must have."

United's social scene was busy.

"We went out to all kinds of places, from swanky Baverdage in Manchester to the Griffin opposite the Cliff in Salford for a bevvy. That would be unimaginable now. We'd go in there with the groundsman. We'd have some great times in Paddy Crerand's pub too. It was well ahead of its time and had continental licensing hours long before they had been introduced elsewere in Britain!

We're The Famous Man United

"When they talk about the drinkers at United then, for some reason I escape the usual suspects. People say Brazil, Whiteside, McGrath and Robson – but never me. I have been right pleased about that, but it's not true.

"My behaviour was sometimes disgraceful when you think that I had a young family at the time. I didn't come home for my Sunday dinner one afternoon. In those days you were not allowed to drink all day on a Sunday so we used to go to a restaurant in Bowdon when the pub shut. I ordered a bowl of crisps and carried on drinking because you were allowed to drink if you had food. It was full of the Cheshire set, all the ritzy women. I was in there one Sunday with Robbo and there was a tug at my trousers. It was my three little kids covered in mud. Because I hadn't come home for my Sunday lunch, my missus had driven to the restaurant, opened the door and thrown them all in. She was really pissed off and I can understand why, but the kids had the day of their lives because everyone fussed over them and treated them to whatever they wanted."

McQueen had met Yvonne, a Bradford girl, in Majorca when he went on holiday with Joe Jordan.

"I don't know how she put up with me in the early years. Some of the lads were sensible, some of them not so sensible. Arthur [Albiston] was far from sensible in the early days, the same with Giddy [John Gidman] and Robbo. Giddy liked a good time and yet he was fit as a fiddle. He had natural stamina and was a real good full-back. He was good fun, a real personality and I've always judged players on their personality rather than their performances. He was always at a party and really easily persuaded.

"I got on really well with Martin Buchan off the field, but not on the pitch because of my indiscipline. His sense of humour and witty sarcasm was similar to mine.

"Gary Bailey was his own man, a little bit different to the rest. He wasn't one of our crowd: me, Robbo, Kevin Moran, Ashley Grimes and maybe Paul McGrath and Alan Brazil, but that's not to say that Gary was an arsehole. I got on with lads who liked the pub and a pint of Guinness. I had a bust-up with Gary at

Nottingham Forest which I apologised for. We were charging at each other and I regret that. I was at fault. Gary was thrown into the team and too much happened too soon with him. I tried my best with him."

McQueen's best was good enough for United fans who used to chant, 'Gordon McQueen, Gordon McQueen, Gordon! Gordon!' to the tune to which the French sing 'Allez les Bleus' – especially when he made one of his runs forward.

"I loved bombing forward and the crowd loved it too. I kept charging up until I ran out of grass or hit an advertising hoarding. I'd run five yards with the ball and could sense that they wanted me to run a bit more. They'd really get me at it so I'd move forward even more. Managers hated it and some of the players hated it. Frank Stapleton, who was pretty serious, used to look at me and I could tell he was thinking, 'Jesus Christ, what the hell is he up to?' I did it because I used to fancy myself as a bit of a left winger. I was always very quick too, despite being 6ft 4ins with gangly legs. I was the quickest player at Leeds and I was the quickest player at Old Trafford when I arrived at the club."

Another player famed for his electric pace who played at Old Trafford was Laurie Cunningham, the former West Brom and Real Madrid forward who made five appearances for United in the 1982/83 season. "Laurie was a fantastic fella," says McQueen. "He had played at Real Madrid where he came on loan to us from, yet did not pretend to be a star. He was supposed to play in the '83 Cup final but got injured." Cunningham died in a car crash in Madrid in 1989.

Another black striker [Cunningham was the first black player to represent England] who came on loan was Garth Crooks, he of the 12-clause question in his current role as a BBC analyst. Crooks played seven games in the 1983/84 season, while on loan from Tottenham.

But no matter who United signed, Liverpool's domination couldn't be broken.

"Liverpool were well ahead of us, the dominant side of the early

'80s," says McQueen. "Their recruitment was second to none and recruitment is by far the most important thing in football."

The two teams met in the 1983 Milk Cup final at Wembley.

"I had a bit of cramp so I was shoved up front. In the last minute of normal time I beat the offside trap and rounded Grobbelaar. There wasn't a Liverpool player in sight. All I had to do was roll it into an empty net. I was going to score the winner – there was no doubt about it – when he absolutely whacked me from behind. I flew right up into the air. It was assault. Nowadays he would have been sent off, no question."

Like the rest of his team-mates, he was feeling vengeful when United met Brighton in the FA Cup final two months later.

"Brighton were not a good side. But they could have beaten us if Gordon Smith had scored. Smith is from Ayrshire too and it was his chance to make history – although he says that more people talk about his miss than would have if he had scored."

As Smith moved towards Gary Bailey in the United goal, McQueen was captured by the cameras screaming "Oh, no!"

"It would have been ridiculous for us to lose to Brighton," he stresses, "so we were totally focused for the replay. There were even more United fans at that game because all the suits didn't take the tickets that should have gone to fans like they did in the first game. We slaughtered Brighton and it was a great night."

In 1985, McQueen missed out on a third FA Cup final with United, injury relegating him to the role of social convener.

"I had been out with a hamstring injury and was playing less and less," he says. "And it was quite a cruel final. Graeme Hogg had played most of the games leading up to it because Kevin Moran had been out injured. Kevin came into the side two weeks before the final and stayed there. I thought that was unfair and cruel on Graeme. Ron asked me to take disappointed lads like Graeme and Arthur Graham out the night before the game around Maidenhead, near to the team hotel. We had a great night but Graeme felt terrible. His family was down from Aberdeen. It was absolutely awful. Graeme was decent, he was quick, had a good left foot and he was strong physically. He gradually took my place by impressing and was pretty much a regular for two seasons. And yet Ron was proved right by the decision because United won the final."

Hogg played 109 games for Manchester United between 1984/88 before moving to Portsmouth and then Hearts.

"I don't think Hoggy was over-bothered by the trappings which surrounded a footballer," says McQueen. "He was an Aberdonian who liked his football and liked life. He'll be every bit as happy now fixing TV aerials [his current occupation] as what he was when he was a player with Manchester United.

"Kevin was a fantastic defensive partner for me too. He was very strong and quick, but blind as a bat. He got cut all the time because he would mix the ball up with people's heads. He wasn't great on the ball, but then he didn't pretend to be. He kept things simple. We both had a lot of injuries, but when we played together I felt very comfortable. We're good friends. We don't pick up the phone all the time but we get on very well."

Moran was rarely off McQueen's abuse radar for other reasons.

"Kevin was the worst dresser at the club, without doubt. Like the other Irish lads who turned up, he wore corduroys which were turned up, big brogues and jumpers and socks with patterns on them."

Moran's dress sense had been noted far earlier in his career. He had made a big impact for Dublin at Gaelic football with his style on and off the pitch, leading legendary manager Kevin Heffernan to say, "He drove a 125 motorbike, wore a multi-coloured woollen pullover and he had a mop of unruly hair and a big grin. You could not but take to the guy."

Thankfully, Moran was better dressed at his wedding.

"Kevin's wedding was funny. It was in the back of beyond in Ireland somewhere. He had about seven brothers and his wife had about seven sisters. We were getting stuck into the Guinness and it was a heavy night. I flew in on a private plane, which was tossed about everywhere, with Ron Wood [a wealthy United fan who was a business partner of Bryan Robson in the Birthdays' card group]. Kevin organised a pick-up lorry at the other end so me and Ron and his wife arrived at a posh wedding in a pick-up truck. We were due to fly back at ten in the morning and I was still drinking at six. I looked around and there was this guy who was absolutely paralytic and crashed out on the floor. It was the pilot who was due to fly us back."

McQueen turned 33 in the summer of 1985, the year he left United. By then Paul McGrath was becoming the dominant centre-half.

"Paul's career at Manchester United was okay, but he made a real name for himself when he went to Aston Villa where they handled him very well," says Gordon. "He was a phenomenal footballer, very much like Rio Ferdinand. He was quick, comfortable on the ball and could play midfield if needed. He was pretty good in the air without being dominant."

McQueen, meanwhile, could look back on a fine career at the top level. Aside from club football, he was capped 30 times for Scotland.

"It should have been a lot more but for injuries," he says. "Playing for my country meant everything to me, more than playing for United or Leeds. I scored against England at Wembley in '77, the first time we had beaten them in a long, long while. It was in front of reputedly the largest-ever away following in British football. There were 60,000 Scots in a 90,000 crowd, but Scotland were never given so many tickets again because the fans wrecked Wembley, invading the pitch, ripping up the turf and breaking one of the crossbars. They wrecked London too. It was a famous day; Kenny Dalglish got the other goal. If I had a pound for every person who claims to have been at that game I would have £410,000.

"Captaining my country aged 22 was special, but that day at Wembley was as good as it got for me as a footballer. My dad wasn't an emotional man, but he was in the crowd that day and I knew that he was a very, very proud man. He never had a drink but he said he could have launched a ship in all the whisky that he was offered on the way back to Scotland."

McQueen's highs in football were punctured by debilitating lows.

"A big regret was missing out on playing a World Cup because of injury."

Gordon McQueen

McQueen did travel in Ally Macleod's squad to Argentina in 1978, hoping to recover from a knee injury for the second round. But by the time he was fit, Scotland were home. And home, for many Scotland players, was England.

"The big clubs in the north of England used to have a lot of Scottish players and United were no exception. Managers used to go up to Scotland and come back with two new players; such was the wealth of talent. That has changed. There has been a huge influx of foreign players in Scotland, even at small clubs at Livingston. Quite simply, the Scots are not playing football like they did at a young age. It's a social issue – parents do not let their kids out on the streets like they used to and kids play on computers. I still believe that there is talent out there though, but clubs like Rangers and Celtic don't nurture it."

McQueen still had a year left on his United contract when he left Old Trafford in 1985. His careers at Elland Road and Old Trafford were almost identical – 171 appearances and 19 goals for Leeds; 184 appearances and 20 goals for United. He could have stayed at Old Trafford and taken the money, but instead approached Ron Atkinson and Martin Edwards on the infamous Jamaica trip.

"I said to them, 'I'm knackered. I don't feel like hanging around for another year. Is there any chance I can have a free transfer?' They agreed. I didn't feel like I was up to signing for another English club, but I'm not bragging when I say that I received an unbelievable amount of offers. I decided to go to Hong Kong to Seiko – the club owned by the watch company – and basically just mess around for a year or so. My legs were a mess; inflammation below the kneecap was the problem. Once you have it you never get rid of it. It still affects my knees now."

McQueen signed a contract as Seiko's player/coach, but Hong Kong didn't turn out how he anticipated.

"I got E-coli and I was really, really ill. I was on drips and it got so serious that the doctors were ringing my mum and dad to tell them to come over. I think I got it from a hamburger, but can't be sure. I was in hospital for five months and the main symptoms were sickness, diarrhoea and weight loss. I wasn't insured and I was in a private hospital, which became a bit scary financially. When I started to get a bit better after a few months, I got my wits about me. The physio would come in and do something with my feet for five minutes. It turned out she was charging £40 for each visit so I told her not to bother coming any more. I had to be on a 24-hour drip to get a certain amount of solution inside my body to clear the infection. It had cost me ten grand by this time. The doctor was Scottish, so I worked something out with him where he let me go home and he would inject me twice a day. Each injection took ten minutes. That was about a quarter of the price of the hospital fees."

After recovering from his illness, McQueen returned to Manchester in August 1987 and lived in a rented house with his family. It seemed inconceivable that McQueen's luck could get any worse. But it did.

"I lost absolute fortunes in the Hong Kong crash of 1987. Manchester United had given me a generous final payment and my wage with Seiko was tax-free. For the first time in my life I had a good amount of money. I met two Scottish guys in Hong Kong and put my money into funds, which started doing great. The United lads came across on a tour and I told them how much I was making with the funds. I even sold my house in Lymm and put the money into the funds, they were doing that well.

"I wasn't overly concerned when the stock markets started slipping, but then Black October happened and the markets just went 'Whhosssh'." McQueen watched his life savings vanish.

"I couldn't sleep, I was sweating continuously. My wife was crying all the time. There was just no obvious way for me to make money again. It wasn't that I was ripped off, a lot of people lost a lot of money at that time.

"I saved a bit," he says. "There was one fund called The Philippines Re-Development Fund which I had pulled out of just a few weeks before the crash. At least I had that and a bit of the shrapnel from the other stuff. Overall though, it was a fucking nightmare."

McQueen now had to give great consideration to something he had never cared about.

Gordon McQueen

"When I had signed for Manchester United and Leeds I couldn't have cared less about the money, I just wanted to play football. But I could have done with some financial advice when it came to pensions. You had to take a footballer's pension which matured when you were 35. I was told that I had to take that money when I was 35, which was nonsense. I didn't need that money at the time and I took it. If that money had been allowed to grow, I could have had the type of pension now that would mean I wouldn't have to work."

The wages of present-day footballers elicit a strong reaction.

"I envy the players nowadays. Never mind all that nonsense about 'good luck to them'. I am pig sick that I didn't earn the money that they are earning, especially those with limited ability. I have never been over bothered about money, but it would have been nice to have been able to look after my mum and dad. My opinion might sound cynical, but actually I'm still happy as a pig in shit and always have been. I love life. I just have a drink and get on with things."

In the summer of 1987, McQueen took the manager's job at Airdrieonians.

"It was a great little club, but a real eye-opener after being at Manchester United. The problem was that it was part-time. I called a few favours in and we did okay. Gary Walsh came on loan from United after his head injury."

In fact, goalkeeper Walsh, who made 63 United appearances between 1986 and 1994, had suffered two head injuries. He was concussed at Hillsborough in 1987 – where United regularly took in excess of 15,000 travelling fans in the '80s – but he played on through the game even though he was later hospitalised. A far more serious head injury followed on tour in the summer, in Bermuda, when he was kicked in the head so violently that the offending striker broke his ankle. Walsh didn't remember anything about the challenge, yet somehow walked off the pitch into an ambulance. The Bermudan striker came to see him in hospital – in a wheelchair. Walsh's mother was so concerned that she tried to talk Alex Ferguson into persuading her son to retire. He didn't. Brave and agile, Walsh went on loan to Airdrie, a stint which he enjoyed. The players made him feel welcome, but he felt embarrassed because the other players were part-timers who would finish shift work and then play, whereas he would fly to games and stay in a hotel.

Under McQueen, Airdrie finished fourth and fifth in successive seasons.

"The teams above us were full-time," he says. "I kept going to the board and insisting that we went full-time. I'd go to board meetings and there would be 12 guys there who would talk about how many pies they had sold after the last game. They would drink huge amounts of whisky until they were absolutely bladdered. The football would come as an afterthought when the chairman would say things like, 'Two of our players have been injured with detached retinas. What are you doing in training because there seems to be one eye injury after another?' I couldn't cope with it any more and they were never going to go full-time, so I packed it in and started doing punditry for Scottish Television."

It wasn't to his liking.

"I found it boring and repetitive and there was no excitement because Rangers and Celtic dominated and teams played each other four times a season."

McQueen's next employment came courtesy of Bryan Robson.

"Robbo said to me, 'If I get a job in football then I'm going to take you with me.' In 1994, he got the Middlesbrough job and kept to his word. We were desperate to do well for one another. Initially, I was reserve team coach and then I became first team coach. It was a real close-knit relationship we had among the back-room staff and that was down to Bryan and Viv Anderson too. We completely and utterly revolutionised Middlesbrough Football Club. Bryan got [Chairman] Steve Gibson thinking in a more professional way. We used to train at a place where the dog shit had to be cleared off the pitch before we started. We brought in a nutritionist and a new training ground was built. Boro are where they are today because of Robbo."

Injuries forced McQueen to give up coaching.

"I started to have real problems with my body," he says. "I had to have my ankle replaced after six operations and I still have a bit of a limp. My new ankle hasn't really worked and the rest of my ankle is a mess. It means I can't play golf as much as I'd like . . ."

But McQueen just takes it all in his giant stride.

"I had a happy childhood. I've had a happy life. I've never been anything but happy."

After Middlesbrough, he returned to television, working for Sky.

"They keep asking me back and I enjoy the people that I work with. I want to do more Sky work and keep friendly with the people I've been friendly with – the people who mean the world to me. I don't see all the lads I played with as often as I'd like. We've all gone our separate ways. But as you get older I think that I'd like to see more of the lads."

Bryan Robson and Joe Jordan, who made 126 United appearances and scored 41 goals for United between 1977 and 1981 before moving to Milan for £325,000, are two he does keep in contact with.

"They are my two big pals in football. Joe is serious and to a lot of people he is dour. I find him good fun. I was the best man at his wedding and he was the best man at mine. He is conscientious and a real hard grafter, someone who is totally dedicated to his work.

"As a player Joe was so determined. He had great aerial ability, timing and was quick. He was fearless too. If somebody did him then he'd do them back, absolutely no doubt. He wasn't clinical in front of goal like Ian Rush, but centre-halves hated playing against him. He was always a really popular player with the fans, even when he played in Milan where he wasn't a regular."

McQueen wouldn't have liked to have played against Jordan, yet found his compatriot Andy Gray to be one of the toughest opponents.

"Andy was a handful. He had two years at Aston Villa where he was fantastic. Kevin Keegan was tough, too, because he was quick, elusive and difficult to pin down. He never got the credit in Britain that he deserved. Yet he went abroad and was European Footballer of the Year twice. If it was Keegan and Toshack then I'd have no problem with Toshack."

He had no problem with United fans either.

We're The Famous Man United

"I had a good relationship with the fans. I don't think I'm remembered as a legend, but I think I was quite popular. I had a lot of injuries, which meant I was never as fit as I should have been, and I wasn't the most disciplined defender. There was a bit of inconsistency about my football as well. But I still loved playing for Manchester United, my days there were easily the most memorable of my career and they are my team, without a doubt. I have a soft spot for Middlesbrough because I worked there for seven years, live near there, know a lot of the people behind the scenes and my son is a season ticket holder, but Manchester United is my team. They get in your blood. I'm glad that I've kept a lovely relationship with a lot of the Leeds lads, more so than the United lads, but I am always treated really well when I go to Old Trafford. I don't know of a club in Britain that looks after their ex-players as well as Manchester United."

If McQueen envies the wages earned by today's footballers, he doesn't envy their lives.

"We had good fun because there wasn't the pressure that players get now, not the tabloid papers. We lived a normal existence. I lived in Lymm the whole time that I was in Manchester, but all the lads more or less lived in Sale as there wasn't the money to live in Prestbury or Hale. We'd all go to the pub together, we didn't have problems with fans and I can't remember a front page story involving Manchester United in all the time I was there. It has changed. The money which footballers earn antagonises fans nowadays. The ticket prices are going up every year and fans feel that players are getting all the money. I think that makes it even more difficult for players now. Supporters don't have the warmth towards the players that we had."

His daughter Hayley, who has just started working for Sky TV, rings him. She's in Eindhoven to cover Middlesbrough's UEFA Cup final and wants to pick her dad's brain. She's also partly responsible for losing her dad's video collection of his career from his time at United.

"I gave them to her when she worked at Boro TV and never saw them again," he says, in a 'that's life' manner.

"It all goes by too quickly," sighs McQueen over a last pint back in the Black Bull. "We were young men from working-class backgrounds who played for Manchester United and travelled the world – the centre of attention wherever we went. We were solid; at least eight of us went to the pub twice a week. Looking back, it was as if we were together for five minutes and then it's all gone."

5
Arthur Albiston

Reliability

"We're all Reds," says Arthur Albiston on the telephone when we arrange to meet for an interview in a coffee bar at his gym in one of Manchester's leafiest suburbs. Given that he works for MUTV and BBC Radio Manchester, Albiston has a career to safeguard and needs to feel he can trust me. Albiston has never been the type to go bleating to the tabloids about the injustices of team selection or a manager with whom he doesn't see eye to eye.

Talk to people close to United about Albiston and they speak well of the Scot who played 482 games between 1974 and 1988, the first United player to win three FA Cup winners' medals. Only six players have worn the red shirt more times. "Good family man Arthur, never a big drinker," says one. "His personality reflects what he was like as a player," another. So I expect him to be dependable, determined and efficient.

Yet Albiston knows that his statement about all being Reds isn't the catch-all it once was. Take his own family.

"Our oldest boy is a big United fan but he has refused to go to the match since the 2005 FA Cup final," he says in a soft Edinburgh accent when we meet. "He was against the takeover and now watches FC United. I was at the 2005 final and trying to get hold of him to meet him in the Hilton hotel before the game. But whenever I rang he sounded like he wasn't interested in meeting me, which seemed strange. I just thought, 'Fair enough, he wants to be with his mates.' When I read the papers the following day, I realised why. He was pictured holding a banner against the takeover.

"Our other lad still goes to United. He asked me to get him two tickets for the cup game at Anfield recently. I could have got them but I wasn't keen on him going. You have to know your way around that ground; it's not a safe place. So I told him that I couldn't get any tickets and he told me that he was still going to go."

Not that Albiston was ever unnerved by a visit to L4.

"People still come up to me and talk about the winner I scored in '81. People can chat about cup finals, but that game is the one that they always bring up."

Albiston likes talking about this match.

"I had no fear going to places like Anfield. I used to love it, in fact. I knew what that game meant to United fans, the 3,000 who used to stand packed in the corner of the Anfield Road. We couldn't lose against them, even though Liverpool were winning everything, and they were European champions.

"We battered the Scousers that day in 1981, battered them," he reminisces. "We should have won by three or four. Kevin Moran had put us ahead in front of the Kop, then they got a penalty – which wasn't unusual – and equalised. There was no way they deserved a draw. With a few minutes left, a ball got played into the box. It came to me about 40 yards out. I'd already had a couple of shots which was unusual. This time I controlled it on my chest and was going to hit it, but then I changed my mind and played a one-two with Frank Stapleton. So I was back with the ball. I thought, 'Let's try something different here and not panic like you usually do.' I was on the edge of the box. I wanted to stay on my feet and win a penalty. Souness came in from the side so I shot. I slipped as I shot but the ball rolled into the corner. I should have done a Gary Neville and ran to the home fans to wind the Scousers up, but I ran straight to the away end.

"A mate of the players called Arthur Jones was watching in the main stand. We'd got him tickets and he was having the banter with Liverpool fans, giving them all kinds of stick. He probably had a bit of back-up, because he wouldn't have done it by himself. He left the ground just before the end and got a load of abuse as he was going. He said that grannies were abusing him. He was feeling disconsolate as he made his exit, then I scored. So he ran back down the steps going mad. He got out alive to tell the tale. The players enjoyed hearing that more than anything because you don't fully appreciate what it's like to be a fan when you play. You don't fully understand the emotions that fans go through. It's only when you stop playing that you start to understand."

Albiston was born in Edinburgh in 1957.

"Like many boys, all I wanted to do was play football. My father was a painter and decorator, my mother did odd jobs. I'm from the west side of the city, a working-class area. Dad was from Leith, near the docks, and was a Hibs fan. They had a great side in the '50s. Hearts was the closest ground to us and all my mates were Hearts supporters. I didn't identify with one team though. Hibs played European football in the mid-'60s and I saw Dino Zoff, the famous Italian goalkeeper, concede five goals against them. Midweek games were better for me because I played on a Saturday and Sunday.

"We had a park which wasn't far from us. Before I played structured football, we used to play there all the time and were split into two age groups. If the older lads were short of players they would get the best of the younger lads to play. I used to get picked a lot, so I realised for the first time that I was quite good. I always seemed to play with guys who were older than me, which really helped my game. You couldn't hold onto the ball for too long because you would get clobbered. So I learned how to pass and move through fear."

Aged 11, Albiston moved to senior school.

"I could have gone to a so-called grammar school, a brainier school, but they didn't play football so I didn't sit the exams. But I probably would have passed the exams. But I went to just a normal working-class school because I wanted to play football and all the guys I played with at the primary school went there."

He may have not been an academic, but Albiston was a grafter.

"I had a great childhood, but my mentality has always been to work for whatever you want in life. Everybody wanted a pair of Adidas Santiagos with screw-in studs, but I knew if I wanted a new pair of football boots then I had to contribute to them because there wasn't enough money going round.

"As a kid I had a milk round which everybody aspired to do – they were much better than paper rounds. But I did paper rounds as well, five of them on a Sunday. The milk round was the elite job though; it wasn't easy to get a milk round job because you had to be recommended. My brother got me the job and I was up at half six every morning and delivering milk from an old Bedford van which had a sliding door. The milkman wouldn't stop because it took too much time so there was an art to lunging onto it. There was a skill to make sure you didn't kick a gate open so it swung back and smashed all the bottles in your hand too."

The money earned allowed him to buy the boots.

"I was so proud of them that after getting changed I used to get someone to carry me over the concrete between the changing-rooms and the pitch because I didn't want my studs getting messed up."

Albiston played for his school team and got into the Edinburgh team at Under 11 and 12, and 15 levels, then Scotland's Under 15 team.

"I played with Gordon Strachan, who comes from Edinburgh, in most teams," he says. "He stood out because he could beat people comfortably, but he was very, very small so he had to show a lot of determination, a lot of heart and he was exactly what he was like when he got older. Neil McNab, who ended up having a spell at Man City, was from the same team."

Only two of that Scotland team were not signed up by professional clubs.

"I never really thought for one minute that I was destined to be a footballer," says Albiston. "Gordon was the one with everybody chasing him, but I was just happy to just play."

Manchester United were the first team to approach Albiston.

"Once United showed a bit of interest a lot of Scottish teams and a few other English teams followed suit. And while I wouldn't say I lacked confidence, I never asked to go on trials at any clubs like Hearts, Rangers or Celtic.

"My dad was approached by Sir Matt Busby's half-brother, a guy called Jimmy Mathie who was United's main scout in Scotland. He asked me to go to United for a trial over the Easter school holidays. The thing which impressed me most was United's organisation. We had an itinerary mapped out and the flight tickets were sent to our house. Literally five minutes after the tickets had arrived we got a phone call from the late John Aston who was the chief scout co-ordinator. I was still looking at the flight tickets and I was so excited. They had taken the time to see that the tickets had arrived. I wondered why United were taking such a big interest in me. My mum was impressed too."

Albiston was also impressed by United's Scottish connections.

"There were a lot of Scottish players – eight of them started in Lou Macari's debut against West Ham in 1973," he says. "The numbers have reduced ever since and that saddens me. But whereas United once recruited from Britain and Ireland, they now get players in from around the world."

Albiston flew alone to Ringway.

"When I got to Manchester Airport I was looking for an imposing guy called John Aston with a shirt and tie. So I was surprised when this guy bowled up, a normal taxi driver from Stretford with a fag in his mouth. He was Norman Davies, who went on to be the kit man for many years.

"We played games in the morning and went bowling or to the pictures in the afternoon. I enjoyed it. We went to a game and saw United lose 3-0 at home to Liverpool at the beginning of April 1972. Kevin Keegan scored a couple of goals. I sat in K Stand and there were 53,000 inside Old Trafford. United were having a ropey spell, but the atmosphere was unbelievable. I wasn't overawed because, without wanting to sound spoilt, I'd seen Scotland play at Wembley and Celtic play Rangers. I once saw Alex Ferguson play for Rangers against Hearts with 45,000 inside Tynecastle. The gaffer would admit that he wasn't the most skilful player, but he certainly put himself about."

The trial was a success and Albiston did meet Aston: in fact, Aston accompanied him back home to Edinburgh because he wanted to speak to his parents. He wanted him to sign for United.

"I went to Manchester with a relaxed attitude and that probably helped," says Albiston. "Being relatively small, I showed that I wouldn't be intimidated by bigger lads. I got stuck in too. I was determined and never gave up. I was a trier. I'd seen United on the telly but I didn't appreciate how big they were and United's league position at the time didn't suggest greatness – Derby County won the league that year. If I had realised then maybe it would have frightened me.

"John Aston told my parents that they wanted me to start an apprenticeship in July. My dad asked me what I wanted to do. I told him that I had enjoyed my week in Manchester. He told me to go for it. There was no pressure.

"I finished school in the summer. I didn't sit an exam and don't have a qualification to my name – which my two boys keep reminding me about. If I had studied and tried harder I would have done quite well, but my thoughts were on football."

Albiston's first contract was worth £6.43 a week, plus a 57p national insurance stamp. He got 50p expenses every time he had to go to the Cliff for a game and a pound for a win.

"Money was irrelevant," he says. "I stayed in digs and switched around quite a bit. First I stayed near Hope Hospital but the lady was too house proud. You had to take your shoes off at the door and pay to watch a black and white telly while she was in the other room watching a colour one. My second digs were closer to the Cliff and there were six of us there. I lived in Chorlton and then Sale where I was re-united with a lad called Jimmy Kelly from Carlisle. He was in the first team squad and made a sub's appearance in a cup game against Peterborough. Then he went to America and stayed there. Jimmy was really into music but I wasn't. I listened to my sister's Motown and Soul collection but Jimmy used to buy the New Musical Express and knew all the cutting edge bands.

"You were allowed to go home once a month, and some of the lads always did this. I didn't. I didn't want to give United any excuse to let me go, so I'd usually stay because I didn't want to miss a game. My parents would come and see me. My dad would come down on the train to watch me play and I'd go home once every two months. You had a two-year apprenticeship and I felt that I really had to prove myself to get a professional contract. I knew that most players wouldn't be kept on so I tried extra hard to make sure that I was one who was."

The work ethic paid off when he was offered a two year pro-contract in July 1974 on £25 a week.

"My parents came down to see me sign and we had a meal in the pub opposite Hope Hospital before they flew back to Edinburgh," he recalls.

Two months earlier, he had travelled to see United at Stoke away for the final game of the 1974/75 season with his mates.

"We were already relegated and I travelled on the train with United fans from Salford. I was an apprentice and one of the other lads was from Blackley and he knew the proper fans. I couldn't get my head round the reception we got from the police at Stoke station. We were met by barking dogs and horses, frog-marched to the ground and treated like crap. You lead a cosseted life as a player and don't see stuff like that. We saw incidents a couple of times in Europe from the team bus, where our fans were getting treated badly. You know what it does? It makes you feel more determined.

"A lot of lads lived in digs in Stretford, Urmston and Chorlton, so we used to congregate in Stretford and watch *Match of the Day* every week in the Bass Drum on Chester Road – which was a bit tricky in those days. We'd then go to a big disco called the Hard Rock which was near Old Trafford cricket ground. When we were a bit older we went to the Sands in Stretford. That was the place. A few of the City lads like Peter Barnes and Gary Owen used to go in there and we got on well with them. Sammy McIlroy was a few years older than us and used to lead us astray. There was a place called Browns too in Stretford. We dressed like Starsky and Hutch with big wide collared shirts, although the club were strict about players not wearing platform shoes in case you went over on your ankles.

"I wasn't silver tongued when it came to chatting girls up. I was quite wary of people until I had got to know them. I met my wife Elaine in the Sands. It was the night of Paddy Crerand's testimonial in November 1975. I was 18. She was a Fallowfield girl from a family of eight – half City and half United."

Albiston had made his first team debut a year earlier in October 1974, aged just 17, against Manchester City.

"I was in Scotland for a Scottish youth team game when I was called back to Manchester," he recalls. "I was disappointed about that. I didn't know that I was going to play in the first team in the Manchester derby. My only previous experience playing at Old Trafford was for the reserves. It was completely different in front of 55,000. I felt so lifted when I ran out. City had the Scoreboard End but the rest was United. Two thoughts hit me: 90 per cent of people here are going home disappointed if we don't win, and, second, we can't let these people down. It really mattered; even at throw-ins, the fans were right behind you. That helped a lot. We were in the second division, too, so a game against City really mattered. Luckily we got a result and won 1-0. I played a couple more times that season."

Later that season, Albiston travelled to Norwich, once again as a fan.

"It was in the league cup and one of the other apprentices had a Volkswagen Beetle. It took ages to get there because the A14 wasn't like it is now. I had already played for United, but I didn't really get recognised. I saw that people went through a lot of crap to get to games. I wasn't a United fan, as I hadn't long left Edinburgh, but I couldn't help get a feeling for the club and that has never left."

Albiston went on to feature sporadically over the next few years.

"I trained with the first team and never felt overawed by them," he says. "There were a lot of Scottish accents which made me feel at home too. Yet I had paid to watch Lou Macari and Martin Buchan play football, and five years later I was playing alongside them. Once they start taking the mickey out of you, you know you are okay. The Irish lads got unmerciful stick – again it was sign of acceptance. They took the piss out of my hair, clothes and accents. I wouldn't have minded, but people who took the mickey were Scottish too!

"In the summer of '75 we went on a post-season tour. Me, Jimmy Nicholl and David McCreery. Steve Coppell finished his exams and then flew out with Matt Busby. Most of the older players didn't want to be on the trip. They were arranging meetings about meetings because they didn't want to be there. They were away from their families for 38 days and played ten matches. There were 14 flights and 32,000 miles to fly. We went to Iran, Hong Kong, Jakarta, Bangkok, Australia. Tommy Docherty had to come on as sub in one of the games. He got sent off. Jim Holton and Alex Forsyth missed the births of their kids. But for the younger lads who were shielded from the arguments, it was a great adventure and we loved the trip. I saw the world at 17 and marked Johnny Rep of Ajax in Bangkok. We had a young inexperienced side; they had Rep and several other stars who had played in a World Cup final. Rep had also scored the winning goal for Ajax in a European Cup final. He was an effective wide player, but he scored goals too. He was a team player, too, who didn't get caught out of position. Rep rarely lost the ball and seemed like a good guy, which added to his popularity. I was young and would have liked to have played against him when I had more experience, to see if I would have fared better.

"It would never happen now, a trip like that, especially as when we got back we had one week off and then we were back in training again."

Albiston was still a young squad player.

"I was happier to play more games each season, but I saw '76/77 as a make-or-break season for me," he says.

It would make him in a big way, when he was chosen to play in the FA Cup final against Liverpool in place of the injured left-back Stewart Houston. Albiston was cast as the rookie, United's inexperienced weakest link. The pundits predicted that Liverpool winger Steve Heighway would quickly shred the confidence of the callow 19-year-old and United would be exposed to the wily European champions-elect. That was the script. Albiston didn't read it.

"I'd actually played 30 or 40 United games. The United fans knew me, yet the media labelled me as a rookie who would be intimidated by the occasion and big crowd. They were wrong. I'd played in front of big crowds before and found it more intense at Southampton or West Ham where the crowd were closer. At Wembley, the crowd were distanced from the pitch and it wasn't an issue.

"And I had had time to prepare for the final. The Doc told me at Bristol City two weeks before the final, after Stewart broke his ankle, that I would play. Stewart had played in every game and scored in the sixth round, so I didn't feel it was right to just come into that game, but that happens in football – players get injured and suspended."

Albiston followed his manager's philosophy of free play that led to the spontaneous attacking football loved by Reds in the '70s.

"Tommy Docherty would say, 'Pass the ball to the nearest red shirt, get it wide and get crosses in.' I got a couple of early tackles in which helped my confidence, but my lasting memory is of Ray Kennedy having a shot near the end that nearly went in.

"It didn't, and United lifted the cup – just as the Doc had promised a year earlier after the 1–0 final defeat by Southampton.

"I didn't feel that I could enjoy it as much as the later cup finals because I didn't feel part of the team. I offered Stewart my medal. I was brought up in a household when if you wanted something you had to work for it. Stewart had contributed a lot more to the run than I." Houston politely declined.

Arthur Albiston

Albiston's relationship with Houston had always been solid.

"Stewart was seven or eight years older than me. I was living in digs in Sale where Stuart had a house and he would give me a lift now and then. I never saw myself as competing with him, but as someone I could learn from. He carried himself well on and off the pitch and was great with the young lads. I simply wasn't a threat to him."

After '77, Albiston did become a threat, although the pair both played many times in the same team.

"I started getting more of a regular game under Dave Sexton. I was fortunate that I was starting the season with a new manager. The team wasn't doing as well as we should have done, but I had just turned 20 and was just happy to be playing.

"I found Dave Sexton was far more into coaching than Tommy Docherty. He wasn't as vocal and had less front. He spoke calmly and didn't like you swearing. After Tommy Docherty that was no good for the media or the fans. United are huge and the media want something every day, something Dave wasn't comfortable with. As a guy, I've got the utmost respect for him. He showed confidence in me and that means a lot to a footballer.

"Dave tried to structure the team differently to the Doc, who had used two young wingers, Gordon Hill and Steve Coppell, with great effect. How many players come from teams like Millwall and Tranmere, join United and then play for England within a season?

"Dave was criticised for getting rid of Gordon Hill and signing Mickey Thomas, who was more of a midfield player than a winger. We were used to playing football off the cuff and that changed a bit. I was used to getting the ball from Alex Stepney all the time and play would build up from the back. It was great as a full-back as you were encouraged to get forward. Dave didn't change the way I played as a defender, but things changed in front of me. People said that the team had their wings clipped, and they had a point. The Doc would build people up and give you confidence. Dave introduced more coaching. He was quite a deep guy. When I was injured he barely spoke to me which was strange."

Albiston's first serious injury in the middle of the 1979/80 season meant he had to have the cartilage from his knee removed.

"It's bone against bone now. After the operation they gave me my cartilage to take home. It was shaped like a squashed prawn and ripped at the end. These days, they would just cut out the bit that was ripped. It still affects me to this day. When I stand up after sitting down I have to rub my knee for five minutes to get it going."

To alleviate the pressure on his knee when he played, Albiston did a lot of weights to build up the muscle around it. "Now, I'll do a lot of swimming and cycling. I keep fit to improve my golf," he says.

Albiston's return coincided with a winning run as United won ten out of 12 games at the end of that season.

"We never considered it a championship race because we were so far behind Liverpool, but we just kept going. We could have won the league had we beaten Leeds away at Elland Road on the last day of the season and Liverpool lost at home." True to form, Liverpool won and United lost. But life off the field was good.

"I had got married in 1978 and our eldest lad Ross, the FC fan, was born in March 1980. Ryan is the United fan. I lived in Sale in a semi-detached house close to Paddy Crerand and Stuart Pearson. A lot of the players lived in Sale then and we used to knock about together. I used to go out in Fallowfield quite a bit because my wife was from there. City fans would engage in friendly banter, but never anything malicious. We'd go in the Little B pub in Sale with the football lads. The Sale rugby union lads used to drink in there too.

"After finishing second in 1980, we were optimistic about the season ahead. We had a young team and several players were in their prime. Then we also had a bit of experience with people like Martin Buchan and Lou Macari."

But United didn't start well, and after defeating Middlesbrough in their first game, didn't win for five matches and were victorious just three times in the first 15 games.

"I don't know what happened," he says. "The pressure was building on Dave Sexton. We finished in 8th position and that's not good enough for a club of United's stature and Dave was sacked.

Arthur Albiston

When Ron took over, I got a bit nervous. We had suffered a few bad results against his West Brom team and I think he had his mind made up about a few of the players when he arrived. I didn't think that he liked me as a player. Sammy McIlroy and Jimmy Nicholl, two lads I had played with a lot, didn't feature much at all. I explained this to my wife and told her that we might be on the move."

However, Atkinson's first season, 1981/82, was Albiston's best for United.

"I felt like I couldn't do anything wrong," he says. "I felt that I was under the spotlight and I worked really hard. I was my own biggest critic. I knew it if I'd played badly. I didn't need others to tell me."

He was wrong about Atkinson in other ways.

"My impression of Ron had been formed by what I'd seen on TV, and before he joined United I thought he was a little bit full of himself. He portrayed the sun-tanned champagne image, yet I never saw him drunk. When he arrived, I got on fine with him in the flesh although he made a point of praising me in front of other players which I wasn't comfortable with. I found it embarrassing and didn't need my ego massaging. When we played five-a-side he would play and pick the teams, and he's always say, 'I'll have the three players who did well last Saturday.' Then he'd usually pick me. But maybe that was Ron's way of encouraging me. I wasn't an outgoing type off the field and perhaps he thought he was boosting my confidence.

"Ron was more of a throwback to the Doc and was into man-management. I quickly found that it was a myth that Ron was all talk. His knowledge of football and his memory were superb. He would know if you made a mistake or contributed to a goal in a match two seasons earlier, before he had even joined United.

"He made mistakes though. Ron liked to be surrounded by people he was comfortable with. A lot of his friends used to come to the training ground. For the 1983 Cup Final, Ron made a big mistake with Martin Buchan. Ron allowed TV crews onto the team bus which meant that there wasn't enough space for all the players. Martin Buchan was one of several players who had to get a taxi to Wembley."

Whether or not this contributed to the team's performance at Wembley, United nearly made a mess of their big show, when Brighton striker Gordon Smith famously missed his chance with the score at 2–2.

"I met Gordon Smith and told him that he had featured in many nightmares," says Albiston of a recent encounter.

Two years later Albiston played in his fourth FA Cup final for United, against Everton, whose line-up included Trevor Steven, one of Albiston's most difficult opponents.

"The greatest compliment I can give Trevor Steven is that he stopped me doing my job. Sometimes you come up against daydreamers who give you time on the ball, but Trevor closed me down quickly and didn't allow that. Like all good wingers, he knew his position in the team. Wingers have to be skilful, but they need to play as a team rather than as an individual. Steven wasn't a dribbling winger who would run at defenders, but he was still awkward to play against. And for that reason he was one of the mainstays in that very successful Everton side of the '80s."

Yet Albiston missed the real drama in the 1985 final, after his attempt to "kick Peter Reid" saw him twist his ankle and leave the field to sit alongside Kevin Moran.

"We had ten men and hung on," he remembers of that day in May 1985, "but Everton looked tired, too, because they'd just had a European final. I was right behind Norman Whiteside's shot, and when it went in I jumped into Ron's arms and wrapped my legs around him. I got hammered for that, especially with my injured ankle. Sometimes you do daft things."

Aside from erratic celebrations, what Atkinson and United fans like about Albiston is that he always appeared to give a hundred per cent and seemed fearless.

"I was never intimidated," he says. "My dad always said, 'Get wired in' [get stuck in]. As a schoolboy, he would keep my feet on the ground by telling me that he hadn't been hearing great reports about me. It taught me to take nothing for granted in football and made me more determined. I used to love playing at Liverpool,

Arthur Albiston

Everton or Tottenham away. I was quick too. I did sprint training as a kid, and my dad knew some athletics trainers in Edinburgh. I used to do sprint training when I went back in the summer. It helped me a lot, taught me how to run properly from a standing start and how to lift my legs properly. I enjoyed it. I never feared pre-season and all the distance running because I liked cross country running. There's no better feeling than being fit. I loved the feeling after a good training session. I'd walk off the pitch feeling like superman, before having a soak in the bath and getting changed."

Albiston was popular with other players, but that didn't protect him from leg-pulling.

"I was frequently set up. On a plane in America I had permission to leave my seat early to catch a connecting flight. When I stood up someone shouted, 'Stop, he's got my wallet.' Three fat Americans jumped on me.

"Gordon McQueen and John Gidman were characters. We wound Giddy up for being a Scouser. Once, we returned from a European tie and we were trying to persuade him to go for a late beer at Paddy's pub. It was about 1.30 in the morning. He wouldn't come, saying that he wanted to get back to Liverpool so we gave him some abuse as he walked to his car in the car park at Manchester Airport. He gave a load back as he climbed into his Capri. His car edged forward and, somehow, flopped onto the floor as the wheels rolled away. Someone had been in the process of stealing them, but hadn't quite finished. Being professionals keen to emphasise team spirit, we left John stranded. He waited four hours to be sorted out."

So the players were too busy playing pranks to win the league in the '70s and '80s?

"Not at all. We were a football club, not a social club. We had a responsibility to the supporters. We liked a laugh and night out, but there wasn't a drinking culture different from any other club. I don't think the drink culture was a problem and Liverpool probably drank more than us. They had a better team than us, a more consistent team at least, which were taken up a level by playing in Europe most seasons and we missed out by not playing in Europe for five seasons.

I used to drink, but I stopped in '87. I could discipline myself if I was injured to stop eating garbage and drinking when I was out. And I remember looking up to Arnold Muhren, who was a great player to have in front of me. His demeanour off the pitch rubbed off on some of the other lads and I really looked up to him, the way in which he carried himself off the pitch and never drank alcohol."

Why didn't United win the league then?

"We had good enough players, we proved that with the results we got against the top sides like Liverpool, but we weren't consistent against your Coventrys. Not winning the league for so long started to weigh heavily on the players, too. That and relying on Bryan Robson. The players sensed that if he was injured, we would struggle. And, unfortunately, Robbo was often injured."

One such injury prevented Robson playing against Everton at Goodison Park on Boxing Day 1986. Albiston was injured but travelled to the ground with the team.

"You feel like a spare part when you are not playing and I wanted to get away from the lads and give them some space. A few of us were injured, not just me and Robbo.

"We were already inside the ground, but we were told we'd have to go back outside to pick up our tickets. This policeman looked at Robbo and said, 'You get to the back of the queue like anyone else.' Outside the ground the Scousers were giving us loads of abuse, spitting at us and stuff. I wasn't frightened because it was laughable. I had been at Rangers v Celtic so nothing fazed me. People started throwing things at us but we couldn't do much because we were so outnumbered. Eventually Everton opened up a door for us and let us into the main stand. I couldn't see Gary Neville having to do that in Liverpool today."

Albiston had recovered to travel to the 1986 World Cup Finals in Mexico, where Scotland were managed by the Aberdeen boss Alex Ferguson after the sudden death of Jock Stein.

"I won 14 Scotland caps between 1983 and the Mexico '86 World Cup, but I didn't perform as well as I could do for Scotland. Frank Gray was in the team in my position before me and Maurice Malpas was younger. Dalglish, Souness and Hansen played in a good side, and it was very hard to get in the squad, let alone the team. In 1986 we were in a tough group featuring West Germany, Uruguay, Denmark and ourselves. I enjoyed being in Mexico with Alex being in charge. He was organised, hungry to learn and made training interesting. I know Alex went to have a few meetings with Sir Alf Ramsey before the World Cup. He knew that Sir Alf had taken England to Mexico in 1970 and wanted to learn lessons from him. People in England don't realise the impact Alex had on Scottish football by breaking the domination of Celtic and Rangers with Aberdeen, a provincial town."

The summer of 1986 was eventful.

"We played in Amsterdam on a pre-season tournament and some of our fans got in trouble on the ferry on the way over from Harwich after fighting with West Ham. The ferry was turned back.

"It was a round-robin tournament over a weekend and we lost our first game 3–0 on Friday night. Ron got wind that a few of the lads had gone out for a beer on the Friday after that one and told the players that we were to eat together without exception on the Saturday night before a game on the Sunday. A few of us went for a swim and a sauna on the Saturday and what we called 'the Madame Tussauds squad' – the sightseers – went around Amsterdam. They were mostly young players looking to make a good impression. Me, Kevin, Robbo, Norman and Paul McGrath stayed at the hotel and played cards. We were down for the meal at 7.30pm, but there was no sign of the magnificent seven. An hour passed and there was still no sign of them.

"Ron said, 'If it was you lot who had gone missing I wouldn't be as bothered, but I'm worried because it was the younger ones.' Soon it was ten o'clock and they still hadn't come back. Ron and Mick Brown were raging. Then three taxis pulled up outside the hotel. The hotel, on the outskirts of Amsterdam, had a garage on the forecourt. Mick went to meet the first taxi. The driver saw him coming and asked him to fill the car up. He thought he was a petrol attendant. Mick was fuming by this time.

"The missing lads eventually turned up very late and were fined."

Although sad to see Ron Atkinson leave, Albiston was pleased when it was announced that Ferguson was going to be made United manager three months later.

"I was playing awfully before Alex arrived because I was struggling with a groin muscle injury. I played in the gaffer's first game at Oxford, but I barely played again that season. He said to me, 'You don't even look like you are walking right, get it sorted out.' I had a hernia operation in December and got back into contention in the spring, but I didn't end up playing much under Alex. I was 30 and back to full fitness, and I knew I was capable of playing for United. Colin Gibson was playing in my position and not playing that well, but I wasn't one to go knocking on doors demanding my place in the team. I wasn't brought up to beg for anything. He was named ahead of me in one team and patted my leg to say 'Never mind' – which really wasn't the done thing to do.

"Colin was so easy to wind up. We played one game at Oxford. The gaffer was paranoid about us resting before matches, to the point where he made a big speech about how he didn't want us to play snooker or golf. But for some reason or another Colin wasn't there to hear it. Gary Bailey had given everyone who played in his testimonial a snooker cue and case, and we knew that the hotel in Oxford had snooker tables, so we told Colin we were going to have a snooker tournament and to bring his cue. The team coach used to pick up lads who lived on the south side of Manchester at Bucklow Hill on the A56 (the rest would get on at Old Trafford). So Gibbo and I were waiting with Robbo, Kevin and a few others for the team coach. As the bus came over the brow of the hill, with Alex and Archie Knox sat at the front, we all stepped aside so Gibbo was left standing by himself with his snooker cue. The manager gave him a right bollocking.

"I don't want it to sound like I am having a go at Colin because we competed for the same position because I'm not. I've got no problem with him; it's just that he was really, really easy to wind up. We watched the 1987 FA Cup Final between Tottenham and Coventry

Arthur Albiston

in Malta on a holiday. It was a great game. We were genuinely pleased for the Coventry lads to win the Cup, but Gibbo was saying, 'Who do they think they are? Who does that Greg Downs think he is?' Later on, some of the lads got the receptionist to do a 'Stop Press' print-out saying, 'Football news. Stuart Pearce has broken his ankle. Greg Downs called up for England.' Gibbo actually stopped eating his meal and pushed his spaghetti away. He was appalled. And it wasn't even true."

Albiston left United in 1988, although he didn't start one game in his final season. "When I realised that I wasn't going to be a regular, I decided that I needed to change to get regular football.

"I went to West Brom on a three-year contract and joined up with Ron Atkinson again, but he left to go to Atletico Madrid. Brian Talbot took over and I played 44 games out of 46, then he told me that he wanted to get rid of me. I didn't want to stay where I wasn't wanted. West Brom negotiated a settlement and we agreed to rip up my contract, but then I went to Dundee and got a better contract."

It didn't work out.

"Dundee was a nightmare. I didn't get on with the manager. Then I got a collapsed lung and three broken ribs playing in a game so I was out for four months. My family had moved back to Manchester and the driving was killing me. It was so difficult, I considered packing the game in. I had a two-year contract but the manager wouldn't play me, even though I was super fit. He was making me lay the kit out and make the players cups of tea. It was demoralising."

With his Dundee contract finally up, Albiston moved back to Manchester and started training with Chester City in August 1991.

"The dressing-room was full of Scousers, but the number two, Graham Barrow, was a big United fan. They offered me £250 a week, a third of what I had been on at Dundee. We settled on £400 and I played every week. I loved it; the craic with players like Gary Bennett was superb. He called me Archie, because I was Scottish. My boys still speak about him."

In the summer of 1992, Albiston played on loan for Molde in Norway, the club where Ole Gunnar Solskjaer would make his name.

"Molde was beautiful, by the side of a fjord. My family, who came out for the summer holiday, loved it and I was getting more money than I had ever earned. The kids learned to fish and had loads of friends. They actually went into a Norwegian school with their new mates. When we left the neighbours held a big street party for us. It was a very humbling experience. I'd like to think that I repaid the people of the town because we finished fifth in the league, which was much higher than expected."

Albiston returned to Chester in 1992, catching the train to training each morning from Altrincham.

"I used to see Norman Whiteside on the Manchester-bound platform opposite at Altrincham station," says Albiston. "He was studying to be a podiatrist. He'd hide behind his newspaper; he wasn't one for being recognised. And I wasn't one for getting his attention. But if he looked up and saw me he'd shout, 'Look how far we've come!' Five years before everything was being done for us."

After Chester, Albiston played for Witton and Droylsden. While at Droylsden, he played with Mark Molyneux, a legendary Mancunian character and former minder to the boxer, Steve Foster. Later, when he was a manager at non-league Trafford, Molyneux made one of his players who was getting a touch 'big time' a 'shit butty' – his excrement hidden by a layer of cucumber. And when the *Manchester Evening News* sent a reporter to Chorlton to gauge residents' reactions to the planned Metrolink which was going right through the yard where Molyneux worked, the pup reporter was confused when Molyneux insisted that he would be delighted when his workplace was knocked down. Molyneux gave a false name for the quote which accompanied the photograph of him smiling while everyone else was angry – 'England Hardiman'.

Molyneux once stole Albiston's underpants after an away game at Barrow and wore them over his trousers in the bar later. He generously told Albiston that he could wear his soiled pair.

Albiston stopped playing after Witton and began coaching the kids at United, which he did for eight years. "I also did radio work, covering United matches, which I still do," he says. "And I coach in

Arthur Albiston

Canada each year and arrange for young Norwegian teams to come over in the summer.

"I watch United a lot. It's better when we are winning things, but I tell my boys that they have grown up only knowing success. Speak to people my age and they can clearly remember United going 26 years without winning the league. It might be a few years before United win the league again. In some ways United have created a monster because expectations are so high.

"Including my apprenticeship, I spent 16 years at Old Trafford. Of course I remember the debuts, and the finals. I actually preferred the semi-finals, though, because they attracted true supporters and were raw, proper games of football as opposed to the big show of the final. I remember doing well against some players and less so against others. Playing against lads like David Rocastle, who was more of a dribbler than Trevor Steven; he was very, very skilful, probably more so than any other player. Some players can be too skilful for their own good, yet Rocastle knew his position in the team and was always closing me down when I was in possession. He would push me back and cause problems when Arsenal had the ball too. It was very sad that he passed away so young.

"I live for the moment," he concludes. "I don't want to have any more regrets. The years pass more quickly in middle age. I have offers, but time is more important to me than money. I've always valued the time I spent with my boys as they grew up. Me and Robbo were the only fathers picking the kids up at the school gate. I know we were fortunate with our jobs, but my family have always come first. I often think back to when I played, remember the last-minute goals and what not. And you remember them, but not as clearly as the everyday banter with the lads. That's what I miss most."

6
John Gidman

The Scouse Flyer

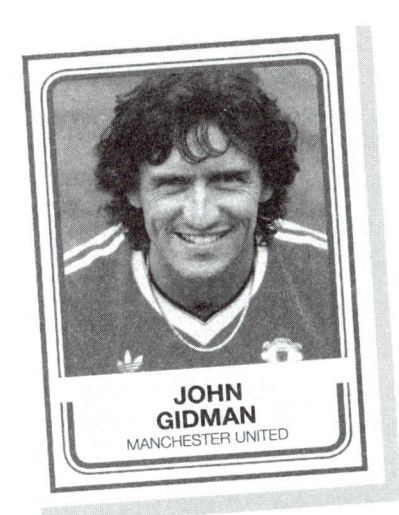

Early March and the weather is glorious in Torremolinos, the most incongruous of the Costa del Sol resorts. John Gidman, the Scouse full-back who played 118 times for Manchester United between 1981 and 1986, sits at the beachside restaurant table, hidden behind black Ray Bans. Gidman is on good form.

"Fancy a bevvy?" he asks. It's 10am. Gidman has agreed to meet here because it's close to Calahonda, his home of nine years, but it's not an area he's keen on or familiar with. "I couldn't live in Torremolinos," he gestures at the high rise buildings which mark the seafront, speaking in a Liverpudlian accent softened by years living away from Merseyside. "Not really my scene, all this."

Gidman's decision to move to Spain was made on holiday in Cuba, where, he admits, his "head was everywhere". After leaving Manchester in 1986, his life underwent more twists and turns than he ever had to encounter marking players like Kevin Sheedy and Glenn Hoddle. Divorce, phone bugs, guns, golf and gangsters, Gidman had been through the lot and he'd had enough.

"Cuba turned out to be the best holiday of my life," he says. "I went with a mate for six weeks and it allowed me to get my head together because I got away from everybody. I'd fallen in with the wrong crowd and I needed to make a break. With two days of the holiday left I sat alone having a beer looking out to sea, just thinking. I thought, 'This is where it started for me, by the docks in Garston, by the sea. I wanted to get back to the sea. I decided that I didn't need anybody in my life and that I was going to live in Spain. I decided there and then to move to Estepona, which I knew because we'd trained there on pre-season camps when I was in Aston Villa. My mate thought I was mad."

Gidman was adamant, however. The memory of Garston took him back to a time when life was simpler and he needed that again. A Liverpool gangster acquaintance offered to help out. "He knew a lad in the Costa del Sol who knew the area so I ended up near Malaga and I've been here ever since. I met my girlfriend eight months after arriving. She caught my eye on the beach, and while I didn't speak Spanish I just took a couple of beers over and said, 'For you, for me.' She told me she was married, but that relationship was breaking down and we got together soon after. She's an air stewardess and we get on. I'm happy after years of madness."

Gidman grew up in one of Liverpool's poorest neighbourhoods by the docks. His dad, a draughtsman for the Post Office, had a season ticket at Anfield and he used to take John to the boys' pen on the Kop.

"My dad was the strongest influence in my life, the man I should be most thankful to. He pushed me and pushed me, although I didn't always like it. The Beatles came home to Liverpool in '68 and everyone I knew was going down to Lime Street to meet them, but my dad wouldn't let me go. I never forgave him for that because I wanted to be a pop star, not a footballer, and I loved the Beatles and had my hair like theirs. At least I did until my dad got me in the bathroom one day and said, 'Enough is enough'. Then he cut my hair. He felt that if I had long hair he didn't have control of me.

"Mum worked hard, selling ice cream in the picture house. I used to get free ice-cream watching Cliff Richard and the Shadows down there on a Saturday. Then she got a job at the ice-cream factory. She came home crying one Friday because her false teeth had fallen into the ice-cream conveyor belt. It took her two weeks to get a new set of dentures."

By 14, Gidman was a regular for Liverpool Schoolboys, until he was dropped for a semi-final against Plymouth.

"I saw the coach of that team last year and called him a twat," he recalls. When he wasn't playing, Gidman watched Ian St John and Ronnie Yates from the Kop. Six months later he was cleaning their boots. Liverpool had offered him an apprenticeship, which included attending a mechanic's course one day a week.

"I've never been academic and never got into the course. All the other lads were doing practical stuff with engines when I was training, while I didn't even know where the petrol cap was on a car and was nervous when my exams approached. A few of the lads asked me if I could get them tickets for Liverpool so I did a deal with them. I got them tickets and one lad allowed me to copy his multiple choice answers in the exam. Liverpool were delighted when I passed; my dad was just confused."

Life at Melwood, Liverpool's training ground, went well for the first seven months until Tony Waiters was appointed head of youth development.

"He didn't like me," explains Gidman. "My face didn't fit." Yet Gidman still had faith in his own ability, so much so that when he was called into manager Bill Shankly's office as a 16-year-old, he was expecting good news.

"I naively thought that Shanks was going to tell me that I'd been called up to the first team. I wasn't. Shanks got straight to the point, saying, 'I've been told that yer shite. We're releasing yer. Son, yer shit' – I'll always remember how he said it.

"Waiters had told him that I didn't have the ability or the

dedication to succeed. Shanks added that I wasn't skilful enough and wasn't the right build. I cried all the way home on the bus because I thought I'd never be a footballer. My contract was to be ripped up, and a letter was sent to my dad which basically said, 'Dear Mr Gidman. Your son is shite!'"

But Gidman's father was no push-over. By then he'd taken it upon himself to go to night school, gaining qualifications which meant a better job and a house in the less impoverished Allerton.

"He realised that a contract couldn't just be torn up, it was simple as that." Gidman returned to Liverpool, where he was put in the lowly C-team, an outcast at 16. But then Waiters accepted a job in Canada and Ronnie Moran replaced him. "Ronnie took me from the C to the B to the A teams. Then he moved me from outside-right, where I'd always played, to full-back. Within a month I was in the reserves. Moran told Shankly to keep me, but Shanks didn't want to go back on his decision and I was released."

Others had monitored Gidman's progress, and in the summer of 1970 he accepted a one-month trial with Aston Villa, whose first team had been relegated to the third division. The move was a success. Within a month he signed a professional contract, and within a year he was in the England youth team with Trevor Francis and Phil Thompson.

"Villa then gave me a two-year contract worth £40 a week, my first taste of money. My life had changed from walking round Liverpool with holes in my shoes to driving round Birmingham in a Morris 1300."

In 1972, Gidman was an FA Youth Cup winner. He made his first team debut in August of the same year, aged 18. However, there were distractions which came with his new-found status.

"Discovering birds was a problem," he admits. "I was moved around several digs and I ended up living with this woman and her kid. She was 31. I ended up in bed with her. She'd lost her husband and just climbed in with me one night. I was going into training with my eyes down by my kneecaps. I was in and out of the first team but I couldn't train. It was taking effect psychologically, like being married at 18. I came clean with the club and told them that I had to get out. They put me in with an old couple in Lichfield."

The kind of discipline his father had imposed was back.

"Les and Barbara kept an eye on me and told the manager Vic Crowe if I came in late."

Gidman settled for less fleshly pursuits, learning to play the guitar. A regular in the first team, his contract was consistently improved and with bonuses he was able to buy a house at 19.

He was content until rookie chairman Doug Ellis replaced manager Crowe with Ron Saunders.

"I didn't get on with him, he was a disciplinarian with a sergeant-major outlook who used to belittle popular players. The first thing he said to me was, 'Who are you?' I said, 'Who the fuck are you?' He said, 'Oh, we've got a smart Scouser have we?' So we didn't get off to the best start. I felt that Saunders would knock me all the time, even if I had a good game. He didn't help my confidence."

Despite this, Gidman was largely happy at Villa.

"Brian Little was my best pal; he had long hair and was well into music like me. I used to think he was on pills, given the way he'd dance. Look at him now, a sensible manager with a sensible haircut. We still keep in touch."

Another player became a long-term friend.

"Saunders rang me and said, 'I'm buying a kid from Dundee. He's going to be good, he's called Andy Gray, can he live with you?' Andy lived with me for a year and we became great mates. Still are. See each other all the time. He's done really well for himself, he's really professional and I'm proud of him. We have completely different lives but we just get on really well. He didn't drink when he arrived at Villa. He did after I'd introduced him to the country pub in his first week."

Villa's centenary season in 1974/75 started well, yet Gidman would miss the majority of it after an accident on 5th November 1974.

"One of the players had a bonfire party. There had been problems in Birmingham with the IRA and I was talking to a QC about it. The next thing, someone accidentally launched a rocket. It hit me in the right eye at 70 miles an hour, putting me through a patio window. Luckily, the club doctor was there. I was haemorrhaging blood, it was squirting out from the centre of the eye. An ambulance came straight away. I was pissed and didn't really give a fuck. They wanted to take my eye out to stop the bleeding, but the club doctor stopped them, saying, 'He's a footballer, you can't.'"

Gidman woke in hospital three days later with his head covered in bandages.

"I shit myself because I thought I was blind. I couldn't see through my right eye at all. The surgeon said it would take about six weeks to see the extent of the damage. All I wanted to know was if my football career was over. He told me he didn't know, but that I had probably lost the sight in my right eye. He said the other eye would adjust, but my central vision would probably be gone. I just had to wait and see."

Six weeks later Gidman was diagnosed as being blind in one eye as the doctor had predicted – but his peripheral vision was unaffected. He could go on playing.

Gidman left hospital and convalesced in a nursing home for two months. He started walking again four months after the accident, training after five. "I had to teach myself to judge the speed of the ball again, with my left eye over-compensating." The dark glasses he wears in the sun now are not an affectation, but necessary protection. To complete a remarkable recovery, Saunders made him substitute for the final game of the season when Villa were promoted behind second division champions Manchester United.

"I got the best reception I've ever had," he recalls. "It was very emotional. I realised that people cared. I played up front with the instruction to enjoy myself as we'd won promotion. I was like Billy Liddell on the wing. Everything I touched went well. I knew after the game that I wasn't finished, that I could be a footballer again.

"All the Villa lads knew I had a dicky eye, and years later at United Frank Stapleton would say, 'Always put the ball to Giddy at the back post because he can't fucking head it. He doesn't know how far away it is.'"

John Gidman

Gidman's career ran relatively smoothly at Villa for the next two seasons. He won a League Cup Winners' medal in 1977 after Villa beat Everton at the third attempt at Old Trafford. The same year he was capped by England.

"I'd been in the squad a couple of times and the QPR right-back Dave Clement, who later poisoned himself, was injured, so Don Revie told me that I was in. He wanted me to mark some fucker from Luxembourg that I'd never heard of. Hearing the national anthem did it for me and I became very emotional. Then I just thought, 'I hope you are watching this Bill Shankly, I really fucking do, because you let me go for nothing and now I'm playing for England.'"

Gidman never did play for England again, which he puts down his behaviour on a trip to the Soviet Union for England U23s.

"Alan Ball got me on Jack Daniels on the way home from Moscow," he confesses. "I'd never had it before and I fell off the plane at Luton airport. If you were a rebel the England people didn't like it. I wasn't a yes man, but my own man. If I see something for a laugh, then I'll do it."

In 1977, Villa destroyed his old club.

"I always felt like I had a point to prove when Villa played Liverpool, although I thought it would be difficult that year as they were about to win the league again. Yet by half time we led 5–0, and Ron Saunders, showing a rare flash of humour, said, 'Get yourself a cup of tea and have a piss.' We were astonished, but he added, 'How can I give a talk when I've just seen you play like that?'" The game finished 5–1 and Shankly later publicly questioned why he had let Gidman ever leave Liverpool.

Villa reached the quarter-finals of the UEFA Cup in 1977/78, before being knocked out by Barcelona. It's a night Gidman remembers well.

"I was paid to wear Puma boots. But before the game in Barcelona some guy approached me in the team hotel and offered us money to wear these new boots from a Spanish company. I told him that we couldn't wear them, that the lads would never all wear new boots, but that we could paint our normal boots to look like his brand. Saunders wasn't bothered, so I took the money and shared it among the lads. We had a photo before the game and everyone wanted to be at the back because they didn't want to be seen in these boots.

"Cruyff and Neeskens were playing and the tackles were flying in. I had my nose broken and the ref wasn't controlling the game. My nose was bleeding, and then I got an elbow in the eye – not my right eye fortunately. I lost it and hit the guy. I got sent off and received a good dig off the police in the tunnel. I left the ground at half-time and went to a bar nearby. I wasn't thinking straight, and I was disappointed because I'd paid for my dad to come and watch the game and he'd never been abroad before. The game was on the television in the bar and I was recognised because of my nose. I had to get off back to the stadium quickly."

More problems lay ahead.

"Not only was I blamed for us going out of the competition, there was a picture of me in the papers the next day fighting – and wearing boots which did not look like they were made by Puma. I got a phone call off the Puma representative, who wasn't happy. He came to the training ground to check our match boots, which had been cleaned by that time. I lied to him that I had worn Puma and it became my word against his. I kept the contract."

Like any dressing-room, Villa's had its divisions and cliques.

"We knew that there was a snitch," recalls Gidman. "Things which should have remained in the dressing-room were getting back to the manager. We'd have a bevvy and he'd find out. If someone was going to throw a transfer request in, then the manager knew before the letter arrived on his desk."

To try and find out, the then married Gidman took the Villa secretary out for a meal, where they cut a deal.

"She left me the players' contracts on the desk and I walked in the office and saw them. I saw that Dennis Mortimer was on a lot more money than me. I was on £300 a week and was gutted to find out how much some of the other players were on because I was one of the better players. Andy Gray and I got bladdered and agreed to put transfer requests in the following day. We were livid and went to see the board with a list of complaints about the manager. It was him or us, we said. The board said that nobody was bigger than the club and that they would sell us. Aside from that incident, Doug Ellis was always fine with me. In fact, I actually liked him. He's probably a twat to do business with, but he always saw me right."

Everton manager Gordon Lee was soon on the phone, with a substantial signing-on fee to supplement the proposed weekly wage of £700. Gidman wanted to move to his home city.

"I had no qualms about playing for Everton as I saw it as a job, simple as that. Yet I failed my medical because Everton realised that my retina was smashed. So they sent me to hospital for a second check. I got friendly with the girl who was doing the test. I explained that my life was in her hands, that I couldn't face going back to Villa because I had pushed things too far."

The specialist was sympathetic.

"She asked me to put a toy plane in a little plastic hangar with my good eye covered. I didn't have a chance of doing that and said, 'Can't you turn your head away and when you look back the plane will be in the hangar?' She laughed and said, 'I'm getting paid to give you a medical.' She let me practise doing it a few times, by feeling my way. When I had perfected it she passed me, but I should never have passed that medical."

Gidman moved for £550,000 in October 1979, a substantial amount for a full-back.

"I got a good drink out of leaving Villa and put it all in my pension."

Yet Gidman felt he didn't justify his fee.

"It wasn't the best Everton side in the world and I struggled to settle. I made my Everton debut against Man United, and when I got cramp Stevie Coppell helped me out.

"There were some comic moments at Goodison though. Mick Lyons was a big Evertonian and used to headbutt the wall to psyche himself up before games. Freddie Starr, the comedian, came in the dressing before one game. He was an Evertonian too and he started taking the piss out of me, showing me his cock to try and embarrass me, acting all gay. Then, after the match, I couldn't concentrate in a television interview because he was mooning behind the camera."

After 17 unfulfilling months at Goodison, Lee was replaced by Howard Kendall.

"I realised that I didn't have a future at Everton when I went to get my number two shirt before a practice game in Tokyo and Kendall asked what I was doing. When I went to the subs bench and he asked me the same question, I knew my time was up. We went out that night in a busy bar. Kendall could be erratic and that night he said, 'The last player with his trousers round his ankles buys the drinks.' So we all moonied."

The Toffees stopped in Los Angeles on the way home, where Gidman received a phone call.

"The hotel receptionist asked, 'Is Mr John Gidman here? I have a phone call for him from England from a Mr Atkinson.' I couldn't believe it – she said it in front of everyone. Kendall had a right go because he thought that I was engineering a move to United, yet he didn't want me. I was obviously interested in signing and Ron Atkinson said, 'Don't be too greedy.' I wasn't, and I was his first signing for £450,000 plus Mickey Thomas, in August '81. I still had the dodgy medical from Everton to prove that my eye was all right too."

Nine hundred pounds a week and a big signing-on fee were not the only perks of the deal.

"I had six bottles of Manchester United champagne given to me too. I drove back to Liverpool and said to my wife, 'I've just signed for the biggest club in the world. This is a dream.'

"And despite not having won the league, I really believed that United were the biggest club. All the players talked about United when I was at Everton or Villa, and I used to get mithered more for tickets for the United game than any other."

Being a Scouser at Old Trafford was a potential problem.

"Steve Coppell warned me that fans would give me a hard time but also told me if you play football they'd appreciate it. The fans were fine."

Coppell was also responsible for Gidman's United initiation.

"I came back to the dressing-room after one game to find that my tie, shirt sleeves and pants had been cut up. I put them on anyway and went into the players' lounge as if nothing had happened. From then on I was one of the lads."

For a player who liked to accelerate with the ball out of defence, go on mazy dribbles and support the strikers, Gidman enjoyed Atkinson's attacking philosophy.

"He'd say, 'If you don't get forward, Giddy, I'll fine you.'"

Fellow Scousers, Atkinson and Gidman got on well, at least initially.

"My first long trip away with United was to Canada in 1982. The film in economy was crap so Atko, who had been knocking back his favourite drink of Jack Daniels and Coke, said, 'Come on Giddy, you know what's going on, let's go to the back of the plane for a drink.' He knew that players were magnets for girls that no manager could compete with, and so I got on the plane's loudspeaker and announced to the whole plane, 'Mayday, Mayday, Giddy and Atko want birds at the back of the plane.'"

I got absolutely bollocked for that by the captain and had a severe dressing-down. I was fined a week's wages, but Atko paid it because he'd been partly responsible."

Gidman played 39 times in his first United season, 1981/82, his biggest number of appearances in any one term at United. Injuries, chiefly a persistent back problem, limited him to just 118 outings in his five seasons at the club. He played just three times the following season and missed out on the 1983 FA Cup final win over Brighton – not that he avoided controversy just because he wasn't in the team.

"I remember my ticket allocation for the 1983 Cup final being wrong," he says. "Each player could buy around 60 tickets, yet I was only given 35. I was told that injured players didn't get the full allocation, so I was surprised to get a phone call saying that my tickets had been found on the black market and the FA knew about it. The 25 tickets from my allocation of 60, which I hadn't been allowed to take, had ended up on the black market."

Gidman's right-back position was usually filled by Mike Duxbury.

"Mick did well. He was younger than me and wasn't injured as much," he says. Duxbury played more games than Gidman for two seasons and looked so settled that Gidman considered his options.

"I thought it was time to either leave United or retire in 1984/85," he says. "I was struggling until I tried acupuncture and after five sessions I was like a spring lamb."

The timing was good.

"Mick Duxbury got injured and I got back in the team, playing the best football of my life in '85. I scored three of my four United goals that season."

Yet when Duxbury recovered, Gidman was dropped for an away game at Chelsea.

"I got a phone call from the *News of the World* the day before the game. We were staying at the Royal Lancaster and they asked for my reaction to being dropped. I couldn't believe it. That was the first I knew and I thought that Atko was unprofessional by going to the media."

Atkinson tried an unusual tactic to try and placate the angry right-back.

"He called me to his suite in the hotel and offered me a two-year contract. I'd got dropped and got a new contract offer, can you believe that? But I was furious. I went straight to the players' lounge during the game and started drinking, which I shouldn't have done.

"I actually wanted Chelsea to win and I jumped up when they took the lead. Everyone looked at me, surprised. I was pissed, annoyed and carried on drinking."

United won 3–1, but the journey home wasn't a happy one.

"Bryan Robson virtually carried me to the back of the coach after the game. I started being abusive to Atko, calling him a 'fat bastard' and a 'baldy headed bastard'. He grabbed hold of me and said, 'If you carry on like this I'll leave you in London.' I got back to Old Trafford and somehow drove back to Liverpool."

Gidman was put in the reserves, yet when Duxbury struggled to regain his form, there was pressure for him to get back in the team – not that he believed it would happen.

"Bryan Robson was on *This is Your Life*. We were told to go to the airport but not what for. I started drinking as soon as I got there. We went to the studios and Eamon Andrews was there with a mad jumper on. He actually called Robbo 'Harry Robson' in rehearsals. A few of us were steaming by the time the show was recorded. I was sat behind Atko, who was wearing a white suit. He'd just had a hair transplant and I was fascinated by it. I started blowing at his hair and he was getting uncomfortable. I said to his girlfriend Maggie, a good Scouse girl, 'What are you doing with a man like that?' Atko pulled me to one side after the show. 'Giddy,' he said. 'I want to tell you something. I want you to sober up and get yourself together because you are playing on Saturday.' That was the first time he'd spoken to me in three weeks. I've got a lot of time for Atko as a manager, but he didn't always treat me well."

Gidman was recalled for an FA Cup fourth-round game against Coventry in 1985.

"I played well and Ron and I were the best of mates again," he says.

Gidman kept his place in the team but the drinking didn't stop.

"We weren't angels when it came to drinking, but I lived in Liverpool and their players weren't either. I was good friends with John Wark, and I'd go out for a drink with Graeme Souness and Jimmy Case, too. Sammy Lee had a wine bar where we used to go. We'd wind each other up about Liverpool and United. United played Liverpool in the FA Cup semi-final in 1985. We drew the first game at Goodison, but that night I went out for a drink with Wark to a Greek restaurant in Liverpool. We'd kicked the fuck out of each other that afternoon, but it wasn't a problem, we were very good mates. People were very surprised to see a United and Liverpool player having a drink together, especially as the replay was the following week.

"I had to be careful being a Man United player and living in Liverpool. I got abuse a few times and I had to be careful where I drank because there was never a shortage of people who wanted to have a go at a United player. It got really nasty in the mid-'80s and I once had to get a police escort home from Anfield. People asked me why I didn't live in Manchester, but I'd had a place built in Liverpool and it was only half an hour to Manchester each morning.

There were other advantages.

"I could go for a quiet drink and get away with it, whereas the lads in Manchester would get noticed if they drank midweek. We were a sociable club but we didn't go stupid because Atko wasn't stupid. He knew if the lads had been out and would punish you by running you for an hour in training.

"If there had been an England drinkers' XI, then there would have been half a dozen from Liverpool and half a dozen from United at the top. I was a drinker, Robbo was, then there were Paul McGrath and Norman Whiteside. We used to say, 'Never trust a footballer who doesn't drink.' Peter Beardsley came to Old Trafford and he never drank. We used to say you couldn't trust a non-drinker because you don't know what's happening in their mind. Ours was an ethos shaped in the bar: the team that drinks together plays together."

Gidman admits, however, that he sometimes overdid it.

"We lost an away game at Southampton on the Saturday and stayed down in Torquay after for a break. We were playing a practice game against Torquay United on the Monday and a curfew was put on us to be in by ten the night before the game. Me, Robbo, Ray Wilkins and Kevin Moran stayed out past twelve and got clocked. There was a cold atmosphere in training the next morning. We had a very long five-a-side game, which was unusual, then Atko called a meeting with the lads who had come back late. He said, 'Come to my suite later because I want a chat.' We went to see him. A bottle of Moet was in a cooler on the mantelpiece. We were all laughing, although Ray Wilkins was a bit subdued. Ron told Ray to open the champagne. We had a game that night, albeit a practice one. Ron poured us all a glass and said, 'Here's to tonight.' Then he changed. He said, 'When I say ten o'clock, I mean ten o'clock. Don't take the piss out of me again.'

"I had a nightmare that night. Atko bollocked me again and again. He slammed the dressing-room door and said, 'Stand up Gidman, you Scouse twat. If you ever, ever, go out drinking before a match you will never play for Man United again.' All the lads went quiet.

He kicked the cups and came right up to my face. He went mad. It was the worst bollocking I had ever had and I couldn't say anything because I was in the wrong. I was made to train with the reserves and Ron didn't speak to me for a week. Then I saw him on the Friday in the corridor at the Cliff and he said, 'All right Giddy, how are we then?' He'd made his example of me."

After beating Liverpool in the FA Cup semi-final via a replay, United reached Wembley for the 1985 FA Cup final against Everton.

"I thought I'd missed my chance of playing in an FA Cup final after being injured in '83 but I had another in '85," says Gidman. "We were the underdogs with Everton going for the treble, but Big Ron told us, 'Don't sit back. Go at them.' It was hot and we took salt tablets. The Wembley grass was long and I used longer studs than usual. When Peter Reid hit a volley, I stretched as far as I could to reach it, convinced the ball was going in. Somehow, my stud clipped it and it went wide.

"It was a shocking decision to send Kevin Moran off and I felt for him, but we still felt confident with ten men. With Frank Stapleton back at centre-half, we aimed for the replay until Norm the Storm did his bit and bent a winner around Neville Southall. I was the first player to congratulate him and said, 'If there wasn't 100,000 people here I'd fuck you now.' After the game, I remember picking my old Villa team-mate Andy Gray up, a tear in his eye, and telling him to keep his head up."

The day after parading the cup in Manchester's Albert Square, the victorious United team left for Montego Bay in Jamaica as a treat from the United chairman Martin Edwards.

"Everyone was happy, not just because we had won the cup but because we were loaded with bonus money, that and money from selling tickets too," says Gidman. "I was offered a new two-year contract on the same money as well.

"Kevin Moran wasn't allowed to pick up a medal at Wembley. He walked up the steps to the Royal Box but wasn't presented with one. The medal was given to the club and was presented to Kevin by the captain of the plane on the way to Jamaica.

We're The Famous Man United

"Jamaica was brilliant. We played a friendly game against a Jamaican XI, but me and Arthur Albiston were injured so we got a few beers and sat on the bench. The Jamaican Air Force were putting a show on and one of their top men stood in the centre of the pitch by a giant cross that had been marked out. He proudly told the crowd of 30,000 that the match ball was going to be delivered to the centre circle by a parachutist, who would land on the cross. I saw 30,000 people look up in expectation and could see the parachutist miles above. I bet Arthur £100 that the bloke wouldn't land in the centre circle. Arthur had it and we watched as this parachutist came closer and closer with the match ball. He seemed like he going to make the stadium until a gust of wind blew him off course and he landed in the car park, breaking a leg apparently. We could already see a second parachutist above him. Arthur said, 'Double or quits', but the poor fucker landed so far away I bet it wasn't even in Jamaica. A third and final parachutist was coming in and we went double or quits again, agreeing that all he had to do was land inside the stadium. The bloke came closest, but became tangled in the roof of the main stand. He was injured, yet all we could do was argue about the technicality of whether he'd landed inside the stadium or not. The game started, only to be stopped ten minutes in when the fire brigade turned to cut the bloke free. I won £400!"

Jamaica was a trip noted for incidents.

"I was sitting on the beach when this little lad came along selling spliffs. I sat there chilling and having a smoke under a palm tree. I'd never had cannabis before or since, but it made me laugh, especially when I saw Ron Atkinson and Maggie walking along the shoreline. All of a sudden, a Caribbean trade wind picked up and Atko's hair piece lifted up like the roof of a Ford Escort Cabriolet, before resting flat back on his head. I was howling with laughter and told the chairman, Martin Edwards. He used to call Atkinson 'Cabriolet' thereafter and Atko couldn't understand why."

With confidence high after the cup final win, United started the following season, 1985/86, with ten consecutive league victories.

"It was our best chance to win the league with United, but I broke my leg at Ipswich in the second game of the season when that prick Cranson did me from behind. The lads kept winning before it fell apart. I don't know why, whether it was nerves, but it wasn't the manager's fault. It was such a shame we couldn't give the fans the one trophy they wanted."

Gidman's broken leg confirmed in Atkinson's mind that he'd have to replace his popular right-back.

"I got wind that something was going on when I bumped into Kenny Dalglish – a good bloke – at Manchester airport. He told me that he had seen Atkinson out in Denmark and that he was buying a new right-back. He warned me that I had to be careful. I was a bit gutted, but then again I was 33, had played in a cup final and had a broken leg. But I shouldn't have found out from another footballer."

United bought Danish international John Sivebaek for £285,000 from Vejle in February 1986, leaving Gidman to weigh up his options.

"I didn't want to play reserve football and Ron was reasonable, offering to pay up my contract and give me a free transfer. I also had to sign a form stating that I wouldn't give any stories out about certain things that had happened at the club. Atko and I shook hands and we left on good terms. I had bought a sports shop in Liverpool and honestly thought that I was going to run that for the rest of my life."

Then he received a phone call from Jimmy Frizzell, Manchester City's manager, that very day.

"Frizzell wanted to sign me. He said, 'We're playing United on Saturday and I want you to play.'"

So I signed and I marked Peter Barnes. He told me to go easy on him, but you can't do that. He was a great lad but a bit of a softie and I told him, 'I'm going to kick fuck out of you for 90 minutes.' They took him off after 40. I had two good years at City but I didn't see eye to eye with the new manager Mel Machin. I swear he couldn't coach a parrot to speak."

Machin had a higher opinion of Gidman and made him club captain.

"He'd use that to try and get me to deliver difficult news to the lads. Once, after playing Bournemouth, the lads had been offered a night out if we won. We won, and then Machin changed his mind and told me that I had to tell them that they couldn't go out. We went back to the hotel and I told the lads to order beers on his room bill. He found out and got the hump. We had a bust-up, not quite fisticuffs. He stopped talking to me and I was let go.

"It was weird playing at Maine Road. Old Trafford always seemed full, yet there were gaps at Maine Road. But City fans were fabulous to me – when I thought I'd get stick for being a Scouser who came from United."

In August 1988, Gidman moved again.

"Mick Mills rang from Stoke, where he was manager, offering a ten grand signing-on fee and £600 a week. I was living in Liverpool and travelled to Stoke every day for five months. I struggled, surrounded by younger lads. One day I was driving down the M6 and I rang in sick from my huge car phone. I turned the car round at Knutsford and went home. I knew I would never play again. The carrot was gone. I just didn't feel the same about football."

Gidman had quit football in his mind, but a month later his old friend Brian Little called from Darlington.

"He said, 'I'd like you to play for me.' So I did. It was hard. My brain was there but my legs weren't. I could see openings that other players couldn't, and when I played the ball no-one made the run. I looked a prat and I thought they were prats for not sharing the same vision."

He lasted three months and played his last professional game in May 1989, before returning to Liverpool, where he had gone into another business.

"Derek Hatton, an Everton fan, had asked what I was up to," says Gidman. Hatton was a member of the Labour Party and the high-profile deputy leader of Liverpool City Council in the 1980s.

"I told him that I was thinking of building a golf range. He offered help in getting land and I bought 26 acres for £10,000 freehold in a good area of Liverpool. I didn't know that the police were onto him and that Kinnock wanted him out of the Labour Party. And little did I know that I was now mixed up in the whole business and that my phone was being bugged."

The flamboyant Hatton's name had become synonymous with the Militant Tendency, a Trotskyite group within the Labour Party. Neil Kinnock waged war on the left-wing grouping, banning them from party membership and expelling Hatton.

"I knew nothing about the bigger political stuff, more that there were some moody people involved in the deal," says Gidman. "I'd never had a gun put to my head before but that happened just before the course opened, when a charlied-up gangster introduced himself as my new partner. That frightened me, coming from the safe football world. A week later I saw on the news that an axe had been put through Hatton's front door.

"Kenny Dalglish, who was manager of Liverpool at the time, had agreed to open the golf range but the day it was due to open, and with all cameras there, Kenny pulled out. He said that he would get the sack if he did it. I gave a false story to reporters that he was off buying John Barnes and got the snooker player John Parrott to open it instead. I later found out that Kenny's chairman knew what was going on with Hatton.

"After six months, eight police heavies arrested me for fraudulent buying of land. The operation was called 'Cheetah' and cost £24 million. The first I knew about it was when they barged through my front door first thing in the morning. Apparently Thatcher and Kinnock had signed for my phone to be bugged. I actually thought it was a joke because I had no suspicion at all. I didn't know the deal was dodgy. I was on *News at Ten*, which I didn't need. They had been watching me for seven months. I was told that I was going down for a long time. They originally tried to charge with me with fraud but it didn't reach court and I wasn't found guilty of anything. They wanted Derek, not me.

"The atmosphere was really bad in the Liverpool underworld. It was getting very heavy. Going into that business was the worst thing I ever did, and not just because I lost money."

A few months after Gidman was acquitted, he received a phone call.

"'Will you meet up with two of the detectives on the case?' asked the voice at the other end of the line.

"'But I thought I was acquitted.'

"'Yes, but you still have a lot of information that we want to know,' the voice continued.

Gidman agreed to a meet at a pub at the end of the M62.

"I was paranoid and asked the detective to strip off to check that they were not taping me," he continues. "He stripped off but insisted that I did the same. So we were both naked in the toilets when this regular walked in for a piss. He saw two naked men. We told him to fuck off. I couldn't believe what was happening to me. I was so paranoid that I threw my mobile phone into the Mersey because I was convinced that people were listening to me."

In 1993, he made another error of judgement when he went back into football to manage King's Lynn.

"It didn't work out and I'm still owed money by them. At this time I was banned from being a company director as I hadn't run my sports shop as I should have done and I was going through a messy divorce. My wife left, citing irreconcilable differences. I had been unfaithful, not for the first time.

"When I was at United, she'd got a private detective on to me. I got caught out when I told her that I was going to Haydock races with Bryan Robson. I did go with Robbo, but with a bird too. I'd just bought a Porsche and I thought I was Jack the lad, drinking champagne and losing a load of money. When she left she had the house wired up and I got caught out big style. I returned home from training one day and my wife handed me an envelope of incriminating evidence and said, 'Get yourself a lawyer.'

"My head was fried in training and I called Mick Brown. 'I can't play. I've been unfaithful and my wife has found out.' To be fair, my wife tried to make it work after that, but hell hath no fury like a woman scorned. The relationship was never the same again and it was my fault.

"I'm not proud of what I did, but I didn't expect to open the door of my house one night to see her sister there with a baseball bat. Then I got done for drink driving. I must have been crazy doing the things I did, but football did that to me. It made me feel invincible and take things for granted – the ability to always get a table in a restaurant, to drive fast cars and be the centre of attention.

"The problem is that you think it will last forever and you think you'll curb your ways and all will be well. Birds followed us everywhere – good ones too. A lot of players from my generation got married early and then divorced after their football careers had finished. The cynic might argue that the women only wanted to be footballers' wives, because the wives never moaned when the money was coming in, when they were staying at the best hotels. They only moaned when it stopped. But there are always two sides with these things.

"I realised I wasn't invincible after football, when your life changes suddenly. You are no longer one of the boys, but alone by yourself. You are no longer part of the tribe that would do things in airport lounges that you wouldn't dream of doing with your family.

"I have happy memories from playing, but I don't live off them. I'm not a lover of football, I don't get totally excited when I watch it, but it gave me a good life and I'm thankful for that. I put a decent pension away from my playing days which I live off. I do some commentary for local radio in Spain, but spend most days trying to get the golf handicap down and playing tennis."

Gidman occasionally meets up with ex-team-mates if they're in Marbella. And he watches United on television.

"For some reason I always bet against United. I don't know why, I just do. I wanted to go to the FA Cup Final in Cardiff in 2005 but United rejected my ticket application. But I don't go on about what I used to do because it's in the past and not everyone likes Manchester United or ex-United players, especially after a drink. It's called jealousy.

"I'm enjoying what time I've got left. Emlyn went, Peter Osgood went and Best went. I don't want to die. I'm enjoying life in Spain. My mates come out from England. Andy Gray was here recently. He interviewed Beckham in Madrid and I rang his mobile and put a false voice on: 'Er, hello, this is Terrance Derby, I'm David's manager and I'm just checking that the interview went OK.' Andy paused. He was only sitting eating with Posh and Becks.

"Usually, I keep myself to myself. I know I should be perfect in Spanish, but I'm only perfect after a few bevvies. I've still got my football medals, but I was thinking of weighing a few things into Christies like my medals and caps. I've not seen them for 20 years and I don't want to. I won't put them out at home in case they get stolen. I've got nobody to leave them to, except my son, who's 26. We've not spoken for a few years. He wasn't happy with an interview I'd done, but I'm not chasing after him. I hope he reads this and realises my side of the story. I was unfaithful to his mum, I was wrong and I accept that. And I wish I had been a bit more sensible in life. I look back at things I did and think that I was stupid. I once ordered a Capri injection three litre as a club car. I went out and got pissed before stupidly driving back to Liverpool. I didn't even know the way back to Liverpool, I was that drunk. I drove across a roundabout near Runcorn and fucked me wheels up. What an idiot. I loved the laugh, but if someone said, 'Don't do that' then I'd do it. That's just me.

"As for football, I suppose I've got to thank my father for the way it all turned out because I achieved what most schoolboys only dream of. I played for the biggest club in the world and I played for my country. And all that after Bill Shankly told me that I was shit. I think I proved him wrong."

7
Clayton Blackmore
Mr Versatility

Of all the players interviewed in this book, only one was still being paid to play football, a remarkable achievement given that he's 42 and supposedly retired over half a decade ago at the acceptable age of 36. Clayton Blackmore was still performing at a sufficiently good standard to be voted Bangor City's player of the year in 2005. The versatile playmaker, christened 'Sunbed' by United fans for his deep all-year tan, has made over 160 appearances for the League of Wales club. In December 2005, he became Bangor's player-manager, replacing another former Red, Peter Davenport.

We're The Famous Man United

"I missed playing," Blackmore says of his return. "It was nothing to do with money. I just love playing football and wanted to play competitively at the highest standard I could. I've surprised myself. I never thought I'd be playing at this age and I'm probably the oldest player in the league, but it's a good league and not full of hackers."

Blackmore arrives well prepared for this interview over lunch at a hotel near his Stockport home. Sitting at the table, he pulls six pages of handwritten notes about his career from his pocket. "I wrote these last night because I wanted to make sure that I didn't forget anything," he says. There's a humility about Blackmore that comes from his background on a tiny estate near Neath, South Wales.

"There were 49 houses and about 15 lads who all grew up together. I had a great childhood and put a lot of my success down to it. We had our own football team and were very successful in lots of sports. Four or five of the lads from those 49 houses played cricket for Wales – I just missed out on the trials. We played whatever was on the television at the time. If it was golf then we'd play golf."

Blackmore had sport in his genes.

"My mum was the Welsh netball coach. She played badminton too. My dad, who was from Surrey originally, played football for Llanelli – who are now in the league I manage in. He wasn't professional, he worked as a foreman at the giant BP refinery, but he did play against people like John Charles. Dad used to be very physical, and he could handle himself, yet he tried to shoulder Charles and just bounced off him. I only saw my dad lose his temper once and that was when he took me to watch Swansea. This car nearly ran me over and Dad snapped and slammed his brolly into the car's windscreen. I played for Dad's pub team when I was 14 and he was 42. There was this idiot playing against us and he knocked me about. Dad waited for him to run down the wing before laying him flat out. I thought it was just a bad tackle and only worked out what happened years later."

Given Neath's status as a rugby hotbed, it was no surprise that Blackmore also excelled with the oval ball.

"I played as a centre. I was pretty good, but some of the lads were massive. At 13, I had to choose between playing rugby and football.

I chose football and played for Neath Boys' Club. I always played in successful teams when I was younger and we seemed to win everything. My family travelled wherever I played, offering great support. You don't realise it as a kid but you need that. We had a Chelsea and a Burnley scout at the Boys' Club. I went to both those places, but I didn't like Chelsea. I didn't like the Cockney 'cha, cha, cha' on the field when I had a trial there. I thought, 'Are we playing football or talking football?'"

By the age of 14, Blackmore had achieved one of his lifetime ambitions.

"I played at Wembley, for Wales Schoolboys. I met Mark Hughes for the first time playing for Wales Schoolboys. He played at Wembley too. He had three England defenders on him and would still get away from them. He was a year older and already signed with United, so he gave me a United tracksuit which I treasured. I played all 11 games for Wales Schoolboys that year."

Walter Robins, a United scout based in Swansea, fixed it for Blackmore to have a trial.

"He died six months after I signed, and it was down to him that I went to United. I used to go to Old Trafford most Saturdays as an associated schoolboy. Big Norm was a star and they used to fly him over from Belfast. I'd played against him for Wales Schoolboys and he was scary. He was seven months younger than me but looked five years older. He was quality, so aggressive, yet he was calm on the ball and moved it around well. He was miles ahead of everyone else – that was shown when he played in the World Cup at 16."

Schooling completed, Blackmore moved to Manchester full-time in the summer of 1981, as an apprentice.

"It took some getting used to," he admits. "I love Manchester now – it's just the right size and the people are great. I've never had any problems with United or City fans. I've bumped into loads of City fans and they've always had a great sense of humour, but it was tough when I first moved there – moving from such a small close-knit community to a big city. I wasn't majorly into music or clothes because of my background – football was what I lived for. I lived with another

United apprentice Andy Hill, who went on to play for City. We shared digs with two young City lads on Derbyshire Lane in Stretford. How mad is that? The house was owned by the mum of Pete Briody – the fan who had a go at Alex Ferguson at the AGM a few years ago. We'd play football on the playing fields near Chester Road most nights. Pete, who was a big influence, would take us out with his mate to Friday's in Didsbury. I've got good memories of that time and we had good laughs. We'd give new apprentices boot polish around their nuts. We were kids being kids. I always remember another apprentice, a local lad called Grant Mitchell. He was a local wide boy who fell out with Big Norm. Norm had him against a wall and was about to smash a metal jug into him when he thought better of it."

There were some calmer figures at Old Trafford.

"The former Chelsea player Ray Wilkins was the biggest influence when I arrived and I learned a lot from him. Ray said I'd made the right decision joining United rather than Chelsea. He was such a nice bloke which surprised me because he was a Cockney! He was the only first team member who would come into all the dressing-rooms and say good morning to the reserve or the youth lads. Mickey Thomas would have a laugh, but he couldn't stay in one place for more than a minute – he's still that way now.

"As apprentices we used to have to clean the first team boots. I once walked into the first team changing-room to get the boots and Martin Buchan was in there. He looked at me and said, 'I didn't hear the door.' So I went outside and knocked on the door. He didn't reply so I gave up and walked away. Martin was like that, but I can see why he did it. I got on with him really well too. We used to be scared of the first team, whereas youngsters these days are very cocky."

Certain events from his days as an apprentice stick out in Blackmore's memory, like a five-a-side youth team tournament at Stretford Sports Centre, which was also the home to United's short-lived basketball team, which played to sell-out crowds of 1,500 in the mid-'80s.

"The competition was between United, City and Bolton. Before we played, the vets of all these teams, people like Bobby Charlton, had very friendly five-a-side games. Then us young United lads played City and it was like a war zone. We had a good team comprising of me, Billy Garton, Norman Whiteside, Mark Dempsey and Mark Hughes. We beat City and we beat them up too, it was fierce."

Fierce was a word that could be used to describe Eric Harrison, the youth coach at United. Like Garton, Blackmore remembers how hard he was on the youngsters.

"Everyone talks about Alex Ferguson being a tough character and a bad loser, but Eric was even worse," Blackmore remembers. "I was so scared of him that he nearly broke me one Christmas. I was close to thinking, 'I don't need this, I'm going to go home.' He was being aggressive all the time and in one session we were training in the snow, just running everywhere. "I've never enjoyed running around for no reason, I was like Brian McClair when it came to that. In later years, Alex used to say to us, 'We're going to do a 12-minute run.' Brian would run 200 yards behind the other lads and then at the end say, 'I've run for 12 minutes.'

"Anyway, we were training in the snow and it was more like army training, when I just wanted to play football. Eric was being really aggressive with me and kept telling me that I had to challenge more when I played. I'd always try to nick the ball off people rather than crunch into them, but that wasn't for Eric. I'd had enough, but I didn't go. The fear factor was daft though. I was that scared of him that when I had the 'flu I didn't dare tell him. We were training in the big gym and it was freezing. My eyesight was going blurry and I finally told Eric how I 'felt. I was out for two weeks.

"Eric was mad, there was no doubt. Norman Davies, the kit man who had been on the bench with many managers, said that Eric was the maddest person he'd worked with. We played Bolton in the Lancashire Youth Cup and we lost 4–0 with Whiteside, Hughes and me. Everything that could have gone wrong went wrong and Eric was furious after the game, saying, 'What have I done coming here from Everton to be with you lot?'"

However, one of Harrison's more unusual ideas did suit Blackmore. "Eric decided to give us a test by telling us that we were to play a game of rugby in the snow. The Welsh lads loved the idea because we knew we would sort the English lads out. We had a game. And we sorted them out!"

Despite the tough treatment, Blackmore has nothing but respect for Harrison.

"Being hard was his way of making us stronger and I learned a lot from Eric. We did well too, reaching the final of the FA Youth Cup in 1982, where we lost 7–6 to Watford over two legs and extra time."

Some players from that youth team would progress quicker than others.

"I always knew that Norman and Mark were ahead of the rest of us. Both stood out. Mark had the name Sparky before he went to United too. I'm not sure where he picked it up from, no-one really knew. My theory is that it's because of the way he played – he was so sharp, so bright."

Reserve team manager Brian Whitehouse was equally tough with players.

"He pushed me so hard once that I collapsed on the pitch at the Cliff. That meant he had to walk the full length of the pitch to see what was wrong with me. He was screaming, 'Get up! get up!' But I couldn't.

"Brian was good with the reserve teams and prepared Alan Davies really well for the '83 cup final. I knew Alan Davies well and his parents were Welsh."

Forward Davies played ten times for United between 1981 and 1984, including the 1983 FA Cup final as a replacement for the injured Steve Coppell. He did well enough to keep his place in the side for the replay, providing assists for United's first two goals in the 4–0 win. Just when his career seemed to be taking off he broke his ankle and tore his ligaments in a pre-season friendly. Davies returned almost a year later, making a goal-scoring comeback in the European Cup Winners' Cup semi-final first leg against Juventus. It proved to be an isolated success and he joined Newcastle United in 1985. In February 1992, at the age of 30, Davies was found dead in his car on the Gower peninsula, near Swansea.

Clayton Blackmore

"It was very sad when he took his own life," remembers Blackmore. "He was a quiet lad. I've heard so many stories about what went on, stories about gambling and that, but I don't know what the truth was. All I know is that he was such a nice, quiet lad. I went to his funeral and it was harrowing."

Blackmore wasn't at Wembley to see the 1983 final, he was in Switzerland with the Welsh Under-21 team.

"There was a sex shop opposite our hotel, but we couldn't be seen sneaking into it," he remembers. "So we waited until a tram stopped outside the shop and then sneaked in behind it to have a look at the porno mags."

Back in Manchester, he moved digs from Stretford to Salford, closer to the Cliff. "Two Northern Irish lads and two lads from the Republic of Ireland lived there. They argued constantly. I would always argue with the Protestant Northern Irish lads and say, 'You are Northern Irish, not British.' But they wouldn't have it and would say, 'We're British.' I'd say, 'But you were born in NORTHERN IRELAND. You're Irish.' They had arguments that nobody ever won. I couldn't get my head around it because I didn't know the issues, so the whole thing confused me."

Blackmore made the first of almost 250 United appearances when he made his debut against Nottingham Forest for the final game of the 1983/84 season, but did not become a serious contender for a first team place until 1985/86.

"I was playing 10 to 15 games a season before Fergie arrived. But I was playing for the reserves too so I felt like I was having a full season. Reserve football may be young players now, but then it included older players too. We played Forest once at reserve level and every single player was a seasoned international. That's what the young lads coming through were up against.

"I thought I might be on the bench for the '85 Cup Final, but Big Ron said, 'I'm going to put Gordon McQueen there because it's his last chance. You'll have more chances.' He was right in one sense, but I should have been on the bench on merit. I was right in line where Norman scored that goal. To do that against Big Nev, who I thought was the best keeper in the world – better than Schmeichel even – was incredible. Mark Hughes had a mental block against Big Nev, that's how good he was. I spent cup final day getting drunk with Gary Robson, Bryan's brother."

Blackmore got married in 1985, aged 21.

"It seemed like the right thing to do, but we were probably too young. Ron liked players to be settled and that was probably an influence on me getting married. It calmed me down a bit, but I went astray and was a naughty boy a few times.

"There were a lot of girls around and they did throw themselves at you. It was easy. We'd go to Saturdays in town [in the Britannia Hotel] and a club next to it called Kicks. We went everywhere – even the Ritz!" The Ritz is a former ballroom and Mancunian institution with an older clientele and said to be frequented by women up for an anything-goes good night out. Every player went out. I always remember Robbo saying, 'I'll drink on a Wednesday after training but I won't drink for two days before a game.' That drilled into my head and I followed him."

Yet Blackmore maintains that the extra attention didn't affect him.

"Becoming a first team player didn't change me at all," he says. "I've never been a bighead. We could always get into clubs in town because of what we did, but I was always a bit shy to say, 'I play for Man United.' I was worried that a doorman would be a City fan and say, 'So what?'"

Blackmore loved being out with the lads, loved the scene that went with being a United player, the jokes and pranks.

"We went to Hong Kong on tour in 1986. Three or four of our England players had to go from Hong Kong back to play for England and, short of players, we went on to Australia and picked up a couple of rookies. Frank Worthington and Peter Barnes guested for us, and it was like the back-heel show. We drew with a full-strength Juventus side. I was a young lad and I missed a penalty in a shoot-out to decide the game. Big Gordon slated me, saying that I had cost United the game.

"Me and Sparky went on a boat trip in Australia on that trip. It was really boring. This boat had XXXX written all over it and we

Clayton Blackmore

didn't have a clue what XXXX was. So we went to get a can of Coke and the fridge was full of XXXX beer. The day improved after that.

"I saw one of the worst things I've ever seen in my life in Australia. We were driving to a training session and there had been a car crash. It had just happened. There was a cyclist crushed underneath a car. Someone was slumped in the back of the car, clearly dead. It made me think how fragile life was. It still crosses my mind, that image. You have to be happy to have your health.

"We played some serious drinking games on that tour," he continues. "One was called fizz/buzz where Big Gordon would tell us how much we had to drink. It was the first time I got really sick through alcohol. I've always been a slow drinker who can last forever, but here I was being forced to down drinks. I threw up everywhere."

United played in Singapore on the same tour.

"We were all in the pool on our knees, pretending to be in the deep end. So Mick Brown (the assistant manager) dived in and hit the bottom. For a while it looked like he had shattered his knees. It was one of the funniest things I've ever seen. We hired jet skis and knackered them up a bit. Kevin Moran ran out of petrol and got stranded. It was a great trip. Dennis Roach, the agent, was on it. It was Mark Hughes' last trip before he moved to Barcelona and Roach was walking along with Martin Edwards. Martin said, 'Where's Mark?' We pointed to the sky, where Mark was paragliding. The chairman was very, very nervous that the player he had just sold to Barcelona for a fortune was doing that."

Yet Blackmore believes that Hughes should never have been allowed to leave.

"Mark was United's top scorer and he was on about £200 a week – about a fifth of what some of the other lads were on. Barca and other teams were coming in for him. Ron, being Ron, tied him up for five years for an extra hundred pound a week in each year of his contract. He would be on £700 a week in five years' time. It was good for the club, but not the player. That's how the game has changed. Mark didn't have an agent. If he'd had one, I'm sure he wouldn't have signed that contract.

"I didn't have an agent either, but I should have. Big Ron told me that I was to get a new contract and told me to come along to the Cliff at six o'clock one Thursday night. We only lived around the corner so I went along. Ron had his own football team who played in the gym on a Thursday night. I went to see him but he didn't have time to see me because he had a game. I ended up walking down to the gym with him, trying to sort my contract. It was a huge thing for me, but he was focused on his five-a-side game. I eventually agreed a deal for about £500 a week, but if I'd had an agent I would probably have left the club and gone somewhere else for more money. City came in for me and offered more money at one point, but I didn't want to leave. I only earned more money once I eventually left United.

"Money-wise, it was always tough when you had come through the ranks. Players who'd been bought in were always earning more. But it wasn't just about money for me. I was getting paid more than the average man for doing what I loved every day, playing football and having a laugh.

"Mick Brown suffered more pranks than most," remembers Blackmore. "He was scared of peacocks and there were lots of them wandering around in the grounds of our hotel in Jamaica following the cup win in '85. They were always shedding their feathers, so four of us started collecting them and stuck them to a parasol, which we attached to a piece of rope. We got into Mick's room through Eric Harrison's, which was next door. We hid the parasol covered in feathers under his bed and waited for him to go back to his room. The chairman was sat with us, giggling. He always wanted to be one of the lads. When Mick walked into his room we pulled the rope, this 'peacock' flew out from under his bed and he shat himself. He wouldn't speak to anyone for the rest of the trip.

"On that trip, I tried cannabis for the first and only time in my life with John Gidman. I can't smoke, but it made me laugh. Ron got to hear about it and pointed to a sign by the swimming pool the next day. It said, 'Please keep off the grass.'

"Big Ron was larger than life, with all the jewellery and that. He thought he was the best karaoke singer but I wasn't bad. I watched

Left. Anyone seen my ducks? Gary Bailey always felt like an outsider in the United dressing-room

Below. Billy's boots. Billy Garton (second right) in action for his beloved United against Charlton

Above. Gordon McQueen, towering centre-back and the club's social convenor, gets to the ball first in the 1983 Milk Cup final v Liverpool

Right. The birth of a legend: Bryan Robson on his Manchester United debut against Manchester City in 1981. Robson was nearly sold to AC Milan for £2.5m three years later

Above. Arthur Albiston: from milk round to Milk Cup final

Left. Having tricked his way through his medical, with his bad eye John Gidman probably didn't even know he was playing in United's rare blue third strip

Clayton Blackmore: still playing in the Welsh League

Alan Brazil: 'The Liverpool lads were drinking just as much as us'

Frank Stapleton (centre) is beaten to the ball by the mighty Paul McGrath, as Kevin Moran looks on against Oxford United

Left. Arnold Muhren didn't drink or smoke, but what was in his secret Dutch potion?

Below. Ron Atkinson and his assistant Mick Brown are introduced to the Old Trafford crowd in 1981 after their arrival from West Brom

Cheers! Ron Atkinson and Chairman Martin Edwards welcome Bryan Robson to United. Never mind the haircuts, if ever you wanted an illustration of just how much the game has changed since 1981 just admire the curtains

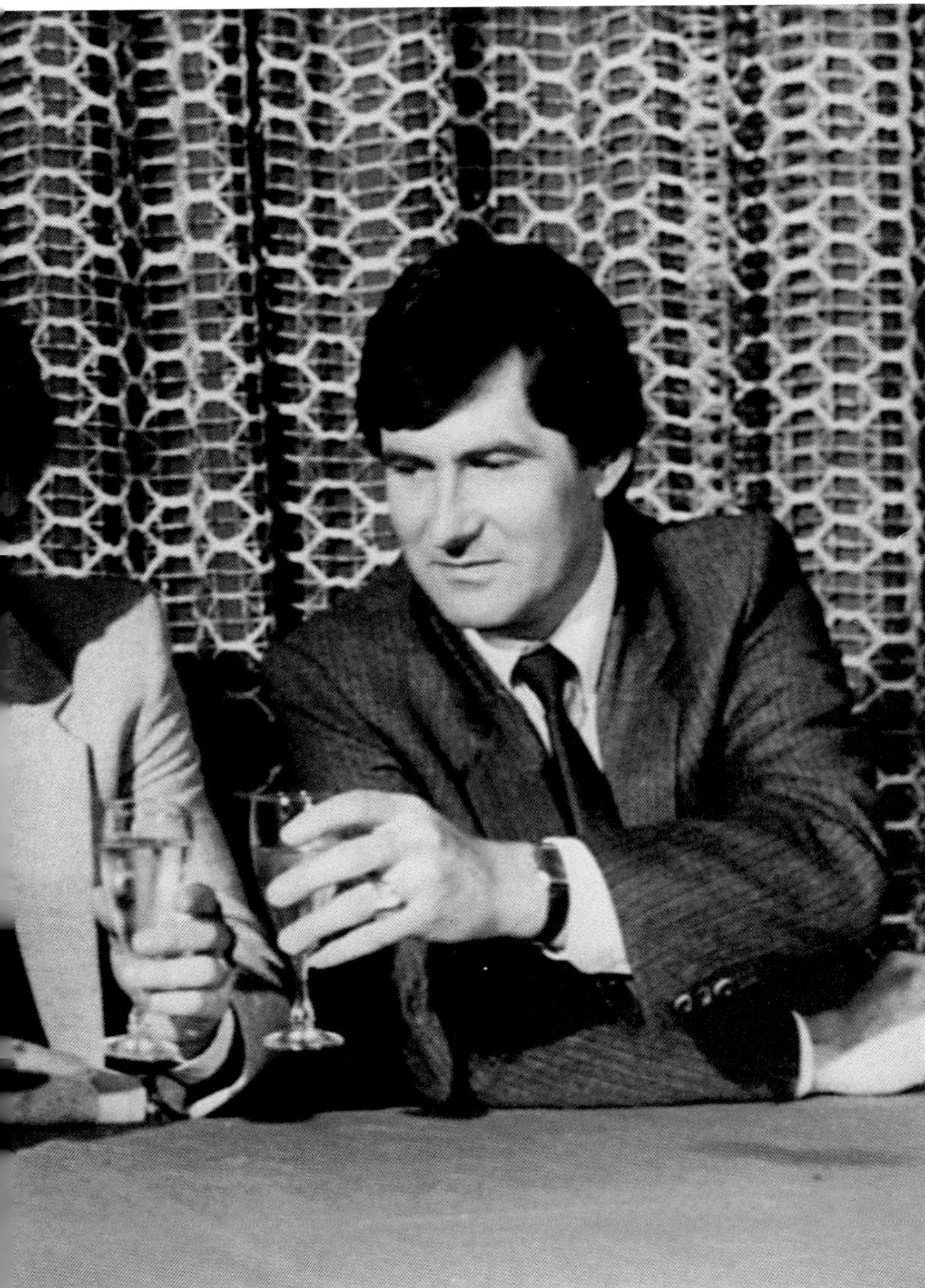

EMPICS

'And Smith must score!' But he doesn't as Gary Bailey makes arguably his most crucial save for United to take the 1983 FA Cup final against Brighton to a replay

EMPICS

No fireworks or sponsors' flags... FA Cup glory '80s style. The United players celebrate their replay victory over Brighton in semi-darkness at Wembley – maybe Ray Wilkins thought no one would notice what he'd done to his shorts

EMPICS

The Shankill Skinhead's finest hour. Norman Whiteside celebrates curling the winner past Neville Southall in the 1985 FA Cup final against Everton as the United fans on the terraces go wild

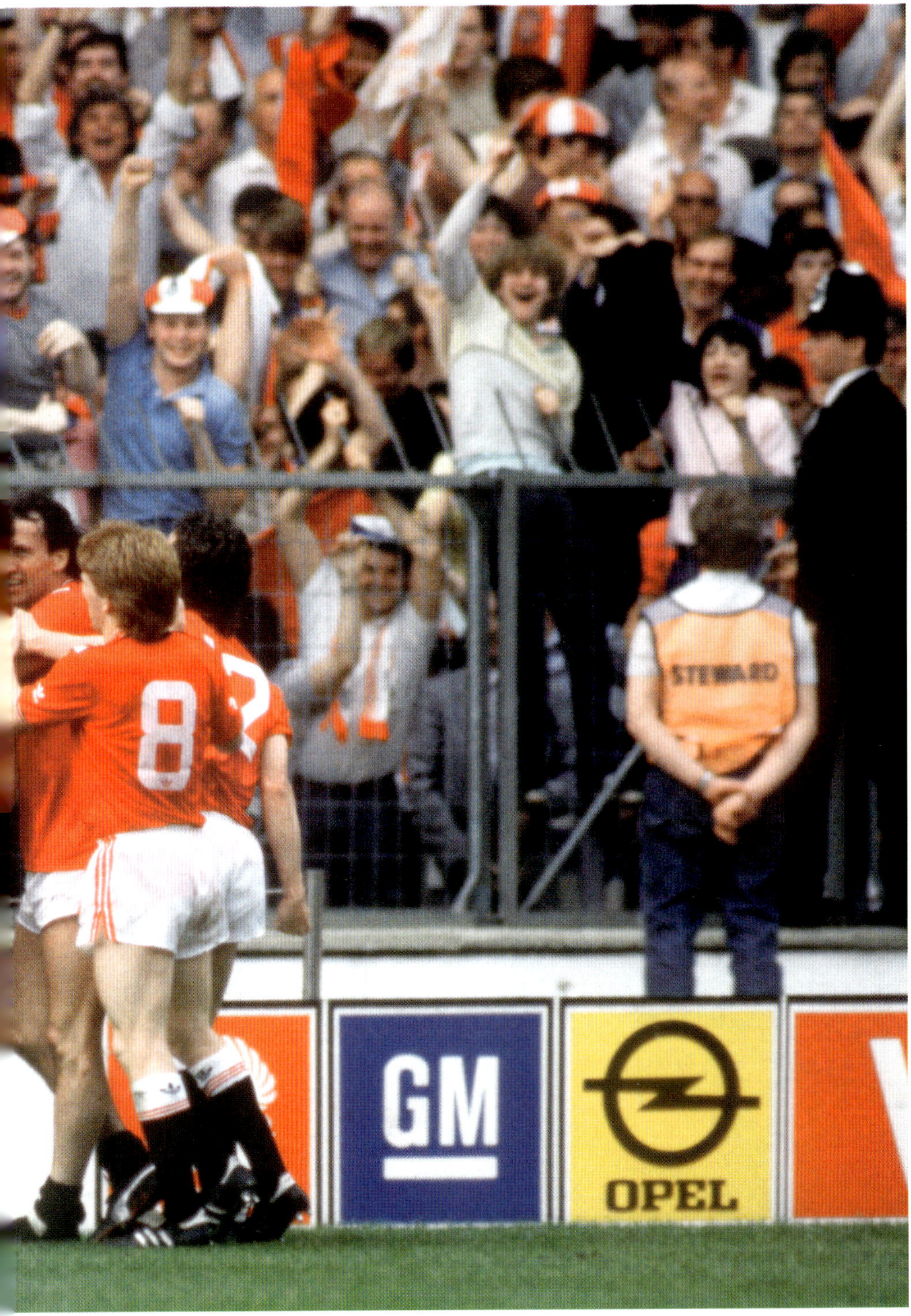

EMPICS

Gary Bailey, TV presenter, back home in South Africa

Bryan Ronson shortly before the end of his reign at West Brom

Billy Garton guiding the kids of California down the correct path in life

Arthur Albiston near his home in Cheshire

Gordon McQueen at home at the Black Bull!

Clayton Blackmore after training at Bangor City

John Gidman on the beach near his home in Marbella

Alan Brazil at work on his breakfast show on Talksport Radio

Frank Stapleton, still the consummate professional

Arnold Muhren at the Ajax training ground

Big Ron, still going strong

one game in the Sharp lounge at Old Trafford with John Gidman. We were both injured and spent the afternoon drinking champagne. We played a team who wore blue, that's all I can remember. After the game we went into Sam Platt's, the pub near Old Trafford. It was full of United fans and I stood up and did karaoke. The fans in there loved that.

"We'd be training on a Friday and we'd look up to see the blue lights of Ron's sunbed. He should be called Sunbed, not me. He'd have the press lads in there and he'd be giving a press conference from under the lights.

"I thought I was dealt some bad hands by Big Ron, though. I had a good pre-season in '86/87 and we played Dynamo Kiev in a pre-season tournament in Amsterdam just after the World Cup. It was the trip where a few players missed a curfew and returned late to the hotel. The club had called the police and people were out looking for us. We didn't realise how serious the curfew had been. One of the lads came in with a black eye and Big Ron said, 'We'll deal with this when we get back to England.'

"The next day we played Kiev. They had ten of the Russian World Cup team playing for them, people like Igor Belanov. We were 1–0 down and Belanov had missed a penalty. They looked so good when they attacked us, and we should have been four or five-nil down. I was sub and Big Ron told me and Terry Gibson to go and warm up. We ran right down to the corner flag because we were scared of coming on. But he chucked us on anyway. It was weird because it wasn't so bad out there. We had time on the ball and I ended up scoring a volley from just outside the box, straight from a corner. We drew 1–1. I changed the game a wee bit."

Next up was a friendly against Real Sociedad at Old Trafford.

"John Toshack brought them over," he recalls, "and I scored again. Things were going well. I played in central midfield as the season started. We played Arsenal away and I hit the crossbar from 30 yards, then they went up the other end and scored. I thought I'd done really well. We lost 3–2 against West Ham at home in the next game, but I had another shot which hit the bar. Then we played Charlton at home, when nothing went right for us. Gordon Strachan tried to pass the ball to one of our players who was about seven yards away. He ended up missing him by about ten yards. But I still did OK. Mike England was at the game and selected me for Wales."

Blackmore was a Welsh international at schoolboy, youth, under 21 and senior levels where he gained 39 caps. "With Wales we'd get ourselves in a great position to qualify for a major tournament but we just couldn't reach one, purely because we didn't have a big enough squad."

Disappointment followed for Blackmore back at Old Trafford.

"Robbo came back from injury a week after the Charlton game and replaced me in the team. I thought that was very harsh. Ron explained to me that he was bringing Bryan back to lift the team, the crowd and the club, and that I was to be dropped. Being wet behind the ears I agreed with everything Ron said, but I shouldn't have been dropped. It knocked me back a bit because I didn't play for a while after that."

The decision still irks him.

"If you leave the players who are playing well out, then it's going to come back and haunt you. I think that happened with Ron. It's one thing that I've learned now that I am a manager – you play the players who are in form.

"That was the difference when Alex came to the club. It didn't matter if you replaced a great name who had played 50 times for England, if you were playing well he would keep you in the team.

Blackmore was in Alex Ferguson's first line-up at Oxford United in 1986.

"It was nice to play in the first game under Alex, even though we lost. He spoke to me in the week leading up to the game about what he was going to do. But his accent was so broad that I couldn't understand a word of what he was saying to me. I just nodded because I really wanted to do well for him.

"Alex's man-management is as good as can be. He has made mistakes, but he's achieved at the highest level for years."

Blackmore has other memories of Ferguson.

Clayton Blackmore

"Alex and Archie Knox would play head tennis at the Cliff. We always tried to avoid being dragged in as referee because you'd end up getting punished either way. If you were ref when the manager lost he'd have you running outside.

"Archie was brilliant. He went to check out the facilities at Milan and came back with some of their ideas, like playing small-sided games in a small area in the warm-up which United still do now. England do it too. It really helps players find their touch before a game."

Ferguson influenced Blackmore in other ways. It's time to order a main course and Blackmore's choice is surprising, especially for a Welshman: haggis.

"I've got to thank Mr Ferguson for my love of haggis. When you hear that it's full of bits and bobs of everything, you don't want to eat it, but it's actually all right.

"We soon realised that Alex was a bad loser," he explains, between mouthfuls of Scottish fare. "He had to get his emotions out and let you know how he felt. You felt like Alex was always dealing you a straight hand, whereas you didn't always feel that with Ron. It was more of a family thing with Alex – everyone was included on equal terms. With Big Ron I always felt that I was going to be treated as a kid. There were different rules for different players – we called Robbo 'Son of . . .' because he was like the manager's son."

Of the 11 players who started in Ferguson's first game at Oxford, only Blackmore remained at the club four years later. Why?

"Probably because I was versatile," he opines. "And the gaffer knew that I loved everything about the club. I'd play for United on crutches in my 60s if I could. Overall, being versatile probably went against me though. I had my best season in '90/91 because I played in one position – left-back. You need a few games to settle into a position and it wasn't always easy switching around.

"I didn't intend being versatile, it just ended up that way. I was like Phil Neville. Managers like players like us. I was played as a sweeper when I arrived at United as a kid because of my size. They didn't want to see me smashed in midfield so they put me there or at right-back."

"Blackmore possessed huge ability but lacked the yard of pace needed to make him truly outstanding in his natural midfield position," was Ferguson's verdict in his autobiography.

"I think that's fair. If I'd had a yard or two of extra pace or been a bit taller I would have been better. I'm a ball player more than anything. World-class players like Giggs can beat players whereas I would rather keep the ball than gamble and take somebody on like Christiano Ronaldo would. I think he will become the best player in the world.

"When you look at Giggs, he's a world-class player, as was Beckham, but purely because of his crossing ability, he couldn't take people on. I used to think of players I'd not like to play against. Giggs would have been my worst nightmare. Beckham, no problem. Ronaldo – no way!

"Yet it was great for me to learn from so many great players. I'd always advise younger players to go to the biggest club they can because they can watch and learn from the top players. Just playing with someone like Cantona was a joy."

Ferguson began rooting out what he saw as an alcohol problem and more golf was played. "Brian McClair and Mark Hughes and I played in Man City's golf day because my father-in-law worked for Brother, City's then sponsors. We were lucky enough to draw one of the best golfers in the North-West and ended up winning City's golf day. It was a bit embarrassing for them when Man United won it. Great for us though."

Despite the new manager's clampdown, the players were hardly expected to be teetotal, especially at the tail-end of pre-season tours when the football had finished.

"I could drink, but Robbo was the benchmark. Robbo used to drink more than us and still train by himself on his day off to run off the drink. I once tried to stay with him in Japan after we had finished our pre-season tour. We ended up in the Hard Rock Café, me and Sparky arm wrestling. There were loads of US Marines in there. I was the champion arm wrestler at the club, well, me and Sparky were. He's bigger than me, but it's about technique, not how big you are. We were turning these Marines over, but I was getting more tired with each victory. They brought this big black lad out. I shat myself and thought he was going to break my arm. It was America v Britain. All the Marines were stood around the table going 'Oooh, ooh, ohh.' He did beat me in the end, sadly.

"We played Everton over there on the same tour. We went out after the game and I had an arm wrestle with Robbo with my left hand. I'd broke it as a kid and it was very weak. He just about beat me after I slipped and my head hit the table, splitting my front lips. I lost a front tooth."

Rather than seek medical advice, Blackmore sought to numb the pain with alcohol.

"Me and Robbo stayed out all night that time. We got back at 7am and went to sit by the pool. We were flying back later than day and just sat there drinking beer, relaxing. The sun came out and Robbo just sat sleeping on his front. He was turning purple but refused to turn over. That was my finest hour in drinking. I'd gone with the best and matched him, but it would be the last time.

"Our Christmas parties were legendary. We'd start on Bury New Road in Cheetham Hill, not far from the Cliff. We'd have three or four hours there and that's when I got introduced to Boddingtons Bitter. On one night Colin Gibson felt that he should be in the England team and he didn't shut up about it. He was always mithering Robbo to have a word with Bobby Robson. He was mithering particularly badly this night, and Robbo, after a few drinks, said, 'You're not good enough to play for England.' Gibbo said that he was going to leave and join a foreign club, to which Robbo said, 'No team in Europe would want you.' Gibbo started crying. I felt sorry for him and said, 'You are better than Stuart Pearce, Gibbo, you're quicker and sharper.' He wasn't, Pearce was a really hard player to play against – I once tackled him at the City ground and got a hole from one of his studs in my shin. But I wanted to cheer Gibbo up. Gibbo brought a lot of the stick on himself because he was so easy to wind up. Denise Robson once chucked a fillet steak at him which hit him on the head.

"We used to give Viv Anderson stick for being a lightweight too. He'd leave the Christmas dos at 8 o'clock. We'd usually have a fancy dress, it would be a military theme or we'd all be dressed as cavemen or something. We'd have them at the Amblehurst [a small hotel in Sale favoured by the players] because it was quiet and we didn't get mithered. We were drinking shorts from a pint glass at one do. Pallister used to drink Malibu and Coke, a woman's drink. I told him that he shouldn't drink that and got him on a yard of wine instead. Pally went outside to get some fresh air and collapsed. We had to carry him upstairs to his room. It was scary because he had passed out."

Blackmore knows the dangers of drink, but he's realistic when it comes to his own players.

"I can't tell my players not to drink because they are semi-professional lads," he says. "They work more than they play football. I couldn't check up on them even if I wanted to, but most actually look after themselves because they take their football seriously."

In 1987, United went on a mid-season tour of Bermuda. The trip became notorious because of false accusations made against Blackmore.

"It was a nightmare, my fault really," he says. "I got married a bit too young and didn't always behave myself. On this trip I was chatting to a girl all night in a nightclub. I was trying to get her to come back to the hotel but she said, 'I've got work in the morning.' She gave me her number and went. Then her mate turned up. I started chatting her up and just as we were getting a bit friendly, the other one walked in on us. She got a strop on. She was not happy with her friend; you could see it in her eyes. Her friend, the one with me, started crying and we all went our separate ways.

"The police station was right outside the club. They left it about three or four hours before the second girl cried rape. I think they decided that they could get a few quid from the papers. The police came into the hotel to arrest me. I was rooming with Mick Duxbury and when the police turned up Mick just turned over. The police come in to arrest his room-mate in the middle of the night and all he can do is turn over. He didn't tell anybody until the next morning.

"The good thing for me was that when I was arrested and put in a cell, the police told me that the girl had done this before. That made me feel better. I was fine at first because I've always been level-headed and I knew I hadn't done anything wrong. Then all of a sudden I was told that if I was charged the trial would not be for eight or nine months. I said, 'What?' I was contemplating nine months in prison in Bermuda for something I hadn't done. The police had made me feel relaxed and then unnerved me. They told me that all the girl had to do was stick to her accusation and I would be detained. However, the girls realised how much trouble I was going to get into and came clean. They dropped the charges and explained that my accuser didn't realise that I was married. It was a wind-up that they realised had gone too far.

"The worst thing was that the papers in England got hold of it. The media were camping outside my house back home and I couldn't get out. It was an awful time. I feel for people who wrongly get accused of being rapists. Opposing fans are always going to use something like that against you. I had loads of abuse but that made me more aggressive and want to do better against that team.

"I had to explain it to my wife which wasn't easy. I was out of order for being with the two girls in the first place. It was drink and having a good time, but it was a stupid thing to do.

"There's so much money to be made now I'd be scared to look at a girl if I was a player. They'll sleep with you just to give a story to the papers."

Blackmore was pleased when his close friend Mark Hughes returned to United in 1988.

"I knew that Alex wanted him back at United because he came to the Welsh team hotel in Denmark to try and persuade him. He can't have been impressed with Mark or me though as we went out all night. Then our flight was delayed the next morning so we hit the bar at the airport. We were drinking shorts on the plane and were well gone by the time we arrived at Heathrow. My car was there and I drove north with Leighton James. It shows how stupid you can be when you are younger. You live for the day. I had a white Capri and I fell asleep on the M6 doing 70 mph. My car hit the crash barrier which woke me up. I pulled over at the next service station and there was a dent right down the side of the car. I was lucky after being very foolish."

Not that Hughes was a negative influence.

"I roomed with Mark for Wales and United and used to say, 'I sleep more with you than I do with the wife.' He was never any good at making tea – I was the tea maid. He was a major sleeper, too, but I wasn't. He'd go to bed on the day of a night game. I'd just watch a film as he kipped. But we're always going to be close because we've been through so much together, we've known each other since we were 14. He's doing well in management; partly because he surrounds himself with people he's known and trusted for years. I think he'll take over from Sir Alex at Old Trafford one day.

"As a player he was superb. Not many people know this but he once played two games in one day. Wales played the Czechs away and we needed a win to qualify for the European Championship in 1988. We played in the afternoon and lost 2–0. Mark jumped on a plane after the game and came on as sub for Bayern Munich the same night, scoring!"

By 1990, the pressure on Sir Alex Ferguson's job was acute.

"The players thought the manager would be on his way," recalls Blackmore. "Man United need to challenge for the league and we weren't." Opinions vary as to whether the manager would have been dismissed, but the 1990 FA Cup success did Ferguson no harm. The third-round victory at Nottingham Forest is famous in United annals as a turning point, but the next round at lowly Hereford United was a potential trip wire.

"I scored the only goal of that game," remembers Blackmore. "I got a lot of stick for being Welsh because Hereford is right on the border. After scoring, I ran to their fans and put two fingers up to them. The picture appeared in the papers the next day – but with my hands cropped out!" Blackmore wore number 7 that day, but he was so adaptable that he eventually wore every red shirt, from 2 to 14.

Like Ferguson, Blackmore was under pressure in 1990.

"I always got on with fans, but I'd been at the club for nine or ten years and it was my turn to be scapegoat. I felt that the fans were against me in '89/90 and I got a lot of stick, in the fanzines and stuff. We used to wonder how some of the stories got out into the fanzines.

"It does affect you if the fans are against you, though. Look at how Jim Leighton was affected. I was surprised that we signed him because I didn't think he was a great keeper, but then I watched him in training and he showed his quality.

"The fanzines labelled me 'Sunbed' which I always took as light-hearted. I used to catch the sun really well in the summer and it would stay around until about November. Mum says I've got Spanish blood in me so maybe I tan quicker. I'd go black as a kid. I used sunbeds, but not very often. I did use them when I was injured to help speed up my recovery. But people who said my tan was a year-round one were wrong; it definitely used to fade in the winter. I find them boring. People still call me Sunbed, but the players never did – they called me 'Blacky' because of my name rather than my tan."

Blackmore got back onside with the fans "by working hard". Season 1990/91 was his best in the red shirt. He played in one position, left-back, and made 56 appearances, scoring eight times that term. One was a vital away goal – a sweetly hit 30-yard volley that was admittedly aided by a fumbling goalkeeper – at Montpellier in the quarter-finals of the Cup Winners' Cup.

"It was my most important goal," he recalls. "We'd drawn 1–1 in the first leg and hadn't expected Montpellier to be so tough physically. They dominated for the first 35 minutes in France. If we hadn't scored we would have lost the game."

Michael Platini came in the dressing-rooms to congratulate the United players after their 2–0 victory.

"I didn't see him. I was having a drugs test and you don't want to miss those."

Blackmore also played in the final against Barcelona in Rotterdam, where he kicked a shot from Michael Laudrup off the line with only a few minutes left.

"It was Clayton's finest moment in a red jersey," said Sir Alex

Ferguson. "As long as there is a Manchester United, that rescue act will be remembered."

"Brucey lost the ball and he still thanks me," explains Blackmore, "I was just there on the line."

In the summer of 1991 United went on a pre-season tour of Norway, where perhaps the worst song ever concocted for a United player was aired by a drunken Norwegian Red. "Clayton Blackmore, ding dong bell, ding dong bell." Nobody understood it then either.

Despite his accurate, powerful shooting, his sweet free kicks and the fact he crossed better than many wingers, Blackmore's first team chances at United would become limited. The left-back spot where he'd performed so well was now occupied by Denis Irwin, the right-back by Paul Parker.

This didn't stop Blackmore loving the life at Old Trafford, especially working with the characters he called colleagues. "Brian McClair was the cleverest player I played with. He'd wind Steve Bruce up, who would say things without thinking. Brian called him 'Empty Head'. Brucey was a happy-go-lucky type, but Brian was so dry and would cane him, really wipe the floor with him. Brucey used to laugh it off.

"Lee Sharpe was a good lad. I went to Ireland once with him through Asics, his boot sponsors. It was like we were pop stars. Girls were throwing knickers at us.

"Paul Ince was always messing around. He once jumped [physio] Jim McGregor and bit his arm. Jim's arm went black with the bruise. Ince once tried to bite me on the neck when I was having lunch at the Cliff. So we started wrestling and he smashed my watch against the wall. I think Incey was surprised at how strong I was. I was fuming and said, 'What are you going to do now then?' We fell out properly for a while after that.

"Remi Moses was one of the hardest players I played with," continues Blackmore. "He once lashed out after Graeme Hogg had kicked him in training. Except he lashed out at me and smacked me one in the jaw. I got out of the way. He was tough Remi, but I'd not done anything. I've never been one to look for fights. If I have to fight I'll fight, but he shouldn't have thrown a punch at me. He found out what had happened and he apologised."

There were countless incidents which remained out of the papers.

"We were in the Midland Hotel in town before a game on New Year's Day," Blackmore says. "We'd always stay in a hotel on New Year's Eve because it was impossible to sleep at home when everyone was having parties. But we'd stay up until 12 and then ring everyone, wishing them well. Me, Mark Hughes and Gary Pallister were together. Pally is a big chocolate head and we went down to reception to get some chocolate from the shop. The hotel was full and we were walking back to the lift when Pally nudged this lad by accident. The lad was as tall as Pally, but overweight. I remember thinking that he must be a mate of Pally's. The lad started following Pally as we walked towards the lift, so I was certain that he was his mate. Mark called the lift. Pally was stood waiting when this lad knocked a carton of Ribena out of his hand. Pally went to pick it up and the lad kicked it away. I still thought they were mates. Pally picked it up and said, 'What's your problem?' The lift came and the lad tried to get in the lift with us. He was starting to get aggressive and we didn't want him in the lift. Him and Pally started fighting. They both fell against a glass case and I thought they were going to go smashing through it. I jumped on the lad from behind and restrained him. Pally absolutely leathered him. The manager came down to see what was happening. The lad then claimed that we started it. Security kicked him out of the hotel. I respected Pally more after that – it was a belting punch."

By 1992, Blackmore's progress at United was being hindered by injury.

"I needed a double-hernia repair and had a year when I really struggled," he explains. "I came back and we won the Premiership. I got my medal and played a few times in the double winning season but maybe it was time to move."

He switched to Middlesbrough on a free transfer in the summer of 1994, becoming Bryan Robson's first signing for the ambitious Tees-siders.

"I regret that decision," says Blackmore. "I should have stayed at

United, got myself properly fit and tried to get back into the side but I saw all these young players coming through and thought it was time to move."

After four years at 'Boro he played for Bristol City, Barnsley and Notts County under Sam Allardyce. "He got me so fit. I'm a big admirer of his. I'd still be playing league football if I played under him."

Then he 'retired'. Except he didn't and he's still playing for Bangor.

"I'm enjoying it. The Welsh league is getting really strong because the big premiership teams only buy foreigners so we're getting really good players."

Blackmore sees his future in football management.

"Mark used to say to me, 'You are bound to be a manager.' I like talking about the game and always watch the moves off the ball. I played in every position for my country and for United so I know exactly what players should be doing because I've done it at the highest level. I feel like I'm coming to the last year of playing though. My dad played until he was 42, so I guess that's a bad omen.

"I've had a good life, but I'd definitely change a few things about my career. Because I was around the fringe I'd always eat as if I was playing – yet I wouldn't always get a game. Maybe if I had the chance again I wouldn't eat so much. Looking back, I would have gone training on a Sunday, too. Being a professional footballer is brilliant – the only thing I'd swap it for is being a professional golfer, but then I'd miss the aggression and the body contact.

"I've changed the way I look at life," concludes Blackmore. "I've still got my parents – my old man scouts for me. He's 67. But I know there are some bad times ahead. Me and my old man have always shaken hands. I've still got to tell him that I love him because I've never done that. But I will do, I've been thinking about that. I think a lot about things when I'm by myself, but I don't tell a lot of people about my thoughts."

8

Frank Stapleton

The Consummate Professional

Frank Stapleton walks into the bar at Players, a new restaurant in the Marriott hotel near Manchester Airport. Approaching his half century, he looks trim, he could still almost pass for a professional footballer. Dressed in a suit and fresh from the gym, the Dubliner who played 286 times for United between 1981 and 1987, scoring an impressive 78 goals, looks after himself as well as he ever did. In the '80s and '90s, Mulligan's restaurant was the favourite drinking hole of the United players, but not Stapleton who was never convinced by nor converted to the drinking culture.

"It was always down to yourself how much you drank," says Stapleton in a soft Dublin-cum-Mancunian accent. "And it was the same sort of guys who used to go out all the time. I couldn't drink like they could at all. We would train on Tuesday morning and then be off until Thursday. The lads would go out after training and would turn in at all hours of the morning. It wasn't for me. I'd have a few beers and then be off home. Certain lads could drink a lot more than I did. I believe that if they had done it less than we could have achieved more with the quality of players that we had.

"People talked about the Liverpool lads being big drinkers. I simply don't believe that Kenny Dalglish and Graeme Souness went on heavy boozing sessions. Hansen or Lawrenson were not in that group either. They used to blow up their drinkers' image and they did have some big boozers, but I don't believe that they were going on binges every second day. They worked very hard at what they did and were together a lot socially but I don't think they overstepped the mark. Whereas our lads often went too far."

Stapleton thinks there could have been a solution.

"If Alex Ferguson had been Manchester United manager in the early '80s we would have won the league, probably three times," he says. "Not only for the discipline side of it, but he would have put a stop to all the drinking."

Stapleton was born in 1956 in Dublin's tough north side, son of a port worker and a housewife in the solidly working-class council estate of Artane, whose renowned boys' band still plays the national anthem at the All Ireland Gaelic football finals. Artane is also famous for a fire which ripped through the Stardust nightclub in the early hours of Valentine's Day, 1981. Eight hundred and forty one people had attended the disco: 48 died and 214 were injured. 1981 was also the year when Artane's most famous son was considered the best centre-forward in Europe – admired for a work ethic instilled in childhood when he was sent to the fields to pick fruit from the age of ten.

"I had a happy childhood," Stapleton says. "But it wasn't easy because nobody had a lot of money. We used to work in the school holidays on fruit farms ten or 15 miles from where we lived. We'd get the train at half seven in the morning and work until six at night for a few pennies. It was a long day but it helped pay for schoolbooks and football boots. I'd pick strawberries, raspberries and blackcurrants. It was hard work but a good grounding. My parents didn't have the

Frank Stapleton

money for luxuries so I went out and earned it myself. It taught me important values that came in useful later in life. Maybe the kids these days don't have it as hard."

Stapleton played Gaelic football at school.

"There was a ridiculous rule in Ireland where anyone who played football wasn't allowed to play Gaelic football," he explains. "Most lads ignored this and still played in Dublin schoolboy leagues. Part of the attraction in playing was that you were not supposed to, but the football was pretty tough and it still wasn't the most popular sport. When *Match of the Day* came on television in the '60s, football became more popular. We used to play on a pitch which was shaped like a horseshoe in our road. A few windows went in and the neighbours would go mad. We'd play until half ten at night during the summers. The parents wanted us out of the house so we were happy to just play football. If I wasn't working we'd go down the beach or to a park in Dublin to play sport."

Stapleton supported United as a youngster.

"There was a great swell of support after Munich and people were really behind the team when United won the European Cup in 1968," he explains. "United were a glamorous team and I was attracted to that."

So enamoured was the young Stapleton with the sport, he decided that it would be his future vocation.

"I wasn't really that good when I started playing football but I told people that I wanted to be a footballer and worked hard at that," he says. "I was playing for a team a year above my age and my big break came when I got into the Irish schoolboys' team aged 14. I started to get noticed more. We played a game against Northern Ireland in Dublin. I played against Jimmy Nicholl, who was centre-half for them. The game was fairly even but I headed a last-minute goal from a corner and we won 1–0. Billy Behan, the legendary Irish United scout who spotted the likes of Johnny Carey, had just passed the reigns over to Joe Cochrane. He approached my dad about me going on trial to Old Trafford. Dad got approached by Arsenal that day too, and there was another offer to go to Wolves."

Stapleton travelled first to Manchester.

"I'd never been on a plane before, never left Ireland," he recalls. "My dad said, 'Enjoy it and do your best.' It was Easter 1972 and I stayed in Salford. I saw the first team play Liverpool at home and was taken into the boardroom after the game and met one or two of the directors. Arthur Albiston was on the same trial as me."

United played a friendly game for triallists such as Stapleton, ironically against the boys of Dublin's Home Farm.

"We beat them 3–0 and I got a couple of goals. United said that they wanted me to come back in the summer, but that they didn't want to sign me straight away. They weren't saying, 'Please sign for us'. I was due to go back and finish school so that wasn't secure enough for me."

After that Stapleton went to Wolves for a week's trial. They wanted to sign him immediately, but he still had the trial at Arsenal to come.

"They had a one-off trial where they got lads in from all over the UK and Ireland. We had one game at Highbury. I knew that their chief scout had watched me play and afterwards he said, 'We'd like you to sign for us'. United were reluctant, Arsenal were definite. I think I made the right decision and my dad agreed. Arsenal had a history of bringing young players through into the first team and that appealed."

Aged 16, Stapleton moved to London.

"It was daunting," he says. "The culture was completely different for me and the training was hell – going full-time really hit me. I would get home and go straight to sleep and could barely get out of bed in the morning because I was so stiff, but things were happening to my body and I was still developing. I was homesick too and missed my family."

Stapleton's perseverance paid off.

"I got 29 goals for the youth team in my first season so it went well. Arsenal allowed us home every six weeks, which was good of them, especially as they paid for air tickets. There was strong discipline at Arsenal which did us well too."

But it still took time to settle.

"With my accent I spoke differently to nearly everyone else. In the early days it was tough in London. There were problems with IRA bombings and you had to be careful with an Irish accent in

Frank Stapleton

public – people were getting slaughtered in Guildford and Birmingham. But there were other Irish lads at the club. Liam Brady had been there a year and David O'Leary joined a year later. There were a couple of lads from Northern Ireland too. Years on, there ended up being six Irish lads in the first team managed by an Irishman, Terry Neill. But I remember Liam Brady was with his girlfriend on the Tube one day when three lads set on him because of his accent."

Stapleton found his own ways to relax.

"You needed to unwind and as soon as we were old enough the players would meet up and have a drink. We had to be careful in case word got back to the club though. I liked girls but I never had a regular girlfriend – I was pretty focused on football. I earned £7 a week, although my digs and travel were paid for. We had luncheon vouchers worth 15p a day too. I try and tell my kids what I earned, but they can't really comprehend it. I learned how to value money though. I sent a couple of quid a week home in the first month to try and help my mum out, but then she told me to stop because she knew money was tight for me."

Stapleton's salary would increase as he progressed.

"I played for the youth team then the reserves and signed pro at 17, earning £32 a week. I wasn't quite ready for the first team when I made my debut aged 19 in the '74/75 season, but they did have injuries to Ray Kennedy and John Radford – the main strikers. My debut was against Stoke and their player Terry Conroy, who played for the Republic of Ireland, came over before the game and said 'Good luck'. I really appreciated that. Arsenal were in the bottom half of the first division and we drew 1–1 with me getting substituted in the second half."

Stapleton played 25 games the following season, 1975/76, but he was playing in an ageing team, the remnants of whom had won the double in 1971. A later addition was Brian Kidd, but he was unsettled and joined Manchester City in 1976. Kidd's replacement was expensive – Malcolm McDonald from Newcastle – which left Stapleton considered third-choice striker with his contract up in the summer of 1976.

"Arsenal offered me £70 a week for six years," he says. "Terry Neill told me to take it or leave it. There was no way I was signing that when a lot of the first team players were on £300 a week. I subsequently heard that Terry Neill had tried to sell me to Luton in the league below for £60,000."

Arsenal's next season started with a 1–0 defeat to newly promoted Bristol City.

"Neill said that he was going to change the team so a few days later at Norwich I started alongside Malcolm McDonald," explains Stapleton. "I scored and he scored two. It took off from there for me, but I still hadn't signed a contract."

Stapleton kept scoring and by October was Arsenal's top scorer. Feeling bullish, he went to see the manager to sign a new contract. "Terry Neill basically said, 'Get out, you're not getting anything.' It was ridiculous. I was Arsenal's top scorer and I couldn't afford to buy a car and travelled to games on the Tube. I scored the winning goal in a League Cup match against Chelsea and the headline in the *Daily Mail* the next day was, 'Tube Ride to the Last Eight'."

Stapleton thought that he had no option but to put in a transfer request.

"I walked into Highbury and handed in my transfer request. There was a board meeting that day at 2pm. I got called in the next day and Terry was very different with me and said that Arsenal wanted to give me a better contract but that they couldn't for various reasons. He said that the chairman had torn up my transfer request. I wasn't interested. I didn't want to leave but said, 'You do something about it or sell me.'"

Stapleton made his Republic of Ireland debut away to Turkey the following month, scoring after two minutes.

"Arsenal suddenly said that my status had changed, that I was an international player and that they could give me a better contract. So I got a contract worth about £150 a week, which was pretty decent – the tax rates were 60% though."

Stapleton became the main Arsenal striker as the Gunners reached the FA Cup final in 1978, losing 1–0 to Ipswich.

"We deserved to lose," he acknowledges, "so we vowed to win the Cup the following season." Arsenal needed five games to get past Sheffield Wednesday in the third round, but they eventually reached the final against Manchester United. "It was a dream cup final for most people – a big southern team against a big northern team and two great cup sides. Individual on individual, we felt that we had a slightly better team. We felt that Pat Rice and David O'Leary could deal with Mickey Thomas, for example. Coppell was seen as United's danger man, an intelligent player. We went to Bisham Abbey for the week before the game and trained hard all week, even though it was the end of the season. Mentally and physically, we were far better prepared than the year before against Ipswich and the disappointment of losing that year had spurred us on."

As United fans don't need reminding, Stapleton scored in Arsenal's 3–2 win, secured in the dying minutes of the game.

A year later, he played in the European Cup Winners' Cup final, when Arsenal lost out in a penalty shoot-out against Valencia.

"My Arsenal contract was up again by 1981. I had scored 20 plus goals every season and Arsenal wanted to keep me, but offered about £600 a week as their top offer and said that it was the best contract that had ever been offered to an Arsenal player. Liam Brady, a great player, had been allowed to leave a year earlier, which maybe said something about Arsenal at that time. I was allowed to speak to other clubs when my contract expired but it wasn't like now: the two clubs had to agree a fee, otherwise it went to tribunal. In June 1981, I travelled to Dublin with my lawyer to speak to Liverpool. We had lunch with Bob Paisley and the Liverpool chairman and they had no problems with the terms I was looking for – about £1,000 a week. Liverpool said that they would approach Arsenal and get the deal sorted. They said they intended to use David Johnson as a makeweight, but then nothing happened."

Out of contract, Stapleton returned to Arsenal for pre-season training, until United approached him in early July.

"I was getting married around the same time to a Salford girl who I had met in Spain on a tour with Arsenal," he says. "There was some acrimony between United and Arsenal about the move. Arsenal felt that United should have approached them, yet United approached me through a journalist the week I was getting married."

Stapleton met the new United manager Ron Atkinson at a hotel near Heathrow.

"My first impressions of Big Ron were that he was flamboyant and showy," he says. "But I wasn't signing for him, I was signing for Man United. If he had been sitting there asking me to sign for West Brom I would have said no. Ron didn't have to sell the club to me. United had great players. I asked him about new players and he told me that United had money to spend to bring some of the best players in. He didn't disappoint in that respect. United were offering the same terms as Liverpool so I was happy to sign, but United and Arsenal couldn't agree a fee. Arsenal wanted £2 million, United offered £700,000. Liverpool came in again at the eleventh hour but it was too late."

Arsenal and United had finally agreed on a fee of £900,000 and in August 1981 Frank Stapleton left Highbury with a record of 108 goals in 299 games to become a Manchester United player. His new manager described him as "the best centre-forward in Europe".

"I read that but it didn't add any pressure on me. I think it was Ron's way of justifying the big fee. I knew that I could play and what my strengths were. I worked hard, I could create and score goals and had decent – not blistering – pace. I was 25 and I was up there with the best strikers in England. Ron used to come out with some unbelievable statements though. He'd say things in the papers that put added pressure on the players. He'd say that United were going to do this or that. Talk is cheap. You don't boast about things until you've done them. It was bravado and people said that's how he was, but I didn't always agree with it.

"For example, we played Liverpool away at the start of '81/82 and beat them at Anfield. We got on the coach after the game and he said, 'Let's stop off and have a drink to celebrate at Haydock Park.' I just wanted to go home. Liverpool wouldn't have gone out for a celebration drink if they had beaten us, so why should United have done the same?"

Frank Stapleton

Stapleton took to living in Manchester straight away.

"You can see that by the fact that I've stayed in the area ever since. It helped that my wife was from the area and my two lads, who are now 23 and 21, are Mancunians. One supports United and one City – probably because the other one supported United."

At Old Trafford, he noticed significant differences in the way his new team trained compared with his former club.

"It wasn't as hard at United and was nowhere near as good as Don Howe's training," he says. "Howe was one of the best though; it would have been hard for anyone to come near him. I can't remember a full day's training at Manchester United whereas they were the norm at Arsenal. At United we very rarely did anything that would prepare us for the game the following weekend, something I'd become used to under Don Howe. He used scouting reports and the preparation was always spot on. Ron used to tell you what he wanted and let you get on with it. That is fine when you are playing well, but when you aren't I think you need to go back to the basics.

"If a player was struggling for form at United then you had to hope that they came out of it themselves. At Arsenal, Don Howe would put on specific training sessions to help you get back to peak form. He wouldn't tell you, but it would work. At United, Ron would look to buy a replacement."

He also noticed a difference in the way the clubs were run off the field.

"Arsenal was a meticulously run club," he says. "Obviously they didn't have crowds as big as United, but everyone was well organised, which wasn't always the case at Old Trafford. Take the respective ticket offices. At Arsenal, people couldn't get past the man on the door. At United, people used to wander in and out of the ticket office because we were allowed to buy ten extra tickets for every game on top of the comps. I'd go to the ticket office and there would be people wandering around with piles of tickets, all friends of friends. Of course, that changed eventually, but it was like that when I arrived.

"The press were free to wander around the Cliff too," he recalls.

"They'd make themselves a cup of tea and they'd see the team sheet for the following day before most of the players. That's how Ron liked it – the openness."

But Stapleton doesn't want to seem too critical.

"United were a great club who fulfilled all their promises. They didn't mess you around on your contract and were really good in helping us settle in the city. Of course my wife was delighted to move back to Manchester – she was doing handstands. She had come down to live with me in London, but she didn't have any influence on the decision to move to Manchester like some suggested."

The fans took to Stapleton immediately.

"There were one or two jokes about me scoring against United in the '79 Cup final, but I liked the atmosphere at Old Trafford and I liked the way that United played too. Until Wenger arrived, Arsenal's play was traditionally built on a strong defence, whereas United were more attacking. We never went for a draw anywhere and Ron really tried to continue that attacking mentality. He believed that the team should never be inhibited and should go for the win, home or away."

Stapleton started off partnering Gary Birtles. "He was a big money signing who was under a lot of pressure," he says. "In training, Gary used to score all the time and his play really flowed. He was a good player with a good engine, but he used to tense up in matches. I told him to relax. He used to wander and drop back deep. I'd say to him, 'Where the fuck are you going? Let the midfield do their job, get up here. People are criticising you for not scoring, you are not going to score any goals from midfield.' I told him to stay up with me which he did. He broke his duck and scored 11 goals that season."

Yet Birtles did not have a future at Old Trafford.

"Gary might not agree with me, but I don't think he had the temperament to deal with the pressure of a big club," says Stapleton, a theory Bryan Robson agrees with. "He was good enough, but being good enough isn't enough for Man United. You have to be able to deal with expectation and people who have been successful for United have dealt with the continual expectation."

Stapleton had a good relationship with most of his team-mates.

Frank Stapleton

"Gary Bailey used to come across as being an arrogant South African, but deep down I think he was a decent lad. I rated him as a goalkeeper and he was very brave. What I found when I joined the club was that some of the players were still blaming him for his mistake in the 1979 Cup Final. They had given up on him. Gary would save us in matches and one or two were reluctant to give him the credit. They didn't like him, it was personal. I didn't have that bias because I'd just joined the club. I formed my own opinion which was that Gary was a decent goalkeeper, Peter Schmeichel's favourite when he was growing up no less. I would have rows with Gary after games but he'd stand his ground and then it would be over.

"John Gidman was an absolute barmpot," adds Stapleton, "a head case and a lovely guy. He lived in Liverpool and used to get away with a lot because of that. I'd see him in training and say, 'You went out last night.' He'd laugh and say that he'd only had a few. Whatever he did, he would still always be at the front in training. I always thought that he was four or five pounds overweight because he enjoyed his life too much, but he was a good attacking full-back. People might have criticised him as a defender sometimes, but you can't have it both ways. Very few people gave Giddy a run-around because he was too quick for them. He was like a right winger. Maybe he was sometimes reckless when it came to defending, but he was a proper Man United player; a player cast in the mould that Sir Matt Busby had set. Oh, and he used to change his car every second week.

"Arthur Albiston was very steady. He worked hard in training. He wasn't a very good drinker. Three pints and he was gone. He hasn't had a drink for 20-odd years. I think he gave it up because of what it made him personality-wise. In the end his wife said, 'Enough is enough.' To be fair to him he stuck with it and he's still a fit lad.

"Ray Wilkins is still a big pal of mine. We got really friendly when I first moved to Manchester. He was a London lad but he loved playing for Manchester United. The criticism that he got from Ron Atkinson was a bit naughty. He called him 'the Crab' because he played the ball sideways – which was rubbish. Ray was a great player, he got 84 caps for England which shows what a quality player he was. The year that he left United he was player of the year and he was absolutely fantastic, but he couldn't turn down the offer to go to Milan. Ray could play with both feet. He wasn't the quickest, but he could play a first-time ball or he could keep the ball. He was a fantastic captain who encouraged everyone and kept the team on a level.

"Gordon McQueen was a funny lad with a great sense of humour. I had quite a big run-in with Gordon when I was at Arsenal and he was at Leeds. We went for a corner together and I got an elbow in the face. I went down, but the ball ended up going out for a goal kick. The physio came on and there was nothing broke, so I made my way back up the pitch. I went for a ball and I saw Gordon coming for it so 'Bang!' – I hit him and split his nose. His white shirt was covered in red. Thereafter we had a respect for each other. He used to come out with some classics, real self-effacing stuff. He'd come in each week and say. 'I'm giving up drinking now' or 'I'm going to lose weight and get properly fit.' Then he'd come in and say that he'd had a couple of beers the night before. He was great in the dressing-room for taking the piss out of people.

"Lou Macari was one for pranks. He once came out after everyone else for training. We knew he'd been up to something – he'd hammered Stevie Coppell's shoes to the bench. There were nails going right through them and he couldn't get them out.

"And we all knew the story about when Gordon Hill was at Millwall and his team-mates did a great prank on him. Hill got a phone call before he went on an away trip, supposedly from a TV company, saying, 'We believe that you play tennis, will you come and do an interview?' A £200 sweetener was offered, to which Hill readily agreed, but the condition was that he turn up to the interview wearing his tennis kit and with his racket. They told him to go down to wait in reception of the team hotel. The Millwall lads were besides themselves as they kept sneaking a look at their team-mate sat in reception dressed for tennis. There was no interview."

Stapleton looks happy and relaxed as he reminisces over a plate of fish and chips. Sometimes he is perceived to be dour and serious on TV, but in real life he is quite the opposite. His memory for detail is astonishing.

"United played a friendly game against Maccabi Haifa in 1986, yet we stayed in Tel Aviv," he says, starting another anecdote. "We drew 1–1 and went back to the Tel Aviv Hilton that night. It was a warm evening and we had something to eat. We were supposed to go back to our rooms as we were flying back to the UK the next morning.

"Two days earlier, we'd had a walk along the beach after we'd arrived to stretch our legs, and we'd seen a giant turtle washed up on the beach. After the meal, someone said, 'Let's get that fucking turtle and put it in Mick Brown's bath.' I said, 'It's dead and it has been dead for about a week.' Undeterred, the lads lifted the turtle between about six of them. It absolutely stank, it was rotten and decomposing and yet they carried it through the hotel. The other guests looked on incredulous. They carried it into Mick Brown's room and into his bath. They put a cap on its head and one of Mick's cigars in its mouth. Mick was down in the bar with Ron Atkinson. The smell was filtering throughout the whole floor. It was so bad that we decided that we had to get the turtle out of the hotel, so we shifted it but Mick's room still stank something terrible. A bit later he returned to his room and went straight to bed. Everyone was waiting for a reaction but there wasn't one, not even the following morning. Mick's nose had been broken years ago and his sense of smell wasn't what it should have been. He hadn't even noticed.

"Martin Buchan wasn't your archetypal professional," says Stapleton, getting back onto the theme of his team-mates. "He was well respected as captain and was just getting to the end of his time when I arrived. He liked things to be done in a certain way – apprentices had to knock on the door of the first team dressing-room at the training ground for example. On a match day he liked to be in control, but he was a good club man and he liked being at United. He was a very good player, a solid, quick, efficient if not spectacular defender. I can't remember Kenny Dalglish getting the better of him too many times. Martin had a wicked sense of humour. He would start laughing at his own joke before he had told the punchline. I still see him and he works for the PFA.

"He was starting to be edged out at United when I was there so he moved after getting a two-year contract under Joe Royle at Oldham. Martin was very principled. At the end of his first year at Oldham, he said to Joe, 'I can't keep doing this and taking your money. I don't think I'm justifying myself and would like to close it here.' He retired and walked away from the security of a one-year contract.

"I didn't play for long with Sammy McIlroy as Bryan and Remi Moses were brought in. Sammy was a very good player and a really nice lad. He was a good trainer, but I think he could see that no matter what he did, it wouldn't be good enough because Ron had made his mind up about changing things. Sammy got a hat-trick against Wolves on the day that Bryan Robson signed and was dropped the next week. Most players realise that the end has to come, but I think Sammy was disappointed that it came when it did and I can understand why.

"Bryan Robson came into the team and settled down easily. He moved at the right time and he wouldn't have got to the level he was at with Man United had he stayed at West Brom. He became the focal point and, eventually, the captain for United and England. He got his fair share of goals and injuries, but the way Bryan played he was always going to as he would go into tackles probably that he couldn't win. He was so brave that he did that. There were times when I'd chase a ball with a defender knowing that I couldn't win it and that if I tried to get the ball I would get injured. So I'd let the player have it. Bryan never saw that – he'd just go for it, even if he only had a 20 per cent chance of getting it. He was the main man in midfield, especially when Ray went to Milan.

"The first time I came across Norman Whiteside was when Eric Harrison asked me to take a session with the youth team in the indoor gym at the Cliff. He told me to watch them and then give them advice on timings and runs. I said to them, 'When I go to make my run, I'll go somewhere else first.' Because if you identify a space and go straight there before the ball comes, you are easy to mark. Norman tried it and we did the build-up again, where balls were crossed in. He went to go straight to a space but I pulled him back and told him to wait for the ball. He waited and he scored. He collared me years later and said, 'Remember when you grabbed my shirt and wouldn't let me go when I wanted to go but you told me to be patient and wait?' The session had left an impression and within a year I was injured and he replaced me, scoring on his debut against Stoke.

"Norman matured very quickly," continues Stapleton. "As he played around better players, his improvement was rapid. He had fantastic ability. When he moved back into midfield he did well there."

Before the 1982 World Cup in which Whiteside excelled for Northern Ireland, United flew to Vancouver and Seattle for an end of season tour.

"After we played the matches we were given a four-day break in San Diego," recalls Stapleton. "It was cloudy when we got there so we decided to go to Palm Springs where there was sunshine. On the way back to San Diego, a friend of Gary Bailey's invited us to a BBQ. I went to the liquor store and got a load of beers in. Norman was only 16. There were about five or six of us around the pool at this guy's house. We weren't training and drank a lot. The season was over and we just wound down. The next day, Norman flew back to Europe and did unbelievably well in the World Cup. His preparation was terrible, yet he did fantastically well."

Stapleton got 13 league goals in his first United season, 1981/82.

"That was the season we played Valencia at the Mestalla in the UEFA Cup. Valencia's main stand is surrounded by bars and our fans were drinking in them. As our bus approached the ground, our fans moved forward to applaud us. All they were doing was clapping and singing. The Spanish police didn't understand that culture; they panicked and thought there was a riot. They charged at our fans with batons and horses. We were leaving the coach and we couldn't believe what we were seeing, but what could we do?"

Back to his 13-goal league haul.

"I wasn't happy with that," he says. "I was capable of getting 20, but the way United played was a little bit different. I was probably more creative at United than I was at Arsenal. I became a better player and set more goals up for people. I would lay the ball off more, especially if someone had a better chance of scoring than me. I benefited from wingers and when Steve Coppell finished I suffered. Laurie Cunningham came on loan. He was a flamboyant boy. Ron thought that he could get him playing again because he'd done so well for him at West Brom. Laurie was a short-term fix to replace Stevie Coppell. He did it for some matches, but wasn't consistent enough. Then Arthur Graham came in and for one season he was devastating."

There were other creative players at United.

"Arnold Muhren was a fantastic player with an unbelievable left foot. If you made a run he saw it and knew where to play the ball. It used to annoy me when people said, 'Muhren can't tackle.' He wasn't there to tackle, but to be creative. He would control a ball that you thought was going out of play with his left foot. He was fit and a very good trainer. I went to Ajax after United when Arnold was there and he was still the best runner at the club. He was such a great player and he never got the accolades he deserved. He could land a pass 70 yards away on a sixpence. He'd play balls to you which compromised defenders.

"Arnold wasn't a drinker. He wrote about the drinkers in his autobiography which was published in Holland, but a Sunday paper got hold of a copy and named names. I think the drinking culture appalled him. If he had a beer then it would be a very small one, maybe a half, which he'd never finish. I would go to his house and he'd have this very light Dutch drink, which wasn't alcoholic. Arnold got his reward in Holland where he won more cups with Ajax and Holland."

Stapleton's first cup final for United came in the 1983 Milk Cup against Liverpool. He ended up playing centre-half.

"It was unfortunate, but Kevin [Moran] had got injured so Mickey Duxbury was alongside me in defence with Lou Macari at right-back. Gordon McQueen had to go up front. We took the game to extra time and were hanging on, but our team was all over the place and nobody was in their normal position. We were hanging on for a replay.

Frank Stapleton

We knew that we just had to hang on, but then Ronnie Whelan tried to slip the ball between my legs. I closed my legs and the ball hit my foot and rolled back to him and he whacked it, curling it into the top corner. That just killed it for us. It was a game with three unbelievable strikes. Alan Kennedy's opener for them was brilliant as was Norman's equaliser. We got a bit of resolve from losing that game."

That resolve would come in useful two months later in the FA Cup final against Brighton.

"The Liverpool defeat made us more determined to win the FA Cup, yet we didn't perform in the final against Brighton. The first game was very disappointing and half the team did not perform. The pitch was really heavy and we went a goal down. We improved in the second half and got an equaliser. Then Ray got the second goal for us, only for us to fall asleep again. They hadn't had a kick. We had loads of chances but didn't take them. Then they got a corner, their first in about 20 minutes. We didn't clear it properly and Gary Stevens scored to equalise.

"There was no doubt that we were going to win the replay," says Stapleton. "We were laughing at the United fans singing, 'Stevie Foster [the Brighton captain who was suspended for the first game], What a difference you have made.' He made no difference as we ran Brighton ragged. They never really had a hope. They'd had that on the Saturday. To be fair, Brighton had been relegated and put up a good performance in the first game, but in the replay they didn't stand a chance. We were two up in no time and the underdogs don't usually get two bites at the cherry."

After beating Arsenal 4–0 to go top of the league at Easter 1984, United won just one game from the last ten that season. "We were unbelievable that day against Arsenal, even though they had a player sent off," says Stapleton. "Yet our next game was against a West Brom team who were fighting relegation – and we lost. We tried to play well but we didn't need to play well, we just needed to win.

"We should have won the first game in the Camp Nou against Barcelona that season too. They got an own goal and then got an unbelievable volley in the 88th minute. Bryan [Robson] had a couple of chances he would have normally just hit, but he tried to chip one and take another around the goalkeeper. We ended up losing 2–0. The Camp Nou wasn't even full so we weren't intimidated by the atmosphere."

United famously made amends in the return leg at Old Trafford.

"Barca had Maradona, Schuster and lot of Spanish internationals, although in truth Maradona was carrying an injury. We knew that the crowd could make a big difference to us that night and they did that. That night was easily the best atmosphere I've experienced. Officially it was 58,000, but I'm convinced there were thousands more in the ground that night. We just knew we were going to win and the Barca players knew it too, you could see how nervous they were. Their goalkeeper fumbled a weak shot from Ray Wilkins and Robbo followed up to knock in the first goal."

Stapleton scored the crucial third goal for United.

"I did, but it was always tight," he says. "Even at 3–0, Bernd Schuster had a chance on the edge of the box. He was played in and he turned the ball onto his right foot and bent it round Gary Bailey. Gary was beaten, but the ball just spun past the post."

With Barcelona vanquished, optimism among Reds was sky high: the Cup Winners' Cup was coming to Manchester. The sublime talents of Juventus would have to be overcome in the semi-final and after a hard-fought 1–1 draw at Old Trafford, United flew to Turin for the second leg. Juve boasted genuine world-class players and few gave United a chance, especially as their players had felt frustrated at their first-leg performance.

Their star Michael Platini recalls: 'We didn't play well. Manchester had two of their best players missing, Robson and Wilkins, and we should have won. I've not always been a fan of English clubs in Europe, but I knew that Manchester would be difficult to beat, that's why we prepared to play our best in Turin."

Stapleton started in Turin, with Norman Whiteside surprisingly made substitute.

"The papers reported that I had a knock but it wasn't true," Whiteside said, when I interviewed him about this game in 2002. "I was dropped and I sat on the bench, frustrated, and watched. The lads were up for it, those big games were fantastic and the atmosphere in the stadium was incredible. The crowd were very hostile, very volatile. In fact, during the warm-up I was frightened of going behind the goal to retrieve the ball.

"Juventus were one of the top, if not *the* top team in Europe," added Whiteside. "A side of internationals, they were very well respected. They were physical and would nip at your heels and tug your shirt. They would body-check you in the box before the ball arrived and try to man-mark you. Rossi was the goal poacher who had done so well in the 1982 World Cup, Platini was *the* best and Boniek was really quick up front. Then there was Tardelli, Cabrini and Gentile . . ."

Whiteside, still just 18, was a target for Juve's main rivals Milan. It was more than paper talk.

"United had accepted £1.5 million for me and Big Ron rang to say that I had to be on a flight to Italy if I wanted to join Milan," he said. "Despite the lucrative money being offered, I didn't want to go as I wanted to establish myself properly at United and I'd just arrived in America on holiday and didn't fancy flying straight back. Playing in Italy was something I fancied later in my career." If only.

The second leg was played in Stadio Communale and 70,000 tickets quickly sold, producing record receipts of £600,000. In an era before budget airlines, a thousand United fans made the journey to Turin. Inside the stadium, many stood bare chested in spite of the cool spring evening. The game started with one end of the ground enveloped in thick smoke from the dozens of fiery flares that had greeted the teams' arrival. As the white cloud lifted, so Platini picked the ball up and spilt the United defence with a mercurial pass to Boniek. The fleet-footed Pole survived a desperate challenge from Albiston and shot accurately past Bailey. Thirteen minutes gone. 1–0

"The difference between the two teams was that one moment of brilliance from Platini when he put Boniek through for the first goal," said Ray Wilkins. "The man was a genius."

Juventus continued to dictate against a side desperately missing

Bryan Robson. The gulf in class meant keeper Gary Bailey was kept busy keeping United in the game with outstanding saves from Bonnini, Rossi (twice), Boniek and three times from Platini. With Juve pressing their dominance, *The Times* the next day would report, "With flicks of pure arrogance and back heels of sheer impudence, the Italians flowed with delightful artistry. As elusive as a blob of mercury, Platini was usually responsible for their dangerous thrusts."

Still, Bailey refused to be beaten and the score stayed 1–0. Then, with 27 minutes left, Atkinson launched Whiteside on for Stapleton with the instruction, "Put yourself about and get stuck in." The antithesis to Platini's elusiveness, Whiteside lit United's fighting spirit with a bang and seven minutes later, the huge scoreboard had changed. It read: Juventus 1 (Boniek) Manchester United 1 (Whiteside). The tie was level at 2–2.

"Big Paul [McGrath] hit a shot across the box," remembered Whiteside. "It ricocheted and came to me and I just cracked it into the top corner. The goal put Juventus on the back foot and subdued the crowd. The game was ours for the taking.

"When Manchester United equalised, jubilation shot through their fans," wrote the American Bill Burford, at the game researching his book, *Among the Thugs*. "Their cheers and songs were suddenly tinny and small in that great cavity of the Juventus football ground, its 70,000 Italians now comprehensively silent. The United supporters jumped up and down, fell over each other, embraced."

With seconds of normal time remaining, the brief euphoria in the United section was cut dead when captain Gae Scirea missed a shot but Paolo Rossi was there to plunder the ball in past Bailey. Brilliant red flares lit the Turin sky and firecrackers exploded by the side of the pitch.

"The exhilaration felt but two minutes before by that small band of United supporters," continued Buford, "was now felt – magnified many times – by the seventy thousand Italians who, previously humiliated, dictated their powerful glee into our corner. The roar was deafening, invading the senses like a bomb." It was a cruel way to go out.

"There was a bad atmosphere immediately after the game," said Whiteside. "But Juventus probably deserved to win.

"On the plane coming home, the boys were playing cards when Big Ron came over and told me that I was playing in a reserve friendly at Barrow the following night. I arrived back in Manchester, had a few hours sleep, and then travelled to Barrow where, bizarrely, we had a guided tour of a submarine. I scored that night and remember thinking of the difference between scoring in Turin and a day later at Barrow."

Juventus went on to beat Porto, who had overcome Alex Ferguson's Aberdeen, in the final in Basle. United, who had been two points behind European champions elect Liverpool before the game, fell away badly in the league and didn't win in the final five games.

"Michel Platini is the greatest player I ever played against," said Norman Whiteside, "Ask Bryan Robson, he'll tell you the same."

After the final whistle in Turin, Whiteside chased Platini to exchange shirts.

"I tell a story that he came up to me, tapped me on the shoulder and said, 'Norman, you've spent 20 minutes trying to pull it off my back, so here's my shirt.' But the truth was he just shook my hand, gave me the shirt and wished me well."

"Remi Moses tried to shackle Platini that night, but admitted afterwards that he couldn't get near him," recalls Stapleton. "I remember Remi saying, 'Every time I got close to him, he'd just lay it off first time or take me out of position.' When Platini did get time on the ball he'd use it intelligently. Remi was a great man-to-man marker, but it was difficult for him against Platini that night."

The run to the semi-finals had provided United fans with some great moments though. Most would rightly highlight the victory over Barca and while Stapleton doesn't disagree, his headed goal in the opening round against Dukla Prague was responsible for United staying in the tournament.

"We drew the first game 1–1 and they had the away goal," he recalls. "It was 1–1 in Prague after Robbo scored a cracking goal with his right foot. One side of the ground was full of United supporters from all over eastern Europe. I had twisted my ankle in the first minute and it was strapped up."

It didn't stop him being effective.

"Arthur Graham went down the right and whipped a cracking cross in. I headed it back across the goalkeeper into the net. It was one of my best goals. They equalised to make it 2–2, so we needed to keep possession and slow the game down, knowing that we would go through on away goals. Except Arthur Graham started steaming towards their box with the ball. 'Arthur, what are you doing?' I shouted. 'We need to score! We're losing the tie,' he shouted. 'We don't, we have two away goals!' I replied. 'Don't give the ball away.' I had to explain to him how the away goals rule worked.

"It was tough to go to Eastern Europe, it always seemed to be bleak. We believed that the ref was going to be against us away from home. We didn't really get to see anything of the cities we played in, apart from a hotel room and what we saw on the coach between the hotel and the ground and we'd be away straight after the game. People used to assume that all the travel was glamorous, but it wasn't."

Stapleton was popular with United fans. Although never prolific, he scored key goals and led the front line with authority, pulling defenders out of position with selfless runs to create space for others. He was never fazed by any big game and, on several occasions, played out of position for the good of the team when he would have rather have stayed up front. When Kevin Moran was sent off in the 1985 Cup Final, it was Stapleton who had to adapt.

"Kevin should never have been sent off, but the referee was on his last game and wanted to make an impact. I had to play centre-half when Kevin went off. I was okay in that position, but I thought that Bryan would have stopped back rather than me. I played alongside big Paul, he marked Graham Sharpe and I had Andy Gray. I knew that I could compete with him in the air and that he would never run me. I just had to make sure that I didn't lose my concentration and that I stayed with him when he wandered into space.

"We were playing well, but when Norman scored the goal, my elation quickly turned to fear. I started thinking that I didn't want to be responsible for any mistakes which would let Everton back into the game. Mick Duxbury kept talking to me. I said to him, 'Keep talking to me Mickey because I'm wandering and following the ball – that was the natural thing for a striker to do.' Fortunately we got through it. I've never seen the '85 cup final since. I might have a copy of it on a video somewhere in the attic."

Flushed with optimism from the cup win, United famously kicked off the following season with ten straight wins. Except that run nearly didn't happen.

"We played Villa in the first game of the '85/86 season and it was 0–0 at half time," recalls Stapleton. "The crowd were actually booing. Then we had the breakthrough in the second half and ended up winning 4–0. We played a tough game at Ipswich and ended up winning 2–0. During that game at Portman Road, Paul McGrath ran off the pitch and straight into the dressing-room. The crowd wondered where he had gone. Paul had the runs."

United still won at Ipswich, but couldn't win the league for the first time since 1967.

"Our problem wasn't the big teams, but the smaller ones, the teams we should have wiped the floor with," says Stapleton. "If you think of every championship side, they have always ground out slender victories. We never learned how to do that. We were an open team who always attacked, but if we got a few defeats our confidence would go. There were games away from home where we needed to be tight. But we'd go to every ground and try to attack. And we found it hard to get out of a rut when we weren't winning.

"We were playing some great one-touch football and nobody could stay with us at the start of '85/86. I think we thought that we could win the league after the great start but then things started to go wrong – the Old Trafford pitch was gone by November and that affected how we played. Liverpool had an unbelievable run at the end of the season too."

Stapleton wasn't surprised when Ron Atkinson was dismissed in November 1986. "Ron's departure was a combination of everything. He was under pressure, you could see that. He became less outgoing and his relationship with the press changed because they had to report what was going on. He had looked after the press, but there wasn't going to be any loyalty when editors were demanding to know what was going on at Manchester United.

"We'd never been consistent in the league and we had a poor start to the '86/87 season. We were not performing and we were all to blame, not just Ron. We were dreadful in some games and that's not good enough for Manchester United."

Stapleton admits that he didn't know too much about the incoming manager Alex Ferguson.

"Gordon Strachan did though," he says. "He warned us about the hairdryer and that he'd be in your face, but there were a lot of positive comments too – like the fact that he wanted to play good football. He changed the whole way the club was, there was no way the press were going to have the run of the place like they had with Big Ron. Training was earlier with Ferguson, too, we started at 9.30 whereas it was 10.30 with Big Ron. I just don't think there was ever a fear factor with Ron. That was the difference, it was too comfortable."

It wasn't long before Ferguson's influence was omnipresent.

"He had spies around town. He would go out himself and got into people, finding out where the players went at night. He used to look at people carefully in the morning to see if they had been out the night before. In his mind, he knew that it wasn't his team and that he had to rebuild because there were quite a few of us in our 30s. We accepted that. But the first thing he had to ensure was that we stayed up, because we were only a bad run away from being dragged into the relegation zone. We were all playing for our futures. I was 31 and had been on a week-to-week contract for a year. The club had offered me a new contract, but it was less money than I had been on in my last year at the club. There was an impasse so I signed a week-to-week contract. I was ready to leave United, but they were looking for a fee. The manager tried to loan me to Man City, but I turned it down. City were struggling and fighting relegation and I felt that if I'd gone there I would have been in a no-win situation. If I helped City to stay up then I wouldn't be popular with the fans when I returned to Old Trafford, and if City went down then I would have been hated by their fans.

"Ferguson almost sold me to Charlton, but I didn't speak to them. It wasn't financially right to move to London. My solicitor spoke to Martin Edwards at the end of '86/87 and he said that United were willing to let me go for free. It was time I moved on from United."

In the summer of 1987, Stapleton moved to Amsterdam after Johan Cruyff signed him for Ajax.

"It was difficult to learn the language," he says. "The football was slower and they tended to isolate you so I hardly got a touch. I roomed with Frank Rijkaard, a fantastic guy and brilliant footballer. He had a row with Cruyff and left to join Zaragoza. Cruyff was very hands-on. You had to make the runs that he told you to make and if you didn't he'd take you off. I didn't give it long enough to adjust."

Injuries hardly helped his cause.

"I got a back injury and only played six games for Ajax. I came back to England to do my rehabilitation and trained with United's reserves for a couple of months. I called Ajax and told them that I was ready to go back, but they wouldn't let me play. I was fit but I failed the tests they put me through at the Dutch FA. And when I did get fit, I wasn't being included in the team – Cruyff had left and I didn't figure."

With the Republic of Ireland about to play in the 1988 European Championships in Germany, Stapleton needed football, so he went to Derby County in March 1988, where he played ten games. He played in Ireland's three games against England, Russia and Holland in Germany.

"I enjoyed that at that stage of my career," he says.

In October 1988 he moved to Le Havre in France for three quarters of the season, before spending two years at Blackburn Rovers, where he played a further 81 games.

"In 1991, I trained with Huddersfield but they had no money and couldn't offer me a contract, but Bradford City rang while I was at Huddersfield and offered me the player-manager's job. I played 68 times for Bradford, which I didn't really want to do. I played in central midfield because nobody would sit there and teams could break against us. I used to play there and keep it simple. Still, it was very demanding for a 34-year-old. I played up front when another lad was injured."

Bradford was a tough management experience.

"We had no reserve team coach so me and Stuart Pearson looked after both sides. We had one chief scout, one physio and a youth team coach. We trained on a council pitch and it was a disaster. We had to sell our best players but we still improved every year. Eventually Bradford was taken over by Geoffrey Richmond and I couldn't deal with that. He was doing things behind my back and doing everything wrong in my opinion. He would say, 'Are you interested in any players?' I'd tell him who I was interested in and ten minutes later the phone would go and it would be the local paper asking me about the players who I had just spoken to Richmond about.

"On the day that he arrived he spent the whole day talking to the press, he didn't come to see me and I was the manager. When I did get to see him, he told me that I had to sack the physio and get a part-time one, and sack the chief scout because he said we didn't need one. He said, 'You've got two weeks to do it.' I said, 'You can give me two years but I'm not doing it.'"

Richmond returned to see Stapleton two weeks later. "He said, 'You haven't sacked those people.' I said: "I shouldn't have to. You fucking do it.'"

The pair argued continuously, which wasn't good for the former Reds in charge of team affairs.

"It was only a matter of time before we were dismissed and he sacked us when we didn't make the play-offs," he recalls. "I'd told Stuart not to be surprised, but he was still devastated. Stuart wanted to pay Richardson a visit and get him back, but I told him not to do that, to get the money that was owed before thinking about any retribution."

That was May 1994.

"My next job was in America where I coached New England

Frank Stapleton

Revolution," says Stapleton. "I quite enjoyed it and liked living in Boston, although I was disappointed by the quality of the football and the politics of the league. And it was quite hard disciplining players when their contracts were owned collectively by the league. I had the lad Alexis Lalas playing for me and he was a real problem. He didn't want to train, he thought he was the big star and he played in a band too. He did promotions for the league as well.

"He wasn't turning up for training so I told the general manager that I was going to fine him two weeks wages. They wouldn't do it, so I dropped him because he was playing shit and his attitude was appalling. That made the news on CNN.

"Lalas started slagging me off in front of the other players and I found out about it. I confronted him in front of everyone and I had a right go at him. I asked him if he was denying it and he said no. I said, 'You're a fucking disgrace.' The owner got on to me and told me that I had to apologise. I said, 'What do I have to apologise about, he's a fucking disgrace and the reason why we're struggling. The young players look up to him and think it's okay to behave like he does.'

"The owner agreed that Lalas was in the wrong, but that we needed to get Lalas playing again as he was being used to promote the league. In the end, I had to go. The Kraft family, who owned the club, paid me my money."

These days, Stapleton keeps himself busy.

"I read books, especially John Grisham," he says. "They might be commercial fiction, but I like them."

He plays golf too and media work provides an income.

"It keeps me busy," he says, "but I miss the routine that football gave me more than anything else. There are times when there are voids with the work and I don't like that. The media work is a good thing for ex-footballers because it can be hard for them. Nine times out of ten their educational levels haven't been that high. It's a competitive market, the television work, because there are a lot of lads who'd like to do more of it. Television stations also tend to like players who have recently come out of the game so that's not great for older players."

Stapleton's other job means he gets to watch United.

"I do the hospitality at Old Trafford too before games. I enjoy that. The people are football supporters who want to know your opinions. People don't get as drunk now and they enjoy the games."

Stapleton's stock remains high among Reds, although one or two have wondered how he calls both United and Arsenal 'we' when asked for his opinions as a guest for Sky Sports News.

"I've got a right to call both teams 'we' because I played for both," he refutes. "If I go on MUTV I'll say 'we' because it's Manchester United we're talking about and I can't remember saying 'we' to describe Arsenal. People always try to draw me on who my team is. You can't win on something like that. I was at the cup final in 2005 and the Arsenal fans were accusing me of being a Man United fan. They were asking me where my scarf was. But I did a piece before that game for MUTV where I said I thought Arsenal would win. Because I did. I spent a lot of time with Arsenal as well as United and it's very hard to separate them. I have an affinity with both. But I live in the North-West, United employ me to do commercial work, as well as MUTV.

"I would like to get back into football on the coaching side but it's not always possible and you don't always get the breaks. I have been applying for jobs, but the longer it goes on the more difficult it becomes. It's like a merry-go-round but I've still got something to offer."

A love of the game for one thing.

"I go to a lot of matches and love watching how teams are set out," he explains, "how they counteract certain individuals. You can tell after five minutes who is going to have a good game. It's very hard for someone to start slowly and then have a good game. I still love football. It has its ups and downs but I've never stopped loving the game I started playing as a child in Dublin."

9

Alan Brazil

The Raconteur

Alan Brazil walks into Langhams, a large Mayfair restaurant barely a Gary Neville throw-in from the Ritz. The girls in neat uniforms on the front desk know Brazil, who seems in his element in the convivial atmosphere. Langhams is popular with football people, not so much current players, but retired pros, journalists, agents and officials. And with the perceived glamour come the ladies who lunch, tables of aesthetically pleasing and immaculately dressed 30- and 40-something uptown girls who look as if the only stress in their lives comes when the Land Rover garage calls to tell them the bill for a new exhaust.

The elegance of Langhams is a long way from Glasgow's Castlemilk, where Brazil spent his first few years.

"I was born in the same hospital as Fergie, over in Govan," Brazil says, as he sits down and orders from a wine list he knows inside out. "Govan is a big Rangers area and Fergie played for Rangers, but I was a Celtic boy."

Castlemilk – sarcastically labelled *chateau lait* by the middle classes in Glasgow's west end – was one of the biggest housing estates in Europe, a failed 1950s peripheral housing scheme built to accommodate people from inner city slums such as the Gorbals.

"It was a bad place," says Brazil. "There was always trouble, murders – horrible. Amazingly there were no pubs. It was a very poor part of Glasgow but it produced a lot of footballers because there was nothing else to do. Like many boys, all I was interested in was football."

Not that the Brazils were a typical Castlemilk family.

"My old man had a couple of shops and made enough to move away so I actually grew up in a more middle-class background near Hampden Park," he says.

Brazil signed for Celtic Boys as a 13-year-old, the first stage in a lifelong ambition to play for the hoops.

"It was great. I stayed there and my captain at Under 16s was Roy Aitken, who went on to captain Celtic and Scotland. At 15, I scored 62 goals, a record in the Scottish Amateur League. That's when suddenly there was interest in me, not in Scotland, but from south of the border. The first club were Ipswich, I've no idea why."

Before moving to Suffolk, Brazil had an unfortunate sequence of trials at bigger clubs.

"I was supposed to have trials with Spurs but had problems with my chest – pneumonia – so I couldn't play. I also went to Everton and pulled my groin so I couldn't play there. I was invited to Manchester United, but they didn't want to see me until August."

So Brazil went to Ipswich.

"I loved it there," he says enthusiastically. "It was totally different from Glasgow, a small town in Suffolk. I had two great years in the youth team when we won the FA Youth Cup. We were a bit like Manchester United's youth team of '92, talent combined with a great understanding and trust."

Alan Brazil

Brazil was a free-scoring forward in the reserve team and had played some friendlies for the first XI, but before playing a competitive game he was sent to play in America, manager Bobby Robson hoping that he would acquire some experience against better players, toughen up and become sharper. The morning after Ipswich beat Arsenal in the 1978 FA Cup final, Brazil flew from Heathrow to Detroit.

"It was make or break time for me. I played for Detroit and against George Best who was at Fort Lauderdale. He was brilliant for them and a lovely guy. He changed with booze, but I've not got a bad word to say about him. I got to know him well in later years when we worked for Sky."

The American move was a success.

"I was only 18, but in America I grew a little, played a lot and got stronger. It was one of the best four months I've ever had. We played in the 82,000-capacity Pontiac Silverdome and, despite being under age, we didn't struggle to get a beer either."

Brazil returned to Ipswich for the start of the 1979/80 season.

"I was chomping at the bit and saying to Bobby Robson, 'Get me in the team, get me in the team.' Then I started to feature. It wasn't easy, but once I'd played a bit and scored a few goals the fans took to me and I grew in confidence. Arnold Muhren and Frans Thyssen came from Holland. They were great for me and for Ipswich. We were a long-ball team, but when great passers like Muhren arrived, the ball came through the middle."

Muhren and Brazil would go on to be team-mates at United.

"Muhren was very quiet. He would always eat the same food – soup with steak. He was a great professional and looked after himself. He always went home after training. Thyssen, meanwhile, was more open and before long he was on the Heineken and owned a snooker cue."

Brazil made his Scotland debut in 1980 and went on to win 13 caps, but it was at Ipswich where he made the most headlines, scoring 70 goals in 143 appearances until he left in 1983. He was in the Ipswich side which beat United 6–0 at Portman Road in March 1980.

"I got two and had a fight with Jimmy Nichol in the tunnel," he recalls. "He thought that I'd done him, but I've never done anyone. We shook hands after. We were the first side to play one off the front two and Eric Gates destroyed Gordon McQueen that day. McQueen said to me, 'He was running through my legs. I was like a fish out of water.' We also missed two penalties that day."

Brazil cites several reasons for Ipswich's success.

"Ipswich had a very good scouting policy. With no disrespect to the southerners, most of our players were northerners or Scots. The cockneys at Spurs or West Ham used to give it the big, 'Here come the tractor boys,' but we weren't Suffolk boys. The coaching was good under Bobby Robson and I loved Ipswich."

Robson, who took control in 1969, had improved Ipswich gradually to the point that in 1980/81 they won the UEFA Cup, finished runners-up in the league and reached the semi-finals of the FA Cup – all in one season.

"We beat champions Villa three times," adds Brazil. "We were runners-up to Liverpool too the following season after they finished the league with an unbelievable run. I'll never forget going to Old Trafford in 1981/82 and scoring in front of the Stretford End in a 2-1 win. Muhren played a brilliant through-ball, I went round Martin Buchan. Gary Bailey came out and I tucked it in. As I looked up, these bitter faces wanted to kill me. I'll never forget that, it was a huge moment for me. All these faces were shouting 'Fuck off!' as I celebrated my goal. Brilliant. Going to Old Trafford was awesome, but we always thought that we could beat United with our team. We didn't think that when we went to Anfield. Not only were Liverpool a brilliant football side, but you never got anything there, no penalties or anything."

Ipswich were getting ambitious, hindsight would suggest too much so. They built the new Pioneer Stand at Portman Road, which was to prove their undoing.

"We ran out of money to finish it," says Brazil. "Fergie's Aberdeen knocked us out of the UEFA Cup; we lost in the FA Cup and had no extra income. Players started being sold and I heard that I was going to be one of them. There were a few rumours coming from Old Trafford, so I was surprised that it was Spurs who came in for me."

Brazil moved to Tottenham with 12 league games left of the 1982/83 season.

"They were mid-table and I scored six, helping them get into Europe. The following year we won the UEFA Cup with great players like Hoddle, yet something wasn't right for me. I never recaptured that Ipswich form and I started to struggle. I was enjoying Tottenham, but not the games. There was a lot of pressure. Everything was done at tempo in training with a lot of ball work. The coaching was very good and I averaged a goal every three games, but I wasn't totally happy because I was in and out of the team. I suppose it was inevitable that I would leave, but it had to be a big club because I enjoyed Spurs. Everything was right about it bar me not playing every week."

Brazil was on £1,000 a week at White Hart Lane.

"United offered me a little bit more and I signed in the summer of 1984 for £625,000. I was at Royal Ascot with Glenn Hoddle when the word came through that a deal had been done with United."

Tottenham made a profit on the £450,000 they had paid Ipswich, but Brazil was more concerned about the football.

"I thought of Stapleton as a target man like Paul Mariner and thought, 'Yes, this could work,'" he says. "I was confident of recreating my Ipswich form where I felt so good I believed I could score against anyone. I was made to feel very welcome when I arrived at Old Trafford by people like Gordon McQueen, Bryan Robson and Arthur Albiston. I knew some of the lads from playing against them and the Scotland squad. There were other Scots, too, like Graeme Hogg a big, dopey centre-half and I don't mean that in a nasty way. He wanted to do well and put his body in the way. He'd struggle in today's game because he wouldn't be mobile enough.

"Me, I just wanted to get in the team, get a good start and do well. But looking back I was a slow starter who picked up injuries, so I was looking for a bit of luck. The fans were frustrated. Merseyside was dominating and the fans were looking for success. United fans weren't daft and some doubted me from the start. They thought, 'He can't get a game at Tottenham so why have we bought him?' and that added to the pressure."

It was a pressure Brazil felt acutely.

"It got to me. Take Everton at home in my first season. I got the ball inside their half and knocked it first time to Jesper Olsen. He whacked a cross in and I hit an overhead kick, catching it brilliantly. It hit the underside of the bar and bounced down. It could have crossed the line but it didn't. That summed up my luck. I came off the pitch and two fans spat at me as I walked up the tunnel. They were kids, but they were still out of order.

"It got to the stage that I used to look forward to away games more than those at Old Trafford, which is crazy. United fans were great noise-wise away from home. It was never so great at Old Trafford and certainly nothing like I was used to from standing on the terraces at Celtic Park. Maybe it was me, though. I felt that if I didn't play well in the first 20 minutes then the whinging and moaning would start. I don't know why people do this because it just makes the situation worse. I didn't like the nasty comments I'd get at Old Trafford, but away from home I scored two against Burnley in the cup. I thought I'd turned the corner but then didn't score on the Saturday after and was bombed out. That happened to me twice. I got two against QPR before the cup final but nothing a week later and was dropped. I was under constant pressure at Man United – as was everyone else. Everything was great about United, but if you are not playing – and playing well – it ruins it."

With Brazil unable to establish himself in the starting eleven, his relationship with manager Ron Atkinson suffered.

"It had been all right to begin with, but as soon as I was out of the side that changed," he recalls. "I might as well have been invisible. When you are out you are out. Soon I was getting compared with Gary Birtles, but I got a goal every three games at United. And I also don't like Birtles getting hammered because before he signed for United he was a very good player in a very good Nottingham Forest side. He probably felt, like I did, that you had to score every time at United."

Off the field, Brazil enjoyed living in Manchester.

"I lived in the Amblehurst Hotel in Sale where all the lads used to go back to after games because it was private. It was great and you were made to feel very welcome. Fergie stayed there when he arrived and loads of others.

"After the Amblehurst I bought a place in Ashley near Hale. Turn right out of the Bleeding Wolf pub and I was near there, out in the country. Lovely place, and I mean lovely. Rumour has it that Paul McGrath wanted to buy my place but that the club wouldn't give him the money and that's why he left. I paid £162,000 for it. Must be worth a million now. I liked a drink, but for all the reputation that I've got for always being out, I never used to drink anywhere but Paddy's place, that's where I was happiest. I liked Mere golf club too. Sunday night was poker night in there. All the rich Manchester businessmen used to get involved in poker schools and I joined one. The snooker player Alex Higgins turned up and he wanted to play so we let him. We were drinking wine and Alex couldn't go wrong, he was making fortunes. There was a former Manchester street fighter playing, a big black guy who was hard as nails. Alex kept winning and it was getting a bit rowdy. The guy from Mere told us that it was time to go. I kept thinking that too. Alex called the street fighter but he didn't have the money and asked to borrow some. Alex wouldn't let him – a mistake. Alex was the stranger to the school and should have let him borrow money. I got up and walked out, but I heard all hell broke loose behind me, with tables going and bottles smashing. Two nights later I was lying on the couch, eyes shut and half listening to the snooker on television. Then David Vine said, 'Poor Alex was kicked by his daughter's pony at the weekend.' I opened my eyes to see Alex black and blue. He'd been kicked all over Mere's courtyard. I've got great memories because I liked Manchester. It reminded me of Glasgow."

Never one to eschew a pint, Brazil puts United's drinking into perspective.

"When I played with Scotland I talked to the Liverpool players and they were drinking as much as the United lads," he says. "And

We're The Famous Man United

Tottenham had more booze on their bus after away games than any club I'd played with. They had crates of wine.

"I'm told that when I left, Norman and Paul were hitting it really bad, but when I was there we were drinking Guinness or beer which you'd sweat out, not spirits. We'd drink at Paddy's pub in Altrincham, even after European away games. I remember banging on his front door at two o'clock one morning after returning from Eindhoven in the UEFA Cup. I'd told the missus that the plane had been delayed due to fog. Paddy shouted, 'How did you play?' as he opened up. We replied, 'Never mind, just open up.' We had six pints of Guinness each then Paddy left us and went back to bed. We liked it there because we never got any hassle."

Brazil also thinks that the drinking helped engender a good team spirit.

"The team spirit at United was great. It was very competitive, but everyone wanted each other to do well, even if we were having a bad time. I roomed with Bryan Robson a lot. He was a great guy and a great Manchester United servant. He always used to encourage me. My nickname was Baz, which I didn't mind. I got Bryan Robson into racing when I took him to York races one day and we both won a few quid. I'd got into horses when I was at Ipswich because Newmarket wasn't far away. The lovely thing about playing football is that you get treated like gods. We looked after the Newmarket lads if they came to watch Ipswich for a big European game and they'd look after us. If the stable lads supported United then we'd get them tickets if United played at Portman Road. I loved the racing. I'd watch the gallops at five in the morning in the summer when we didn't train. It wasn't just about having a bet, I loved everything about it.

"Robbo loved that afternoon at York, not just the bet but the social side. Peter Reid was there, Sam Allardyce too. We talked about football over a glass of champagne between races. Robbo's done brilliantly and he deserves it. He wasn't an excessive drinker like people said. I live in London and see people drink more than Bryan Robson every day, lots more. Bryan played hard and trained hard – and was entitled to have a few bevvies after.

"Bryan Robson became a big buddy. We used to take the kids swimming at Mere on a Sunday. It's difficult now with Bryan because he's still in the game and I have to give opinions on radio. And whatever they say, they don't like it if it's negative. I don't mean any harm and if I can help an ex-team-mate I will, but sometimes you have to tell the truth and give your true feelings. People shouldn't take to heart what I say on radio."

Brazil was fond of his other team mates too.

"Gordon McQueen was one of the funniest footballers I ever knew. He used to throw up on the pitch before games because of nerves. Paul McGrath? He used to beat Jesper Olsen in sprints. You didn't see too much of Big Paul in the pubs. On the training ground, he was always the fastest. It surprised me when I heard that Paul had problems through booze. I think there's a fine line between someone who can drink a lot and be okay, and someone who drinks a lot and has to depend on it. Arthur Albiston was a lovely bloke. He loved a drink but it got on top of him, so he knocked it on the head. Arthur got so pissed up one night he couldn't walk. McQueen and I took him home and delivered him to his wife. His wife gave him the ultimatum. He was always the first to get pissed, but he loved that togetherness. He was a very steady player, Arthur, very good full-back, without being spectacular. He was quick enough though. Gordon Strachan would have a few but not a lot, the same with Jesper Olsen. Big Norman loved a pint. It was to do with your background. Look at George [Best], from Belfast."

Brazil is warming to his theme.

"People talk about drink cultures, but it's there in black and white – look at who ruled Europe in the '70s and '80s. I know doctors will tell you differently, but what was wrong with our diet then, our booze? I'm adamant; it's an absolute load of bollocks that you shouldn't drink. I eat now what I ate then, steak and chicken. Although I was weighed one day at Old Trafford and was 13st 10lbs. I must admit I had the shock of my life. I'm heavier than that now because I can't exercise. Sometimes the kids want a bit of pasta and all that. I'd have that with a bit of white wine now and then, but I've never changed."

He claims that as long as players performed, managers would turn a blind eye to the drinking.

"Ron was no different," he says. "I would have a few, sometimes on a Thursday when I shouldn't have, but I'd still do well on a Saturday. You needed to unwind sometimes. Because you were naturally fit and training every day the beer just naturally flowed out of you. I've forgotten what it's like to be fit now, but when you feel properly fit you feel so great within yourself that nothing is a challenge, nothing. You feel so good that sometimes you overstep the mark and get a little arrogant. Now, my back is knackered and even swimming hurts my knees. I do a lot of walking with my dogs at the weekend, but that's it."

Despite his problems, Brazil is aware that he could be in a far worse condition physically.

"I'm pretty lucky that I don't have a lot of problems, because you see some players from my era and it's horrendous, some of them can't walk. Mick Channon's hips and knees had gone at the end of his career; Tommy Smith had all kinds of problems. I'm one of the lucky ones because I made another career. A lot of the other guys haven't."

And those who didn't tended to sink financially.

"Some of them feel embarrassed about how little they earn. I know former England internationals who are struggling financially, who wouldn't have £50 in their pocket. I know guys who were heroes who are now driving vans for a living. Maybe it was a blessing that I retired from football at 27 because I had a bit of time to do something else."

"I'm always aware of sounding like an old fuddy-duddy who complains about how much the players earn these days. But then I'll watch a game now and see players who earn £30k or £40k a week and they are average. But because the top guys are on £100k a week, you have average players on £30k a week. Sometimes that's hard to take, bloody hard. I know former players who don't earn half the amount in a year that players now earn in a week."

Alan Brazil

Brazil's views are not for the politically correct.

"I don't like it when clubs keep buying foreign players," he says. "That money goes out of the country. Real Madrid have more English players than Arsenal. That's scandalous. The big clubs used to buy off the Rochdales and the Peterboroughs and keep the money in the English game. It's not the case now. Managers tell you that the value for money is abroad, because of Bosman.

"It was different when I played and I've got no complaints about the boys I played with. Football is small. It's like a private members club. You don't have too much outside interference and you are much happier talking to people inside that club. It's strange. Now, the players, especially the foreign ones, train and go home."

Brazil was on the United bench for nine of the ten winning games at the start of the 1985/86 season.

"They used to call me 'the Judge' because I was always sitting on the bench," he cackles. "I came on now and again, but I could have no complaints because the team was winning. And don't forget, suddenly Mark Hughes had come onto the scene and he was sensational. Sparky was very strong – very quiet in the dressing-room but awesome on the pitch, hard as nails. Nine players out of ten would come off worse if they tried to tackle him. Sparky had played in the first team when I was at Tottenham, but obviously Ron didn't fancy him and that's why he signed me. That was added pressure on me. I cost a lot of money and people expected me to be better than the home-grown kids. Yet my goalscoring record was never bad."

Whiteside was a player he rated highly too.

"Whiteside was clever as anything for a young kid. He had the head of a 25-year-old. He was nasty and looked after himself on the field. Strachan was a great player while Bryan Robson was the driving force. Frank Stapleton was a top professional. He would go home straight after training and rest up. He was moderate on booze and didn't abuse his body. I used to think that he did extra training at home.

"I was different. I'm an outgoing guy, a sociable guy who loves people's company. I was always scared of missing out on something and I still am. I can't sit in and watch the telly at night; I've got to go out. I'd rather watch football in the pub than sitting in my flat. I'll never change.

"We once went to Benny's nightclub in Bury on a coach. The management had agreed to a lads' night out. There was a little bridge just before the club and the driver got out to see if the bridge would take his coach. John Gidman then got in his seat and tried to drive the coach over the bridge but the coach got stuck. This bridge was the only way into the nightclub and no one could get through. Gidman was a nutter. He used to reckon that he could play the guitar. He was a hippy who thought he was Paul McCartney because he was from Liverpool. But he wasn't. In fact he was crap! But he would play Beatles songs on pre-season tours and the lads would sing along together. Yet get Giddy on form down that right wing and he was brilliant."

Given the hours spent in Paddy Crerand's Altrincham pub, it's no surprise that Brazil can recollect some anecdotes from there.

"One Sunday morning I left the house at 11am. I was in the dog-house with the wife, an Ipswich girl, because I had been late out in Paddy's the night before. The kids shouted, 'Where are you going dad?' as I walked out. I got down to the pub and knocked on the door. McQueen opened it. He had pals down from Ayrshire. I said, 'What are you doing here?' He said that he was in the dog-house with his wife and I said 'Snap'. At midday, Kevin Moran came in with his brother, who was a surgeon at the Royal Liverpool hospital. He couldn't believe that we were already on our third pint.

"Kevin was a hard player. I was heartbroken for him at the cup final. I scored two against QPR a week before and was hoping to be named on the bench and I was rooming with Robbo, hoping for the best, but I found out that I wasn't to play from Dickie Davies off the television, not Big Ron. That wasn't good – wasn't professional – finding out through the media. I'd remembered seeing Eric Gates get dropped for the '78 Cup Final. He was miserable as sin, even after we won the final. I could relate to that. I felt deflated because I wasn't part of it. We returned on the train and I was with my father-in-law. He came on the train with me and he wouldn't put the FA Cup down.

"Another time back at Paddy's pub one Sunday morning, Bryan Robson turned up with his dad, a long-distance lorry driver. It wasn't all-day drinking then so the head barman had to go to the cash and carry to get some more drink in. We stayed until ten thirty at night. We were all ready to go home when McQueen shouted, 'I'm Hank Marvin, who fancies a curry in Manchester?' For the good of the team in training the following morning, fortunately only him and his mates fancied it."

By late 1985, Brazil's United career seemed to be on the wane.

"Ron was fair, but he started to ignore me towards the end and I didn't like the way he said, 'You're going.' I was playing for the reserves against Blackburn. The coach Mick Brown said to me, 'You're not playing.' My immediate reaction was, 'Oh, brilliant. Am I getting a chance on Saturday?' Then I spoke to Ron. He said, 'Don Mackay has rang. We've done a trade and you're going to Coventry.' I said, 'I'm not.' He said, 'You are, because you'll never play for me again.' In the end I thought, 'Oh, bollocks, I'm wasting my time here.' I could have been awkward and stayed, picking up a wage, but I wanted to play football. I'll never forget the way I was treated though.

"I've spoken to Ron since. There's never been a problem, but he's never apologised. That's football and that was the decision he made. Don't forget that Ron was under serious pressure. My main criticism of Ron was that he was almost scared about what the punters thought. If he heard the crowd getting on a player's back he'd take them off. He was very aware of the pressure – that people expected him to bring success to Manchester United. Yet Merseyside dominated. They probably had better players. Everton had a great side with Trevor Steven, Graham Sharpe and Andy Gray. Ron Atkinson will hate me for saying this but I don't give a shit. United didn't win the league because they bought big name signings. Players like me. Liverpool won it because they bought players who fitted their system.

"You've got to understand that Ron's a showman," continues

Brazil. "Always has been, always will be. He loved the attention of the media and still does. Fergie's the opposite. When he was at Aberdeen, Fergie used to come and watch Ipswich pre-season. He was fascinated with us playing one off the front two."

After just 24 United starts, 17 more appearances coming off the bench and 12 goals, Brazil signed for Coventry City in January 1986. Terry Gibson arrived at Old Trafford in the exchange deal, with Gibson valued at £600,000.

"I enjoyed Coventry. I played with Cyrille Regis and we hit it off right away but my back was getting worse and worse. Coventry were really good to me. The manager John Sillett said, 'If we win the FA Cup final I'll give you a testimonial game.' I looked at him and said, 'Thanks, but I can't take that. I've not been at Coventry that long and I'd be embarrassed to take money off people.'"

Brazil moved to QPR in June 1986.

"They played on plastic, which wasn't ideal for my back. But I loved London because there's always something happening. People think I'm Champagne Charlie, who is always about everywhere, but I'm not. I'm just very sociable."

A back injury forced Brazil's retirement from league football in January 1987, three years shy of entering his fourth decade.

"I missed six or seven years earning decent money," he says. "The most I got as a footballer was £1,500 a week, when I was at United.

"After QPR, I played some non-league which was good fun. I went to Australia for four games and enjoyed that. As long as I wasn't training every day my back was okay. I had a spell in Switzerland for a year. I'd only train once a week and had to be careful. When I'd finished, I intended to walk away from football. I wanted a clean break, I was sick of it."

He got into the media by chance.

"Someone asked me to do some commentary. I did and thought, 'I like this.' It was for BBC Radio Suffolk, and I was often unbelievably biased towards Ipswich because it was only for Suffolk. This was in 1989 and from there I went to Five Live. I've no idea why I was good at it."

His media work would bring him into contact with the United fans who once paid his wages.

"I don't think United fans remember me as a legend and there have been some incidents over the years which I have not enjoyed. United were playing Rotor Volgograd in the UEFA Cup in 1995. I had a long lunch at the Moss Nook near Manchester airport. I was working for Five Live and I really didn't fancy going to Russia but I was booked to go. We were flying late at night, but after a few more beers I decided not to go, yet I was forced to by the BBC. I was the last on the plane, a charter for journalists and fans. As I walked down the plane, fans were saying, 'Oh, no, not you.' My seat was right at the back and I wasn't enjoying the situation. The nutcases were at the back of the plane. The abuse I was getting from United fans was horrendous. The plane took off and soon after the stewardess said, 'Would you like a drink, Mr Brazil?' I asked for a red wine but she said, 'I'm sorry, but this is a supporters' flight and there is no alcohol.' This guy was kicking the back of my seat and I was fuming. Then he whispered, 'No, I'm not one of them idiots; just get yourself some coke and a load of ice.' Then he said, 'Ignore these pricks.' So we had a drink. The idiots were shouting, 'You should have never worn a United shirt,' and stuff like that. They were really pissing me off. We arrived in Volgograd at dawn. Out of the corner of my eye I could see a big, fat, bald guy giving me abuse. I shouldn't have said anything but I was gone by this point. He came over and said, 'You can't even tell us your greatest memory playing with United because you haven't got one.' I told him where to go and he walked off.

"Another time, I went to Coventry to cover a Man United game, although this isn't really about me. I was in the press box with Frank Stapleton and Paddy Crerand. It got hairy and the Coventry fans felt hard done by. These nutters kept looking up at the press box and having a go at Paddy. It all kicked off and these four guys came to the back of the press box. Paddy was like, 'Come on then, if you think you are big enough.'"

After impressing with Five Live, Brazil was offered a better contract working for Sky, where he did five years, following Football League games as an analyst. In 1999 he joined the revamped TalkSport radio station, where he has remained.

"I get up at 4.45am each morning. We're on air from four minutes past six until ten, four hours. It's hard work. People disagree with me all the time, but that's what it's about. My radio show is like being in the pub."

Just like his football career, life as a presenter hasn't always run smoothly. In 2004, he was sacked after failing to appear for a breakfast show during the Cheltenham Festival after a drink too many the night before. He was reinstated three weeks later after an outcry from listeners. As a caveat to his reinstatement, he was told to forfeit a week's wages – around £5,000 – if he missed a show during that week. In August 2006, he got in further trouble after using the term 'Nips' when referring to the Japanese live on air, during a supposedly light-hearted discussion about hunting whales. Brazil's right-of-centre opinions have raised eyebrows too. He considers homosexuality to be wrong and suggested that the 2005 French riots should be curbed by the police adopting a shoot-to-kill policy.

But Brazil's style is undeniably popular. His show gets a million listeners a week who tune in to hear him say 'Why?' as a reflex answer to most questions, often repetitively. He likes the word 'whoosh' too. And upon hearing a location, Brazil will usually say 'I've never been' or 'beautiful', depending on whether or not he has visited it. A caller may ring in from Stoke – and Brazil will happily give him directions to his home city – as if the caller needs them. This excess enthusiasm for life has made him an award-winning presenter.

"I just won Best Radio Show, beating *Today* on Radio Four," he says proudly. "It felt fantastic, but nothing compares to scoring the winning goal at a big ground. That's the best moment in life. That moment when you look up and the crowd are there, like the Stretford End in 1981."

The impact of TalkSport never ceases to amaze him.

"All the cabbies want to talk," he says, "and we get 1500 emails an hour on air. I get recognized more than ever. The kids can't believe it."

Alan Brazil

A true *bon vivant*, Brazil leads a hectic life. "I'm always busy," he says, while recommending the best desserts in Langhams. "I like being busy. I live life to the full. I've never been at a loose end; I'm always looking around the corner. Some modern footballers have too much done for them and struggle to adapt to life after playing. My advice is: roll your sleeves up and get off your arse. The harder you try, the luckier you become."

Media work means that he sees how United are treated from the press perspective, rather than that of a fan or player.

"United don't get a fair hearing in the media because people want to hit United as they are so massive. It could happen to Chelsea. I watch Chelsea a lot because most of my friends are Chelsea fans, but I'm not. People envy success. Players want to beat United more than any other club. I know I did at Ipswich. We used to travel to Old Trafford and say, 'Bring it on!' There was something magic about playing there."

Brazil's passion for horseracing remains undiminished.

"I've got a racing club – Alan Brazil Racing – where we've got about 600 members paying £5 a week for football tips, racing tips and the chance to come and watch our horses. Mickey Quinn is one of my trainers. We've got flat and jumps," he explains, breathlessly.

"I earn much more now than I ever did playing football. I'm lucky; some people I used to play with work their bollocks off to earn £20k a year."

Brazil has few regrets in life, but where United are concerned he has some.

"My only regret is that I didn't play regularly at Tottenham or United. I would have loved to have been a star at United. Loved to. Really. I even changed my game a bit when I went to United because I wanted to impress fans. I used to go chasing balls and try and get my foot in. Yet my game was about waiting for the right time and making a run. I should have been getting behind centre-halves. But I can remember almost every goal I scored for United and running to the crowd after scoring against West Ham, or after a toe poke against Everton. If I was playing how I played at Ipswich I'm sure that I would have started every game. But with what I know now about my body and my back, I accept it could have never happened for me. I didn't realise that my back was knackered when I got to United, but I should have known that something was wrong when I couldn't keep up with Arnold Murhen in training.

"I had wear and tear problems on my bottom discs, the most important discs for your mobility, and mine are shot away. I should have them fused together but it's a horrible operation and I don't really want to have it. But when I played nobody diagnosed things like that. These days you have specialists and scans. Not then. In the '80s racehorses were treated better than footballers."

10
Arnold Muhren

The Dutch Master

"The rain falls hard in a humdrum town." April 2006, and Manchester's greatest musical export Morrissey is in Amsterdam as part of a European tour. Much as I'd like to see Stephen Patrick strut his stuff, I'm in Holland's biggest city to meet the former United player Arnold Muhren, now a youth team coach at Ajax.

ARNOLD MUHREN
MANCHESTER UNITED

"Now you can see why I settled so easily in Manchester," says Muhren, pointing to the raindrops running down the big glass windows which overlook several pristine football pitches at Ajax's training ground. At 55, he looks lean, much as he did in 1988 when he was the grand old man in the only Dutch team to have won a major international football trophy.

Muhren has particularly intrigued me ever since the former

We're The Famous Man United

United director Maurice Watkins described him as his favourite ever player in a *United We Stand* interview. It's not like United's former legal eagle is a major authority on the game, but he's watched the Reds for four decades and singled out Muhren from any number of great names.

Fifteen years after United's victory in Rotterdam, some Ajax die-hards are selling their fanzine outside the ArenA in front of murals of Marco van Basten and Frank Rijkaard, heroes of yore. The sellers speak well of Arnold Muhren – who played and roomed with both the aforementioned Dutch masters. Closer to the turnstiles, brassy girls in lycra are handing out a free supplement called *Sportwereld* – its pages dedicated to the exploits of Dutch clubs in Europe. Aside from the obvious, Ajax, Feyenoord and PSV's European Cup wins, and the obscure, like Bradford City's 2–0 victory against RKC Waalwijk, the name Muhren crops up in a feature on FC Twente Enschende's UEFA Cup victory over Juventus in 1975. A Twente fan had been asked: 'De beste speller?' [Who was the best player?]. 'Arnold Muhren,' was his answer.

Muhren walked into an insular and alien foreign culture when he arrived to play in Britain in 1978. His British peers were intrigued and confused. John Gidman had said, 'Never trust a player who doesn't drink,' when interviewed for this book, a statement he quickly qualified when it was pointed out that Muhren never drank. 'Except Arnie,' backtracked Gidman, 'Arnie was all right.' Alan Brazil had claimed that Muhren used to have a Dutch soft drink imported and that none of the Ipswich lads knew what the mysterious liquid was. Maybe that was the key to the longevity which saw the lithe left midfielder play for so long at the highest level – a magic potion?

Muhren, wearing an Ajax tracksuit, laughs out loud when he hears these two stories.

"I've got lots of nice things to say about Alan Brazil, but he's wrong on that on. I didn't import a special drink from Holland."

Muhren then recounts his life story so far.

"I grew up in a family of nine children," he says, describing his childhood spent in Volendam, a pretty fishing village of 18,000 which

Arnold Muhren

has a reputation for creativity and craftsmanship. It is also one of the few Catholic enclaves in Holland.

"My older brother was a very good example for me as a footballer. We played football in the streets of Volendam, day in, day out. I started off in goal but could never stay there; I was always running all over the place and eventually my brother said that I could play outfield with him and his friends. We weren't exceptional, because everybody could play football to a very high level. If you couldn't play football, then it was bad luck, you had to go in goal. If it was raining we played in the bedroom. We played with anything as long as it was round – rolled up papers tied with string, a tennis ball. You develop great technique like that. Only the richer families could afford to buy a proper ball. The ground was hard in the streets so you didn't want to fall because it hurt – that made you have good balance. My father was a director of a big company which made belts. He was football mad. He said, 'I'll give you everything so as long as you are serious. If you want to play football I'll give you shirts and boots. But if I get the impression that you are not giving football 100 per cent then I'll not give you anything any more.'"

Muhren's father had another reason for encouraging him to play football.

"My brother, who was five years older, was already doing well at football. I can remember people asking me when I was five or six what I wanted to do when I was older. I always said that I was going to be a footballer. I was very definite. People said, 'You can't only say that you are going to be a football player.' There were not a lot of professional footballers when I was a child so I can understand why they said that."

Muhren supported Real Madrid as a boy because they won trophies and played attacking football.

"Then I started liking Ajax because they won trophies and played great football. When I eventually moved to Ajax, I ended up playing alongside the players I had idolised, people like Johan Cruyff and Johan Neeskens."

Muhren started out at his local club Volendam, who played in the Dutch second division.

"My aim was to get into the first team. I reached that aim and did quite well as we won promotion to the first division. The celebrations were great. We lived near a harbour and when we won the league we went on a dyke on a kind of boat with wheels on it. That was a tradition there."

Volendam were relegated in their first season, but they bounced straight back up. By that time, Muhren was in demand.

"Ajax had wanted me to play for them when I was 17, but that would have been in their reserves, so I stayed at Volendam. I didn't have a driving licence either so it would have been difficult going there every day."

Muhren joined Ajax when he was 19, the year he met his wife.

"They had just won the 1971 European Cup beating Panathinaikos in London. I played there for three and a half years and I was in and out of the team. They had such a good team, a team that won three consecutive European Cups was very difficult to get in."

All players at good clubs face competition for places, yet few find themselves with a dilemma like Muhren's.

"The person ahead of me in my position was my brother Gerrie!" he says. "He had more experience and was just the right age, like most of the team, about 25. I was 20. But I went to Ajax to learn a lot at the highest level, that was the only reason, and I did learn. I was also substitute in the two European Cup final wins."

Playing an average of 15 games a season for Ajax, Muhren began to feel that his future lay elsewhere.

"I wanted to play every week and I had an offer to go to FC Twente who were a top-four Dutch team, a very good side who played regular European football. I had a very good season there and all of a sudden Ajax wanted me back again. I told them that I wanted to stay at Enschede for one more year and then go back to Ajax. Twente said to me, 'You can go to Ajax for 400,000 guilders in one year.' Ajax agreed. There was nothing written on paper, which was my mistake. I didn't have an agent because there weren't really any then."

Arnold Muhren

Muhren's form was even better in his second year at Twente.

"I broke into the national team and Twente did well in Europe, beating Juventus. When the year was finished I was preparing to go back to Ajax. I put my house up for sale, but then Twente told Ajax that they wanted 800,000 guilders for me, not 400,000. Ajax rightly said that they had agreed to buy me for 400,000. I had a big argument with Twente and told them that I did not want to play for them any more because I didn't trust them."

Muhren went back to live with Volendam, training with his old team. He didn't know what to do.

"Then," he says, "all of a sudden Mr Bobby Robson came to see me. Ipswich were playing a tournament in Bruges which featured another Dutch club, AZ Alkmaar. Robson asked the Alkmaar manager if he knew a left-sided midfield player in Holland who could do well in England. He recommended me and that's why Robson came to see me."

Flattered as he was, he decided to wait a little.

"After my bad experiences I needed an agent," he says. "But Mr Robson told me that I had to come to Ipswich and sign before the deadline to play in European competition. Ipswich paid for a private plane and I flew there with my wife and my dad. I couldn't believe what I saw in Ipswich. There were so many people and photographers, I thought that Paul McCartney was coming to town. But they had come to see me! I was the first Dutch player to play in England – the first foreign signing, I believe. I was surprised that so many people were interested in me."

Muhren was interested in Ipswich too.

"Mr Robson was a sort of a father figure," he said. "He showed me everything in the town, but I told him that I didn't want to make a decision until I had an agent as I didn't want to repeat the same mistakes as last time. He offered to pay me more money. He wanted to sign me before 12 o'clock and the deadline. But I wouldn't do it. Finally, he gave up, saying, 'If you ever want to play for Ipswich just let me know.'"

Muhren returned to Holland.

"I spoke about it with the missus," he says, a phrase he definitely wouldn't have picked up had he stayed in Holland. "I said that Ipswich was a great club, similar to Volendam. Maybe it wasn't Manchester United, but Ipswich then was a great club. So, we decided to jump in at deep end. I only knew a little bit about English football but I decided to join Ipswich."

Muhren's arrival marked the beginning of what we now know as the "foreign invasion". Muhren's successors were not only the likes of Jaap Stam, Ruud van Nistelrooy and Edwin van der Saar, but every continental player who has raised the standard of the English domestic game in the past two decades. Holland still exports a greater number of good quality footballers than any other nation of its size.

"We're a small country but we produce very good players," says Muhren, whose position as a youth coach at Ajax helps preserve the Dutch game's great secret – its education. "One of the reasons is that we start very young. If you don't start at an early age, you don't have a chance. I was in England for seven years. English schoolteachers can't teach kids to play football. In Holland they start at six years old on the streets. In England they started later, cleaning boots and dressing-rooms."

Muhren had missed the deadline to play in Europe for Ipswich, but he had taken his time over the decision and was comfortable with it. He flew back to Suffolk and readied himself for his debut, against Liverpool at home.

"I remember it very well," he says. "Everybody was saying, 'You are playing against Terry McDermott and he's a runner, you have to stay with him.' So I ran all afternoon and none of us touched the ball. Initially, I thought I had made a mistake coming to England. I was the type of player who wanted to see the ball and yet I had barely touched it. The game was completely different to Holland. How could I show what I could do?"

Dutch journalists had warned Muhren against the move, saying that English football would be too physical for him, that the midfield hardly saw the ball. After a few games, he was convinced that they were right.

Arnold Muhren

"There were doubts in Holland. I was not one of the strongest players and I was going to a league that was physically very tough. I went to see Mr Robson and said, 'If you want to use me properly, then I have to have the ball, otherwise you might as well have the groundsman playing. I want to be an important player for your side and I can add something extra to your team, but if I don't get the ball you might as well buy another player.'

"Robson talked with the squad. He said, 'We've bought Arnold from Holland, he's a technical player with a good left foot, technique and vision. You have to give him the ball.' From then on it changed a bit. I did a good job for Ipswich and one of the reasons was because I wasn't a typical English player. I had reasonable technique, good vision. If you use your brains in the game, it makes things easier. I gave the side something extra."

Muhren's reverence for Bobby Robson is clear, as much for the person as for the manager.

"I liked Mr Robson. He would try and make me feel welcome. All the time he would say, 'How is the missus?' 'Where is she shopping?' 'Which street does she go to for clothes?' 'How are your children?' 'Are they doing well at school?' 'Where do you buy your food from?' He realised that if me and my family were happy then I would pay him back on the pitch. I was a little bit concerned about my family, if I am honest. Concerned that they wouldn't like the English way of living, but we had to adapt to the English style of living, not the other way round. My attitude is that if you give something 100 per cent of your effort you'll succeed. I could have gone to live in Algeria or even Zimbabwe and survived. But it wasn't always easy for my family."

A few months after Muhren had arrived in Ipswich, Robson asked for his assistance. "He said to me, 'I would like a right midfielder from Holland. Do you know any?' He wanted to sell Brian Talbot and I recommended Frans Thyssen. Frans wanted to play in England and I told him to expect a phone call."

Ipswich's reward would be the greatest period of the club's history, including championship challenges and victory in the 1981 UEFA

Cup. Muhren and Thyssen revolutionised the way Ipswich played, adding poise, intelligence, a different dimension and skill.

"We changed completely. Everything went through midfield, partly because of us two, but also because we had a team good enough to play that way. We had a very good balance, and players like Terry Butcher, George Burley, Mick Mills, John Wark, Eric Gates, Alan Brazil and Paul Mariner. The English players had things I didn't have. They were strong in the air and good tacklers. They can run all day too. If you combine the best from the British and Dutch you would have the best footballers in the world.

"I had a very good understanding with Alan Brazil. When I looked at his eyes I knew exactly what he wanted to do. I assisted a lot of his goals. I liked him as a player and a person. He was fast with tremendous skill. He was superb in a one-on-one situation. We did very well in the league and came close to winning it but our squad wasn't quite big enough and we suffered if one of our regular players was missing. Aston Villa won the league and the European Cup the following year – yet we had beaten them three times in 1980/81. I am still under the impression that we were the best team in England that season. Everyone said we were the better team, but we got tired in the end. Our problem was that our squad was not big enough and we played too many games.

"We played in the UEFA Cup final of 1981 against AZ Alkmaar," whose coach had recommended Muhren to Ipswich, "and we beat them 3–0 at home. But away from home we lost 5–2. If the game would have been 15 minutes longer we would have had a big problem because most of our players couldn't run any more."

Ipswich won on away goals, but the threadbare nature of their squad had come close to being exposed.

"We played Cologne in the semi-final," adds Muhren. "We played on the Saturday at home and on Monday against Norwich. We travelled to Germany straight after the match. It was ridiculous and I remember an interview from Toni Schumacher, the Cologne goalkeeper. He said, 'We're going to take these tired Englishmen.' They didn't. We beat them 1–0. Terry Butcher scored with a header."

Arnold Muhren

Given Ipswich had the quality to win away at places like Cologne, their players were not fazed by trips to Old Trafford in the league.

"We were a better team than United so we had no problems with our confidence when we played at Old Trafford, but it was always special to play there because of the huge crowd. United were hard to beat, but I think they were more afraid of us than we were of them. We felt invincible."

Muhren spent four years at Portman Road. After his third year, he was offered deals to return to the Continent, speaking with Dutch clubs and Club Bruges of Belgium, who had been strong enough to reach the European Cup final in 1978 against Liverpool at Wembley. In that year, Holland illuminated the Argentina World Cup finals with their total football. Muhren missed out on selection. His time in orange would come. At club level, Ipswich thought they were going to lose another one of their better players.

"I think Mr Robson thought that I wanted to go back to Holland because there were rumours. But I'd never said that. I knew that Manchester wanted me. They had Ashley Grimes on the left side of midfield, but they wanted me, maybe because I had done well for Ipswich when I played against United."

Muhren was 32 when United made a formal approach to Ipswich in January 1982.

"I thought that it was probably my last chance to play for a big club. United asked if I wanted to play for them and I said that I did, but that I wanted to finish the season at Ipswich, where I was playing very well. But I travelled up to Manchester by train with my agent John Hazel for talks. I had to look at houses too. Everything had to be a secret – nobody could know that I was going to Manchester. So we booked into the hotel in Manchester as Mr and Mrs Hazel. The receptionist looked very funnily at me because I am not a lady!"

In any case, Muhren's cover had already been blown.

"As soon as I got off the train at Manchester after the long journey from Ipswich I was approached by a Manchester United supporter. He asked me if I was signing for United. I told him that I was not Arnold Muhren, but Mr Hazel. The supporter didn't believe me."

Muhren was able to leave on a free transfer.

"That meant I got a pay rise at United, but the most important thing for me was not the money, but that I could play for Manchester.

"United really made me feel at home. I was quite impressed by the way the club dealt with me. After I returned from Holland in the summer, I found a club car waiting for me at the hotel where United had booked me into. A Ford. Somebody from the club showed me ten houses, and I picked one in Wilmslow, Fulshaw Park. My family and I were used to the English way of life, but it was important that we integrated when we arrived in Manchester. My wife joined in with neighbours and invited children from school to play with our children. Our home was near Mr Atkinson's house – his garden backed onto mine. Sometimes he would come to see me, crossing from his garden to mine. I could hear him coming before I saw him because he wore lots of jewellery. He would talk about Manchester and my role in the team. He said, 'You are the missing link.' I was impressed because he seemed to know a lot about me. He thought I was a world-class player and that flattered me. Of course, I had played against him when he was manager of West Bromwich as well as Manchester United. He told me he had wanted to sign me for West Brom.

"My first impressions of the team were positive, but I didn't think they were better than the Ipswich team I'd left," says Muhren. "I knew that Bryan Robson and Norman Whiteside were very good players and we had good national and international standard players, but maybe only Robson was a world-class player, one of the best around. He was captain and a perfect example for the rest of the team. Ray Wilkins was a very good player, as was Remi Moses. We had one problem – Liverpool were just a little bit better. They had world-class players."

Off the field he was less impressed by the social scene.

"I was quite surprised at the drinking culture," he says. "In Holland we'd have a drink after a game on a Sunday evening. But you can't do that too often and at United there were a couple of players who went drinking during the week as well, which is not the right way to do things. On Sundays there was not a lot to do in England and a lot of players went to the pub. I didn't go out with

Arnold Muhren

them and the other players never put me under any pressure to have a drink with them. I never felt an outsider. They saw me not as a foreign player, but as a team-mate. Maybe they thought that if I didn't drink then I'd play well.

"That's the only reason I played so long. I didn't drink because I lived for my sport. I ate lots of fruit and vegetables – my diet was focused on my football career. I didn't smoke and I went to bed early, about 11. Sadly, I couldn't say the same about all the players I was with in England."

He did find a kindred sprit in Frank Stapleton.

"Frank was similar to me," explains Muhren. "He didn't drink a lot and we shared the same view about the players drinking, that the players had too much time because they were free from 12 o'clock. That was fine for me because I had a wife and three children, but not for younger players. On several occasions I was concerned after smelling alcohol at training in the morning. But I realised that I couldn't change the culture on my own, nor could me and Frank change it. You needed the majority of players. Frank was one of the best pros I'd met in my career."

Having been at Ipswich for years, Muhren realised that the drinking was not exclusive to United players.

"Liverpool had a lot of drinkers and they were European champions," he adds. "And to be fair to the United players, they always gave 100 per cent in training, but I realised that they couldn't drink and play football beyond the age of 30. Norman Whiteside, who used to call me by my full name every morning (he used to shout, 'Good morning, Arnoldus Johannus Hyacinthus Muhren'), was an example of someone who could have played much longer. He was the youngest player to play in the World Cup finals and did very well for Manchester for a couple of years. He did well after he moved to Everton, too, but he wasn't the Norman Whiteside we'd known before. If you play just on strength, then what do you do when the strength goes because you haven't looked after yourself as well as you could have done? It's a pity because Norman was such a good player and a tremendous guy."

Despite his serious approach, Muhren loved the camaraderie and jokes of the United dressing-room.

"Gordon McQueen was the joker, but lots of the lads had good humour; the English have the best humour. Look at the programmes from television like *Only Fools and Horses* – all the best humour programmes come from England."

On the field, he settled immediately too. While he had few physical advantages, his range of passing and vision was superb, his left foot one of the best seen in M16. Muhren could split a defence with a perfectly weighted pass and fans immediately took to him.

"We won the FA Cup in my first year, which was fantastic. When I joined Ipswich, they had just won the FA Cup. Mick Mills said to me, 'Don't go back to Holland until you have played in an FA Cup final.' We never won the FA Cup with Ipswich – City knocked us out in '81 and I was so disappointed. I remembered what Mills had said in 1983."

It shows just how highly regarded the FA Cup was then.

"I played in the final of the European championships for Holland in 1988, but the FA Cup final in England was a bigger event, mainly because of the build-up. For more than one week, every day in the newspaper was dedicated to the cup final. For instance there was a girl on page three in the *Sun* wearing a United scarf and describing her favourite player. It wasn't me! Everybody was involved, from the linesman to the groundsman at Wembley. If you read that, day in day out, then you really want to play in the final."

His memories of that final day against Brighton are vivid.

"I can remember the coach from London to Wembley. There was a camera on the coach from the BBC. There were helicopters flying above the coach. Then we saw thousands of people on Wembley Way. Everyone in England sees it as a day out, even people who don't like football wanted to be at the game. That was sad in some respects because a lot of the real supporters, the fans who watched United week in week out, didn't get tickets for the game.

"My family came over from Holland. Everybody was asking me for tickets in Wilmslow and Holland. They showed the FA Cup final live

Arnold Muhren

in Holland too; it was known as a big occasion. The dressing-rooms were old fashioned but full of history. There was a nice atmosphere on a sunny day.

"I remember the game and Gary Bailey's tremendous save from Smith when the score was 2–2. So the replay was on a Thursday. That wasn't right. The English FA Cup final should be played on a Saturday, even the replay. We beat them quite easily 4–0. The Brighton fans gave us a standing ovation; it was incredible, very sporting and would never have happened in Holland."

Muhren scored one of the goals, a penalty. Before he took it he flicked an imaginary fringe.

"I did? I don't know why!" he says. "Steve Coppell was the regular penalty taker, but he was injured. Before the game the manager said, 'Who wants to take penalties?' It was very quiet, so I volunteered. Bryan Robson had scored twice by the time the penalty was awarded. I said to him, 'Bryan, if you want to take the penalty then I understand because it will get you a hat-trick.' He said, 'No, before the game we decided that you would take the penalties and that's how it should be.'

"There was a little bit of pressure because nobody had missed a penalty in the cup final before. But I was confident because we had won the cup anyway. I scored and Gordon McQueen kissed me on my forehead."

The cup win had masked another season without the title. Improvements were expected in the league in 1983/84, yet United slipped a position to fourth and were humbled further, knocked out of the FA Cup at Bournemouth in the third round.

"That was a very disappointing day for us. We were quite humiliated and just did not play well," says Muhren.

In March 1984, Muhren was injured. So telling was his contribution to the team that a realistic title challenge faltered as a shapeless United won just two of the last ten league games.

"At one point I was in plaster because of problems with a tendon. The plaster was removed but the problem wasn't solved so I had to wait a week for an operation, but the problem never really went away."

Muhren never reclaimed a regular place in the side and played just a dozen games in his final season, 1984/85. In the summer of 1984, Muhren's former Ipswich team-mate arrived at Old Trafford.

"Alan Brazil was a great player, but we never saw the real Alan Brazil at United," he says.

Muhren's form was also badly affected by injuries. More pertinently for the Dutchman, United paid £700,000 for Ajax winger Jesper Olsen, a former bank clerk from Denmark, with Ron Atkinson saying, "Olsen will be the most exciting player seen at Old Trafford since George Best."

Far from being worried by the acquisition of a new player in his position, Muhren had recommended Olsen.

"United asked me about Olsen and I told them that they should buy him because he was one of the best players in the Dutch league. I didn't feel threatened because I was 34 and thought that I didn't have long left playing. Plus, I wasn't thinking about myself, but about United."

Muhren remains unconvinced that United got the best out of Olsen.

"Jesper was a completely different player to myself, always running at defenders, but United didn't see the good Jesper Olsen," he opines. "They used him in the wrong way. He played as a winger at Ajax, but at United he played more as a left-sided midfield player, and he was always too far from the opposition goal to cause real damage. United should have played him closer to goal, because when he got to the edge of the penalty box he was tired."

As his time at Old Trafford came to a close, Muhren's relationship with Atkinson suffered.

"At the start Atkinson was very good to me, but when I played well and scored important goals in my final year, a week later I wouldn't be in the team. That made me very disappointed. The manager had his own mind and explained that he had bought Olsen. He had to be fair to Jesper, but Jesper was not playing well and he should have changed the team. I felt I could still do a good job for United but the manager didn't agree."

United still offered Muhren a new one-year contract.

Arnold Muhren

"I think Mr Martin Edwards saw me as an example to younger players. I knew I wasn't going to play every week, but I liked the idea of working with younger players. I had given Mr Edwards my word that I would sign, then all of a sudden Johan Cruyff called me up from Ajax. He asked me if I wanted to play for Ajax again. I said, 'But I'm 35 now.' He said, "I don't care how old you are, I know your character, that you can do a job for me and I just want you to play for us.'"

The move re-launched Muhren's career.

"When I came back from Manchester to play for Ajax, everybody was saying, 'Hey, he's 35 now and at such a big club. Why?' But Cruyff was the manager and he knew me as a player and as a person. In fact, when Cruyff left Ajax to manage Barcelona, his wife told me that he wanted to take me to Barcelona, but at 38 maybe I was finally too old! For Ajax, though, I played well and there was a gap at left-midfield for the national side. All of a sudden Rinus Michels, the Dutch manager, called me."

Old enough to have been a contemporary of several in Johan Cruyff's 1974 World Cup runners-up and Ruud Krol's 1978 losing finalists (he made neither squad), Muhren found himself considered young enough to line up alongside Ruud Gullit, Frank Rijkaard and Marco van Basten.

"I was nearly 38 in 1988," he remembers, "but I was very serious; didn't smoke, rarely drank and lived like a monk."

The 1988 European Championships in Germany would bring Muhren his highest honour. Van Basten kicked it off, leading Holland's 3–1 defeat of Robson's England, and his exquisite volley was the champagne moment in the victory over the Soviet Union in the Munich final. Muhren provided the cross for the miracle goal, his calm, perfect technique excelling at the highest level.

"Everyone said it was the best cross I ever made, but that's nonsense," says Muhren modestly. "Marco made a not very good pass look very good. Before the ball reached my feet, I saw him running near the penalty area. If I'd controlled the ball, there would have been another situation, so I decided to play it first time. I was trying to play the ball about two yards in front of him. I thought he would control the ball and bring it back into the penalty area. But he finished it! I've never seen anything like it. Everybody talked about Marco because he scored so many goals, but we had five world-class players – van Basten, Gullit, Ronald Koeman, Jan Wouters and Rijkaard. I thought Rijkaard was the best all-round player in 1988, playing in a sort of centre-half position. He did it so well. He was good in the air, a strong tackler; he was fast and had such good technique."

Muhren and Rijkaard had been room-mates at Ajax, and the friendship continues. Muhren remembers how the young Rijkaard, now in charge at Barcelona, would shake his head at the idea of a career in management.

"He was more interested in business. But, you know, people change."

Muhren remains close to both the English clubs for which he played.

"I get invited over for dinners and although it is difficult to attend during the football season, it's always nice to be back in England," he says. "People don't forget you if you did a good job and I was lucky to have played for two such good teams in England. We played continental football, which suited me very well. I had a tremendous time, working with great players."

And he's still having a tremendous time working with potentially great young players.

"I don't want the limelight," he concludes, as the skies outside darken and yet more rain lashes Amsterdam. "I've had that for 30 years, so now I enjoy doing something in the background, putting something back into the game that I love."

11
Ron Atkinson

The Manager

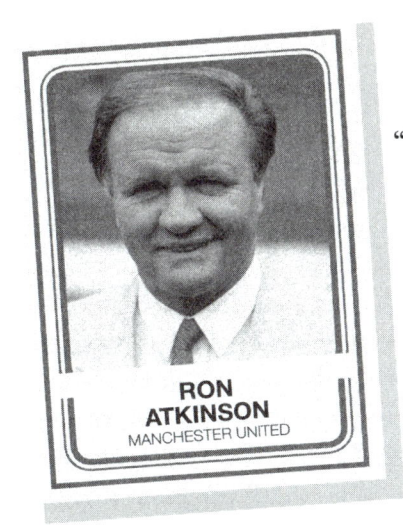

"Not for a single moment did I ever think of myself as a United manager destined to be in control for ten years, 20 years or even life. Nor did I ever want to." Ron Atkinson pauses to sip his cappuccino. "I had other plans, different ambitions. I was never cut out to be the dynasty-type of manager; an ambition that always seemed close to the heart of Alex Ferguson. That particular notion wasn't ever a consideration on my professional agenda. Not my style, to be completely honest."

Big Ron has agreed to meet in a Bromsgrove hotel close to his home. Despite being a regular, his presence causes a stir. He doesn't shun the attention but happily engages in banter with the girls on reception, complaining about the car park prices. Impeccably dressed in a shirt, jacket and elegant Cartier watch, the man who oversaw the most successful United period since Sir Matt Busby has aged well. He seems undiminished by his recent set-backs. Sacked in disgrace from his position as the country's most renowned television football pundit, then put into intensive care by a blood disorder contracted on holiday in Barbados. Now someone he doesn't know keeps ringing his mobile.

"Sorry about this," he says as his mobile trills again. Ron deals with the call swiftly and shakes his head as he puts it back in his jacket pocket. "Someone has put my number on that internet and I keep getting stupid bloody calls."

Sackings and unwanted phone calls. It must remind him of that time two decades ago when Manchester United dispensed with his services.

"Thursday, 6th November 1986, at dead-on 10.09 a.m," he says. "That was the exact time my car phone rang as I motored in for another day at one of the biggest clubs in the world."

On the line was Pauline Temple, secretary to Martin Edwards.

"'Ron,' she said simply, 'could you pop into the ground? The chairman wants to see you. Right away, please!'"

Atkinson swung the wheel of his big Merc and, instead of nosing past the Salford tower blocks towards the Cliff, headed towards Old Trafford.

"Already the brainwaves were crashing against my skull," Atkinson recalls. "I tried to figure why Martin should need to see me with such haste. Talk about being caught wrong-footed and on the blind-side as well. I had ignored what should have been blindingly obvious. I should have recalled a grapevine whisper from football's always alert inner circle that had reached my ears some months earlier at the World Cup in Mexico. The warning couldn't have been plainer or more prophetic. Alex Ferguson, then in caretaker charge of Scotland and firmly in the manager's chair at Aberdeen, had already been tapped up for my job. That information, which came from Lawrie McMenemy, proved to be startlingly correct.

"The United job had been an immense and demandingly exciting experience for me, disturbed by just a few disjointed weeks of poor form, crucial injuries, and a less than impressive league position at the start of the 1986/87 season. Nothing, I felt at the time, that couldn't be swiftly countered by another push to the top of the table by Christmas, just as we had done the previous season. But 48 hours before I entered the unemployment statistics, we got whupped 4–1, courtesy of a 17-year-old called Matthew le Tissier, in a league cup replay against Southampton at the Dell."

But despite the drubbing at the Dell, as Atkinson nursed his car onto the Old Trafford forecourt, he insists it never entered his head that he might be in any kind of jeopardy.

"Until I spotted my number two, Mick Brown," Atkinson remembers. "Mick was clearly very concerned. 'What's going on, Ron? The chairman has just called me over to see him.' For the first time so was I. 'Tell you what, Mick, if those boots of mine aren't laid out ready for the five-a-side this morning, I can predict one thing: we won't be getting those six-year contract extensions.'"

Atkinson went to the boardroom to see Edwards, who was sitting alongside Maurice Watkins, the club's solicitor and United director.

"Business was brief in the execution chamber that morning. They told me that my contract, which still had two years to run, was terminated immediately. They clearly expected a response. But with their decision irrevocable, I merely explained that I would leave all the arguments on financial settlements to my legal people. They nodded agreement. And then, as my last request, I asked, 'Is it okay, Chairman, if I still use the indoor gym on Friday nights? Get the old internationals in for the usual seven-a-side.' Martin could barely believe it and seemed taken aback. Here I was, having just been sacked by the biggest club in the land, and all I wanted was the free hire of their facilities for a kick-about team. I smiled when I made the request but I was being serious. And fatalistic. If they had decided that I was history, that was it. Two or three months of dodgy results, nothing more, and here I was out on the street."

In Atkinson's eyes, there were genuine reasons why this minor crisis in the club's fortunes had ended up being portrayed as a national fiasco under the unrelenting focus of the media.

"Five of my most productive, essential and senior players – Bryan Robson, Norman Whiteside, Arthur Albiston, Gary Bailey and Gordon Strachan – had returned from the World Cup to face operations. Hardly the most encouraging medical news before the launch of a new campaign to resolve, even remedy, the increasingly annoying failure of the season before when United had been ten points clear in the autumn of '85, yet failed to win their first league title since 1968."

In fact, Atkinson had offered to pack his bags in the spring of 1986, an hour after a defeat to QPR when it became clear that United were not going to win the league. After five years at the club, he wondered whether it was time to go and had questioned whether the target of the league championship was unreachable. Two years earlier, his fortunes had been so different.

"Shortly after we had knocked Barcelona out of the Cup Winners' Cup, the feelers started to come my way from Barcelona. My answer, discreetly passed along the grapevine, was simple. 'Sure, I'm ready to talk; just name the place.' I met the Catalan delegation at a London hotel. I confirmed that if everything regarding my United contract could be resolved with them, then I would be willing to move to Barcelona. To be frank, apart from the clearly exciting professional opportunity, it offered the perfect escape route from the domestic upheaval that was then brewing in my private life. I could have gone, closed a page and been spared so much hassle from the news boys as my first marriage broke up and my second, with Maggie, started. Just let me make the career jump, I thought at the time, and let me get the hell out of it. Oh, and my salary would have quadrupled.

"During the initial discussion the only stumbling block was that Barca wanted me to join them on a two-year contract, which is the usual practice abroad; I countered that proposal with a demand for an extra year."

As Atkinson awaited more talks, events took another twist without his knowledge.

"Bobby Robson, a long-standing friend of the Barca hierarchy, was apparently asked for his opinion on my potential appointment.

Ron Atkinson

Apparently, without any malicious motive and with the best possible intentions, he told Barca something along the lines of, 'I don't think Ron would ever want to leave United. I suspect he is using this to secure his position in Manchester and maybe he wants it as a lever for a new contract.' At the time, I was mystified why the contact with Barcelona suddenly petered out. The next I knew about the whole affair was when Terry Venables landed the job, ironically enough recommended by my old mate Robbo."

Atkinson stayed at United and in the summer of 1986, months after he had offered to resign, he told chairman Martin Edwards that he was ready to give it another crack after some serious reflection.

"I can't decide whether I planted the seeds of my own downfall after I offered to go following that QPR game," he says.

At the start of the 1986/87 season, Atkinson bumped into Alex Ferguson at a game in Glasgow.

"Alex and me had always been fairly close. We got on fine, always enjoyed a joke and a bit of banter, and regularly talked on the telephone. If there was any manager in Scotland in that period that I regarded as a pal, it was Fergie. But this time he was very sheepish, more distant than I had ever known him, and he really didn't want to look me in the eye. Gordon Strachan was with me at the time and couldn't understand the stand-off that I got from Fergie. I could. And I had a quiet chuckle at his obvious discomfort. Why was he so uneasy? Because he knew that I knew that we both knew his arrival was a pending item for the in-tray at Old Trafford."

The warning signs had been there even earlier, at Ron's first United board meeting after the Mexico World Cup.

"As soon as I broached the planned signing of England's centre-back Terry Butcher, certain people on the board put a fairly hefty boot solidly through the idea. When Mark Hughes had been reluctantly traded to Barcelona for £2 million, the understanding was that the money from the deal would be stashed to one side, primarily to secure the signing of Butcher and, we all hoped, the capture of Kerry Dixon as Sparky's quality replacement. Later we were priced out of that second objective. But, yes, Butcher was always cast as our number one priority. So I was staggered when press reports trickled out that United just hadn't the cash to afford him. I didn't pay the speculation too much attention. Already, Butcher was sounded out. We had spoken in Mexico and there was a loose agreement on what he wanted to do. The night before the board meeting when my strategy was shot down, Terry – rooming with Gordon Strachan – called me from Pasedena where he was involved with a World Eleven. At the time Glasgow Rangers were pressing him to put pen to paper. He was still buying time, holding out for the outcome he still wanted, to join us at Old Trafford. He told me he was 'desperate' for the move. My answer, 'No sweat, Terry, we'll sort it.'

"I went to confront the directors on the subject – and the roof fell in. 'Gentlemen,' I said during the manager's report, 'let me raise the long-standing issue of signing Terry Butcher.' Immediately, with the final word barely dropped from my lips, the opinion was voiced that Butcher was no better than the first-team defenders already within United's squad. I wasn't having that for a second. I replied, 'I don't care who you have as manager of this football club, whether it's Terry Venables, Graham Taylor, Alex Ferguson or me, I don't think any of us would be too unhappy to have Butcher alongside Paul McGrath for the next five years at the heart of this defence.' I also added a rider aimed at Bobby Charlton, 'He might just have been good enough, Bobby, to have kept Preston up when you were briefly there as manager.' Maybe it wasn't the most diplomatic comment to make friends and influence people, but the nit-picking had got to me by then. The words ricocheted around the room like a sniper's bullet.

"Martin Edwards very quickly stepped in to cool the discussion. 'There is no argument,' volunteered the chairman, 'that Butcher is a good enough player for United. The fundamental problem is that we haven't got the money to buy him at the moment.' Naturally, I countered with the Hughes transfer fee which should have been set aside as the Butcher bank roll. Martin responded that the money had already been earmarked for United's new museum. Being cruel, you might suggest that the country's biggest club was investing in the past, not the future. Actually, being serious, I see the museum now as part of the 'bigness' of United. But I still insist that the financial constraints should not have blocked the Butcher transaction. He would have helped considerably too, in seeing us safely through the team problems that very rapidly cost me my job."

In Atkinson's judgement, United needed players to strengthen certain positions. Liverpool had always invested in reinforcement when they were on top, whereas United had failed to do this after winning the European Cup in 1968, leading to a downward spiral.

"Butcher, I would submit, was part of that failure. At £750,000, he would admittedly have been an expensive acquisition, but also a very sound and proven investment. The irony is that close confidants at United have told me that, apparently, when Alex first took over my position, he said: 'I cannot believe a club of this stature allowed Terry Butcher to sign for Rangers.' And it was pointed out to Fergie, very quickly and from within his own new dressing-room, that that costly decision was reached within the boardroom and not at management level.

"But I haven't lost any sleep over the shenanigans surrounding my premature departure and I don't blame Alex one bit," continues Atkinson. "It's all part of the management game. Somebody is inevitably waiting to nick your boots, whether as a player or manager. If I was ever chairman of a club, I, too, would operate by the same unwritten rule: always have a reserve waiting to take over, just in case. And I'm not going to deceive the world that the tapping up routine hasn't benefited me. I have taken several jobs during the last 25 years thanks to a similar, shall we say, invitation. It happens, it's soccer's jungle law, if you like.

"Once my sacking was confirmed, it didn't take long for the back-up system to be put into operation. I'm told that within an hour of Martin delivering the dreaded words, he and Maurice Watkins left in a private jet for Aberdeen for the formalities with Fergie and his Scottish employers. Even as I arrived back at the Cliff, to summon the senior players to my office and inform them what had happened, United's negotiating contingent were in the air and laying preparations for the next boss. The following morning, Alex was squarely positioned in my barely vacant chair and meeting the media world. As for myself, it was a case of a bit of tidying up. I called a few people who needed to know, shared a quiet drink with the United squad and then headed off home for what should have been a consolation gathering of old mates and odds and sods. Instead it turned into an all-night rave with more than a hundred people packed into the house. It lasted until about five o'clock the following morning. Just as dawn was breaking I got a panic call from Gordon Strachan. He had been at our place with his wife Leslie, but had left a couple of hours before. 'Ron,' he said urgently. 'I'm outside a football ground and don't know where I am. It could be Maine Road.' It turned out to be Elland Road, a prophetic destination when you remember where Strach ended up being sold by Fergie. The pair of them had taken the wrong carriageway on the motorway and ended up in Yorkshire instead of Cheshire where the Strachans lived.

"Quite a few of the players were aggrieved when I was handed my cards. Apart from Gordon, Bryan Robson turned up with Norman Whiteside at my impromptu sacking party. But I would like to stress that it was never a case of revenge: an act of football sabotage with United's top-ranking players before the Saturday game. The big-time bunch were all out of contention at the time due to injury.

"I have always held my conviction that if certain delicate matters concerning my future had been left in the hands of Martin Edwards, I would have been given more recovery time at United. Even when he was saying farewell, the impression I had was that he was being pressured into the decision. Certainly I harbour no bitterness towards Martin. He has my utmost respect, and I wouldn't change my view that there was no better club chairman in the game. He was always extremely supportive towards me, an outstanding professional colleague as well as a good friend. Later, Martin was to prove outstandingly supportive towards Alex."

If the end of Atkinson's United career came as a surprise to him, his appointment, in the summer of 1981, had had a similar effect. He didn't consider himself in with much of a chance of the United job, the general understanding being that Lawrie McMenemy was

Ron Atkinson

the leading runner. That changed when Atkinson, on a post-season tour of Florida with his West Brom team, was approached by Frank Worthington, then playing for Tampa Bay.

"He leaned over my shoulder and said, 'I know who is going to get the Manchester United job,' says Atkinson. 'Don't we all,' I replied, 'No big secret in that – it's Lawrie.' Frank knew Lawrie, and also that he had turned the job down. Then he filled me in a bit more. Naturally, I picked up the waiter's tab."

Shortly afterwards, a contact called Atkinson to ask if he would be interested in the United job.

"I told him to leave the jokes to Tarbuck," he says. "But he was serious and we made a definite arrangement for me to meet Martin Edwards at the house of an intermediary in Cheshire. Martin tried to interview me, but it quickly turned into a different type of conversation with me asking most of the questions. Quite early in the meeting it was apparent the pair of us could get on well together."

With a three-year contract rapidly agreed, the deal was done. Apart from the club car.

"Martin pointed out that my predecessor, Dave Sexton, had a Rover. 'Well, I've got a dog called Charlie, Mr Chairman, but I thought we were talking cars.' On the spot he agreed to replace the car I already had, a Mercedes coupe, for an up-to-date model."

Atkinson then switched his priorities to sorting the United team out and within days of arriving at Old Trafford in June 1981, he met Brian Clough.

"There was an urgent task to perform when I arrived: the sussing out of prospective targets with the United board, establishing the financial clout at my disposal and, then, the swift move to make signings for the new season. One of the first was a speculative double deal built around the departure of goalkeeper Gary Bailey and Garry Birtles to Nottingham Forest in exchange for the England pair, Peter Shilton and Trevor Francis, bolstered by a cash adjustment. The four-part swap had already been aired when, along with Dennis Roach, the agent for a couple of the players, I was lured into one of the most peculiar, off-the-wall meetings I have ever experienced."

We're The Famous Man United

The rendezvous was set for the Midland Hotel, Derby, in the midsummer of 1981.

"I showed early, so did Roach, and we ended up locked in small talk and hanging around the foyer. Out of the corner of my eye, I spotted a car roll up, in it were Brian Clough and Peter Taylor, Clough's right-hand man. Taylor clambered out, skipped up the steps towards us in an open-neck shirt, nonchalant as you like, to ask, 'Have you seen my mate around here?' Having worked in the Midlands area with West Brom, I was fully aware of the methods of operation mastered by the deadly duo from Nottingham, so I buttoned the lip and waited. Five minutes late Brian came bounding into the foyer. Picture the scene: usual green casual sweater, shorts and covered squash racket strapped to his back. He completely ignored my presence and headed straight for Taylor without a nod, never mind a word. Then he delivered this amazing monologue, 'How are you, son? Where've you been? What kind of summer have you had?' I thought to myself, 'He must think we are both crackers; I've just seen them in the same car together.' It was Clough's attempt at being smart.

"Next a conference was arranged, and dear old Brian waited until everyone was scattered around in various positions before he grabbed the loftiest seat in the place. Then, in the belief that he had established the seat of power, Clough tried to bully the whole transaction through in his particularly idiosyncratic way. By that stage Bailey was out of the equation. I had worked with him for a few days at United, and rapidly my long-distance assessment had changed. He could do a job for me at Old Trafford, no question. So the deal on the table was a two-way swap: Francis to us, Birtles back to Forest, plus a cash adjustment. The finances couldn't be agreed, but during the stalemate Clough accused me of leaking potential transfer business to the press. I leapt to my feet, loomed over Cloughie, jabbed my finger repeatedly in his chest, and bawled, 'Brian, don't ever accuse me, don't come the old soldier with me, we all know who let that one out of the bag.' Clough backed off and shrugged. It was my first important battle with Clough and one I had to win."

Yet changes were needed if United were to improve.

"Influential stars like Martin Buchan and Lou Macari were reaching the end of their United careers. To a lesser extent so was Gordon McQueen. And on the day I had walked in, Joe Jordan had walked out, off to join Milan."

Atkinson drafted a blueprint, arguing that United had to buy several top players rather than recruit in dribs and drabs. The board agreed to this and set him a spending budget of £3 million. And there was a condition, that more than half of that was to be dragged back within an agreed period.

"The first player I spoke to officially was Glenn Hoddle. He was out of contract at Tottenham and I came within a whisker of signing him, until he told me that if he didn't move abroad he would stay with Tottenham.

"Mickey Thomas called to see me almost as soon as I had been appointed. He started twitching and was hyper, crossing his legs, scratching his nose and fidgeting like a five-year-old. He blubbered, 'I want a move.' Shake of the head and then the only possible reply, 'Thanks, Mick, I have only been in the building a matter of minutes and you want out. That's really giving me a chance.' He looked back at me and said, 'I've got to go, boss, I need the money.' Gambling too much, trouble with the missus? 'No, boss, I just spend more than I earn.'"

Atkinson knew that Howard Kendall, who had just taken over at Everton, wanted Thomas. In turn, Atkinson wanted the Everton full-back, John Gidman. An exchange was agreed.

"Next was Frank Stapleton, an equally forceful replacement for Joe Jordan. His contract with Arsenal had finished and his wife happened to be a Lancashire lass, so that made it easier for us to sign him."

David Armstrong of Middlesbrough was another target, but 'Boro demanded too much money. Mark Lawrenson of Brighton was approached, but the defender went to Liverpool instead. Which left Atkinson to spend the rest of his money on the big one – Bryan Robson.

"I have been fortunate to work with some exceptionally gifted footballers, many of them magical, world-class talents. But Robbo, without a doubt, is the finest, the greatest, the most rounded and accomplished footballer I have ever worked with. He was a magnificent technician, superbly aware team player, not a great captain but a good one, and a tremendous driving force in any famous shirt he wore."

Robson had barely impressed Atkinson when he first set eyes on him at West Brom in 1977. The man who would become known as Captain Marvel wasn't even in the first team, but stuck in at centre-half in an FA Cup replay against Manchester United, Robson "obliterated" Joe Jordan as West Brom won 3–2. Robson was 19.

"Personally, I don't think he got any better," says Atkinson. "The truth is he reached such a high plane as an immature, inexperienced player and never descended from it. He achieved greatness at an early age."

While at West Brom, United had sounded out Robson.

"I prised it out of him that United wanted him. Apparently, he had been having a few discreet words with their players inside the international camp. 'There is only one way, Robbo, you are going there,' I promised him, 'and that's if I am there as manager.'"

The morning Atkinson was appointed United manager, Robson called him, saying: "Remember what you said, boss. Just keep that promise."

Atkinson kept his word and, after being stubborn in negotiations, West Brom agreed a deal for Robson and young midfielder Remi Moses in an overall package worth £2 million. Robson's fee was £1.5 million, a British transfer record.

"Barring Moses's desperately unlucky injury record, he would have become a clear favourite to replace Robson at the heart of the England team," says Atkinson. Liverpool had a solid midfield with Souness at its heart, now United had Robson and Moses.

Yet one man did not agree with the size of the transfer fee for Robson. Sir Matt Busby, without any public fuss or posturing, resigned from United's board over the Robson deal. Busby never doubted Robson as a player; he just couldn't accept the size of the transfer fee.

Ron Atkinson

"Robbo and I had a close relationship both professionally and privately," says Atkinson. "He was my greatest signing, but there were others who were not far behind in my estimation such as Gordon Strachan, Arnold Muhren and Frank Stapleton."

Atkinson tried to sign Kevin Keegan for £100,000 before his career renaissance move back to Newcastle in 1982, an opportunity he wished he had pursued more rigorously. Another ageing player, Frank Worthington, was considered, until the flamboyant striker panicked that United were not interested and moved to Leeds on a free transfer.

"They were the two that got away and, in Keegan's case, an important influence on my decision to sign Arnold Muhren," says Atkinson. "I was unsure about taking both players as they approached the veteran stage, but I plumped for the Dutchman because he was blessed with a well-proven creative ability and played wide on the left. It was a position I had always found hard to solve. I tried for a while to persuade Sammy McIlroy to go for it, but he could never be tempted. He preferred to play central midfield, and there he had to take on the in-club competition of Robson, Moses and Wilkins, which struck me as not the smartest move. So I took Muhren. He was heaven-sent and came on a free.

"I don't think Arnold ever collected the credit he deserved from United's followers, He was a superb technician who made a revolutionary impact on our game with his total football education. He helped Robson no end in the art of passing. Arnie didn't have to pass to feet, not when he could cause more destruction by passing into space. People used to have an image of Arnie as a laid-back, maybe even lazy, strolling type of player. Far from it. He was a highly competitive trainer, a complete football nut, and never out of the top three in any of our training runs. When he left, I wanted him to stay another couple of years. But Johan Cruyff, his own hero, lured him to Ajax.

"When Gordon Strachan dropped in to play a testimonial game for Martin Buchan I got the vibe that he might be on his way from Aberdeen. You could detect the friction, even at a long range, between him and Fergie. Apparently Fergie believed that although Gordon was only 27, he had been flying down the wing on just one trip too many. Fergie considered him burnt out with nothing left in the legs. It was a suspiciously similar script when he shipped him off to Leeds. My judgement was that Strachan was worth signing for United at a price of £500,000. There was just one snag – he had already taken it upon himself to sign for what appeared to be half the clubs in Europe as well."

United paid £70,000 to one such club, FC Koln of Germany, to free Strachan from a pre-contract agreement that carried his name. In his first season, 1984/85, Strachan scored 15 league goals.

"Sure, a fair few were penalties, but then he won plenty of them as well. He got so overexposed in TV playbacks that revealed his technique, it blew Strach's mind and he started missing them. He had, it's true, earned himself a reputation as a rag doll merchant, but for me he made the most of his attacking opportunities. When that now famously recorded ten-point lead went down the pan it was tied to a dislocated shoulder suffered by Strachan when he collided with a post at West Brom. In roughly three years at United he always looked like he was in the very place he was born to play."

Those United fans who watched him score the equaliser at Anfield in 1988, before smoking an imaginary cigar in front of the Kop, will not disagree. Strachan had arrived to replace Wilkins, who left for Milan.

"I rated Ray highly – despite the popular theories that have been put about. Originally Robson was Milan's target. No deal. The next name they mentioned was Wilko. Less of a problem for me, obviously, because United had a fair number of central midfield players. Ray, in a system where he was our sweeper and cleaner, had just played his best ever season for the club and was headline material. I told Milan we couldn't allow him to leave for less than £1.5 million. Cheeky, considering that Arsenal had offered £400,000 for him that season, but worth a try."

The negotiation was fixed for a Saturday night meet at the Midland hotel in Manchester.

"I told the chairman I was prepared to be a bit bolshie and show them a lorry-driver's aggression if they stalled. Repeatedly, I kept hearing the £750,000 figure. It transpired that the middle-man had sounded out various managers in England about their valuation of Wilkins. I blew my top. Later they upped it to a million and, by this stage, Martin Edwards seemed ready to grab the money and run. He was really straining at the leash but I persuaded him to sit tight. Ten days later they came up with the million and a half and everything went sweetly."

Atkinson is proud of his record in the transfer market at Old Trafford.

"I spent a little over £7 million, and recouped £6 million of the investment. It was called balancing the books and I was made very aware of the hard financial rules from the first day I arrived. Then there was the youth development, a facet of United's game rightly emphasised in Fergie's era. I was quite proud of what happened in my time. You don't get much better than Norman Whiteside and Mark Hughes as home-produced talent. The only difference is that after my departure United made great play with the general public about their production of super kids. It was not such a high-profile topic when I was in charge and it was never meant to be. But nobody will ever convince me that the massive change from my decade to Fergie's wasn't all about finances. I don't want to give the impression of jealousy about the money that Sir Alex Ferguson has at his disposal, but with him United didn't need to count the pennies any longer because they had bank vaults full of the stuff. And they were prepared to invest it in the finest players around. That was the significant mind shift that transformed everything. When I wanted Mark Lawrenson we lost out because the money wasn't immediately available. And I missed out on Gary Lineker in the summer of '85 before he joined Everton because we needed to balance the books. Lineker fancied the move to United but I needed to try and trade off Frank Stapleton to help with the funding, but Frank wasn't interested in going. Cash flow, you might say, effectively made sure United would never benefit from a torrent of Lineker goals."

Atkinson reckons that the one asset his team lacked was a prolific goalscorer.

"Most of the other units functioned just fine. We were blessed with a good team balance, had abrasive and creative factors in the midfield, were sound enough at the back. The only thing missing was a truly instinctive predator. Stapleton, unquestionably, was an impressive line-leader, arguably the best centre-forward in the land for a time. Young Hughes was very similar, a link-man and linchpin of the attack who created the spaces for other people. Neither was, though, the out-and-out goal poacher I felt we needed. So the goals had to come from various sources: Robbo piled in with a few, the wide men contributed too, and Frank and Sparky offered the team their ten or 15 apiece. Oh, for a Lineker. A footballer able to turn candidates into champions."

If Lineker is a player United missed out on, then future England captain David Platt is one that got away – one Atkinson let go.

"I never considered it like that and quite a few people in the game would support my view," he says. "Platty is an example of the young lad who never looks like he is going to make it, and then turns himself into a superstar. Yet even now, I see Platt's departure from United as the right decision at the time. Consider the facts. He was a young centre-forward, not a midfield runner capable of nicking important goals. And he was in a queue behind a whole bunch of more promising youngsters. Hughes and Whiteside were the big two, but there was a lad called Scott McGarvey and another, Nicky Wood, regarded as a major star in the making. Sadly, that potential was to be wrecked by injury. David deserved a break at another club where the ladder might have been easier to scale. I did a ring round for Platt's benefit. Oldham, his home town club, didn't want him, then, after some persuading, Dario Gradi took him at Crewe. Dario, well-respected in developing youthful talent, remained unconvinced. Then, right out of the blue one summer, the lad arrived for pre-season and simply blossomed beyond belief – the classic later starter."

Peter Beardsley was another class act who was allowed to leave United after playing just 45 minutes in a league cup game against Bournemouth in 1982.

"I regret Peter going, in a way, but again special circumstances

Ron Atkinson

prevailed against him staying. I first saw Peter playing for Vancouver Whitecaps when we took them on in a summer friendly in 1982. It was immediately plainly obvious that he was something of a player. I took him on a three-month loan. Unfortunately most of the time he figured in the reserves. Once again the key factor was the log-jam of forwards ahead of Beardsley. So, too, was the £500,000 fee demanded by Vancouver. Brian Whitehouse, the reserve team manager, counselled me with the sound advice: 'Pete's a very handy player, but it's still half a million. I already have a lad here who is as good, if not better and he cost us nowt. Sparky will do that job, just give him the chance.' When I first saw Hughes he was coming up to 16 and whacking a ball about in United's indoor gym. I was less than knocked out. He looked morose and unenthusiastic and his football was even worse. He was downright slipshod and lazy, just the opposite of the bright and lively kids I loved to banter with in training. I had almost given up on him when, in an instant, he left me gobsmacked. Playing for the youth team against a powerful Leeds team, he picked up the ball, beat four defenders as if they didn't exist and smuggled the ball for a Whiteside goal. In a few seconds, Hughes had shown me the kind of quality that was later to become his trademark at the highest level.

"Sparky emerged so quickly that he was only picking up £250 a week on a reserve team contract, a deal that was due to expire within eighteen months. We needed to act fast and we did. A new pay deal was put in place and Hughes signed for another five years. There was just one snag, a real crippler at that. His agent insisted on a buy-out clause being inserted, which compelled United to allow Hughes to consider his options should a foreign club pursue him with an offer of at least £2 million. What could the club do? We were over a barrel. If we backed off, Hughes could quit for buttons. Sign him up and at the very least it was £2 million – then a British transfer record by a considerable distance. And that is exactly what happened."

Within two seasons of breaking into the first team properly, Barcelona wanted Hughes.

"I didn't want him to leave and did everything I could to persuade him to stay," says Atkinson. "But money talks. I tried to convince him that it was too early for him to move abroad. He had less than two years' experience of top-flight football; he wasn't married and would have been a well-paid recluse in Spain. Most of my warnings, unfortunately for him, would prove uncomfortably true. But there were massive temptations for Sparky, not least being the financial rewards. At United his contract was now worth £1,000 a week. Barcelona offered him £10,500 a week – basic."

Hughes' contemporary at United was Norman Whiteside, who had signed apprentice forms on the day Atkinson joined United in the summer of 1981.

"With another yard of pace, he would have been the greatest player in many generations," ventures Atkinson. "As a schoolboy he looked about 30 and played with equal maturity. The sad thing was that within days of becoming an apprentice he was packed off to hospital for a cartilage operation on a knee that ten years later would bring a permanent end to his career.

"Whiteside's game was all about intelligence, awareness and the perceptive pass. At times, his skill was astonishing like the Wembley goal in '85 where he employed an Everton defender as a screen to fool Neville Southall and bend that FA Cup final winner past him. Big Norm always saw the bigger picture. He knew exactly the position and availability of every player on the pitch at any given moment. He could always pick team-mates out with uncanny accuracy to punish the opposition. Yet, wrongly, that was not always the image of Whiteside presented to the general public. Too often, and in a serious distortion of his talent and contribution to United, he was cast as no more than a thug. Norman was tough, a strong and very powerful opponent, but he was never cut out to be a hatchet-man – you could always see him coming a mile off and that was the only part of his game that was predictable.

"Norman could look after himself though. In one game at Anfield, I remember a certain Liverpool player calling him a coward. Frank Stapleton questioned his sanity and urged him not to say it again –

in case Norman got to hear it. Frank was an international team-mate of the player in question and I think it was very sound advice."

In Bryan Robson's absence, Atkinson made Whiteside United's captain at the age of 20.

Another striker purchased by Atkinson was Alan Brazil.

"People said that Brazil was a panic buy in my final season at the club, but he should never come close to being mentioned in that category. He scored 13 goals in 29 first-team appearances and I would never condemn that record as a poor return. My reasoning for wanting Brazil had been straightforward. I figured that he would be a useful foil for Stapleton. I knew that he had been the beneficiary of Arnold Muhren's midfield supply at Ipswich and I believed the partnership could surely blossom again; and, finally, he had a proven record for goals. In the end he lost out for two reasons.

"Number one was that he was rendered redundant as a serious candidate for the front line by the emergence of Whiteside and Hughes. Basically, the pair of them made it impossible for me to pick him. The other reason, as time went by, was that Brazil just couldn't cope when the United crowd turned nasty and started hounding him. Possibly, I didn't help, either, when I presented him with his debut at the expense of Norman, already something of a cult figure on the terraces. Poor old Brazil was a come-lately outsider. He seemed to allow the crowd reaction to upset him so deeply that, eventually, as a sub it looked like he preferred to warm up in the tunnel. There was no rhino hide to protect him from the barbs."

Unable to cope with the crowd's venom, Atkinson decided that Brazil had to go.

"We arranged a swap with Coventry, the first intention being to recruit Cyrille Regis in the exchange. That was sabotaged by an injury scare, with our medical experts insistent that it was too risky to take Regis on board. Pity, that. So in the end our transaction revolved around Terry Gibson. I considered his extra pace might provide attacking variation for us. It was a theory that never had a chance to prove itself. In truth, the whole scene was just too big for Terry. He couldn't handle it and, if I had to hold my hands up to one transfer gamble that failed, it would have to be the signing of Gibson. Not Peter Davenport, though, whom I recruited around the same period. Dav was a good player and capable of operating in a number of positions. At United, he boasted a record of one in three which is always respectable. He cost £570,000, spent three years at United and then the club sold him at a profit."

Davenport moved to Middlesbrough in 1988 after 95 United games. His first goal for his new club enabled them to beat United 1–0 in January 1989.

Atkinson's most extravagant foreign investment was Jesper Olsen, the Danish winger who signed from Ajax in 1984 for £500,000.

"After an encouraging first season, Jesper looked like he would deliver huge dividends for the side. I figured he might develop into a contender for footballer of the year in the next season, yet his promise was undermined by serious injury. Jesper was an extremely gifted winger and a nice enough bloke, but the Danes considered him to be a fiery and explosive player. We were to find out why soon enough."

Arthur Albiston delivered Atkinson an early warning about Olsen's suspect methods on the training field within days of the Dane's arrival.

"It's going to go off out there, gaffer, unless you watch carefully. Jesper is definitely a bit naughty," said Albiston. In the next session, Olsen made a tackle that almost wiped out Remi Moses. Big mistake, as Moses adopted his best Marvin Hagler stance and, in Miles Platting parlance, battered the fuck out of Olsen.

"Blood was spurting all over the place and Jesper was in a sorry heap on the deck," says Atkinson. "It wasn't necessary to intervene as the one-sided contest was well and truly over."

Two Danish reporters who had witnessed the event made sure that it became front-page news. Moses was fined two weeks' wages and Olsen never again make a reckless challenge on him in training.

Atkinson considers Eric Harrison, his youth team coach, to be one of his best signings.

"When I was shown the door, Eric stayed and had a masterful influence on the likes of David Beckham, Nicky Butt, Paul Scholes and the Neville brothers. He might never have featured in a back-page headline in his life, but Eric was a coach whose contribution to United should not be underestimated."

Atkinson is highly complimentary about Sir Alex Ferguson, but they had their run-ins, one when he was manager of Sheffield Wednesday.

"He picked on me once and he picked the wrong target," says Atkinson. "He accused me of leaking a story to the press about Gordon Strachan's impending transfer when, eventually, he finished up at Leeds United. I was innocent and I was angry. I can remember the exact response I bawled down the phone: 'Alex, you can forget anything like that. If you don't shut up, I'll be across there to shut you up. You are not talking to one of your silly footballers so I suggest, for your own safety, you shut up.' Later that day, to be fair to the fella, Alex rang back to apologise. The transfer leak, he had discovered, had nothing to do with me. The incident was dead and buried. That's Alex. He blows hot at times, and he is a very passionate man. It's what has made him the most successful and revered United manager.

"Me? I have never felt, in all modesty, that my own record was too bad. In the early '80s, when Liverpool were blessed with the capacity to boss most teams around, we sorted them out more often than not."

Atkinson once memorably described a trip to Anfield as like being in Vietnam.

"I said it after we went there for a league game and they tear-gassed us. We got off the coach and all of a sudden something hit us and everyone's eyes went. I thought it was fumes off new paint or something, but it was tear gas. Prior to the game there were a lot of fans in our dressing-room, Liverpool fans too, kids, all sorts, eyes streaming. Clayton Blackmore was so bad he wasn't able to play. I was in an awful state. I'd run in and there'd been two blokes standing in front of the dressing-room door and I couldn't see who they were. I was blinded and I'd pushed one of them up against the wall. Afterwards, Mick Brown said, 'What have you done to Johnny

Sivebaek?' I said, 'What are you on about?' It turned out that Sivebaek, who we'd signed the week before and didn't speak much English, in his first game, against the European champions, had been gassed as he got off the coach and then hurled against a wall by his new team manager. No wonder he didn't perform that day.

"I had five years in charge at United, spent a few quid and did enough shrewd business to get most of it back," concludes Atkinson. "And I left United with the best record, at that time, since the great Sir Matt Busby. We never finished below the top four in the First Division, won two FA Cups and lost in the League Cup final. We were involved in European competition every year, something that had never been achieved since Matt's days.

"We also did it with a certain amount of football panache and style, living up to United's finest traditions. So it wasn't all so bad, was it?"